Story House
2.85

Edmund Burke
and the Natural Law

Edmund Burke
and the Natural Law

PETER J. STANLIS

Ann Arbor Paperbacks
The University of Michigan Press

TO

DR. JOHN C. H. WU

Defender of the Natural Law

First edition as an Ann Arbor Paperback 1965
Copyright © by The University of Michigan 1958
All rights reserved
Published in the United States of America by
The University of Michigan Press and simultaneously
in Toronto, Canada, by Ambassador Books Limited
Manufactured in the United States of America

Foreword

"History," Lord Acton wrote near the end of his life, "hails from Burke, as Education from Helvetius, or Emancipation from the Quakers." Acton meant that Burke's high imagination gave to modern writers a true sense of the past, and restored an understanding of the Middle Ages and of the great continuity which joins Christian and classical civilization. As Professor Herbert Butterfield remarks, "It was Edmund Burke who—having recovered contact with the historical achievements of Restoration England—exerted the presiding influence over the historical movement of the nineteenth century."

Yet the philosopher-statesman who thus transformed the writing of history has himself been badly neglected and misunderstood by the rationalist historians. No statesman or writer of the past two centuries has more profoundly affected the spirit of the age than did Burke; and it is surprising, then, how little has been written about his life and his mind. As a great rhetorician and leader of party, rather than as prophet and philosopher, Burke has been studied in schools and universities. The specialization of our modern educational system has had a hand in this: the political historians hesitated to discuss Burke because he was a man of letters, the teachers of literature because he was a philosopher, the professors of philosophy because he was a statesman, and so round the circle. The very breadth of genius may bring neglect, nowadays. Yet perhaps it is well that a proper appreciation of Burke has been reserved for these years, two centuries after he entered upon public life, that (like the period following Burke's assault upon the Revolution) constitute an epoch of concentration, in which thinking men endeavor to restore order and justice to a bewildered society. The publication of Burke's correspondence in a scholarly edition of many volumes (now just commencing), and the appearance of Professor Hoffman's edition of Burke's letters to Charles O'Hara and of his letter-book as agent for New York, are beginning to give us a better understanding of Burke the man.

Dr. Stanlis' book does more than any other study of this century to define Burke's position as a philosopher, relating the convictions of Burke to the great traditions of Christian and classical civilization. Indeed, *Edmund Burke and the Natural Law* is the first full-length endeavor to examine the philosophical postulates of that intellectual giant. Only some few perceptive essays have touched upon this field before, notably the introduction to Hoffman's and Levack's *Burke's Politics*, and the remarks of Professor Basil Willey in *The Eighteenth Century Background*. Books like MacCunn's *The Political Philosophy of Burke* and Cobban's *Edmund Burke and the Revolt Against the Eighteenth Century* have left unexamined, or have merely glanced at, several topics of the first importance for the understanding of any great thinker; now Dr. Stanlis searches these subjects. Burke's concept of human nature has here its first thorough consideration; Burke's understanding of international law, scarcely mentioned by any other critic, receives here a good analysis; Burke's real convictions on the relationship of Church and State, so often misrepresented or shrugged off, obtain from Dr. Stanlis a sympathetic exposition. As a study in the history of ideas, *Edmund Burke and the Natural Law* amounts to a conservative reform of scholarship—uniting, as Burke himself aspired to do, an ability to reform with a disposition to preserve. It is a most temperate book, and a most illuminating one.

Just as Burke revived an appreciation of the Christian and medieval past, so he revived, in his later speeches and writings particularly, the apprehension of Natural Law doctrines, submerged during the age of absolutism. As Dr. Stanlis proves in *Edmund Burke and the Natural Law,* the grand Natural Law tradition of Cicero and the Schoolmen, though battered by Hobbes and confused by Locke, re-emerges in all its strength in Burke's reply to the French revolutionaries; and through Burke, in large part, it nurtures today whatever is healthy in our civil social order.

After more than a century in which Burke was confounded with the utilitarians, the real nature of his concept of Natural Law is being recognized. Dr. Leo Strauss touches upon it in his *Natural Right and History*, Lord Percy of Newcastle in his *The Heresy of Democracy*, and Dr. Ross J. S. Hoffman in his *Burke's Politics*. For all this, the average professor and the average student remain unenlightened upon the question, so that a Harvard professor of history—Dr. Oscar Handlin— actually can state in print, "Intellectually, the weightiest attacks upon the conception of a natural and universal law took their points of departure in the writings of Burke and Montesquieu. . . . " A misunderstanding so complicated requires a book for its remedy; and Dr. Stanlis' admirable study is just that book.

Edmund Burke, the chief formulator of the English and American positive concept of civil freedom, Lord Percy writes, "has been, until quite recently, almost persistently misunderstood." Burke's great accomplishment as a political philosopher was the restoration of the primacy of true Natural Law, as distinguished from "the Rights of Man." Burke's party pamphlets, Lord Percy continues, "have been taken as sound history, while his anti-revolutionary philosophy has been dismissed as a crochet of old age and declining powers. This is almost the exact reverse of the truth. Burke was a Whig partisan, no more reliable as a witness to contemporary fact than any other party politician. But, as other such politicians have not seldom been shocked into statesmanship by war, he was shocked into philosophy by, first, the American and, then, the French Revolution." It might be more strictly correct to say that Burke was forced to *express* his philosophy coherently by the revolutions; for, as Dr. Stanlis shows, the same assumptions concerning the Natural Law run through Burke's whole career as are expressed in the *Reflections* and later writings. "It would be near the truth," Lord Percy adds, "to say that his philosophy began and ended in the re-vivification of the two ancient ideas of dualism and of covenant."

Just so. Perceptive scholars, and serious journalists such as Mr. Herbert Agar, Mr. Walter Lippmann, and Mr. Russell Davenport, recently have been reminding us that our whole fabric of justice and order depends upon the acknowledgment of a body of Natural Law; and they have recognized Burke's great accomplishment in describing the chain of right and duty which joins the dead, the living, and those yet unborn. Now Dr. Stanlis, in a work of the most painstaking and lucid scholarship, examines the cast of Burke's mind, and the significance of his thought, in a fashion which ought to put an end, once and for all, to the sorry notion that Burke was somehow a Benthamite, or that Burke, in exposing the fallacies of Paine and the Jacobins, was undoing the true rights of men. No one who hopes to understand modern politics can afford to ignore Dr. Stanlis' remarkable study.

Dualism and covenant: these ideas suffuse Burke's interpretation of Natural Law, and give that abused phrase meaning in the twentieth century. "The little catechism of the rights of men is soon learned," Burke wrote, "and the inferences are in the passions." To save us from silly little catechisms of rights without duties; to save us from ungovernable passions aroused by inspiring men with expectations that cannot be gratified in nature; to save us from sham and cant—this was Burke's endeavor in his splendid assault upon the *philosophes* and the Jacobins. "I have laid the terrible spirit of innovation which was overrunning the world." These are the words of Napoleon, whose coming Burke prophesied. But it was Burke, rather than Napoleon, who in truth exorcised the fierce spectre of Jacobin alteration. Natural Law, Burke knew, is no mere body of "theoretic dogma"; it is not fiction, but reality; and Professor Stanlis' work is a model of scholarly accomplishment. "A good book, a very good book," George III (who had small reason to love Burke) said of the *Reflections*, "and every gentleman ought to read it." So say I of Dr. Peter Stanlis' book.

RUSSELL KIRK

Preface

From the publication of Buckle's *The History of Civilization in England,* which appeared in 1857–1861, until the present it has been the almost universal conviction of utilitarian and positivist scholars that Burke had a strong contempt for the Natural Law and that the ultimate basis of his political philosophy was to be found in a conservative utilitarianism. The classical expression of this conception of Burke's political thought was written by John Morley in two books on Burke. Benthamite and positivist scholars such as Sir Leslie Stephen, William Lecky, Charles E. Vaughan, Elie Halévy, John MacCunn, Harold Laski, George Sabine, Fossey J. C. Hearnshaw, and so on, have merely followed and extended the original path laid out by Buckle and Morley. The common conviction that Burke was an enemy of the Natural Law has been repeated constantly in many contemporary textbooks on political science and history.

It is the thesis of this study that far from being an enemy of Natural Law, Burke was one of the most eloquent and profound defenders of Natural Law morality and politics in Western civilization. In every important political problem he encountered, in American, Irish, Indian, and domestic affairs, in his economic principles, and in the great crisis of the French Revolution, Burke consistently appealed to the Natural Law and made it the basis of his political philosophy. It should also be evident from this book that as an exponent of Natural Law or traditional "natural rights" Burke was in the great classical tradition of Aristotle and Cicero and the Scholastic tradition of St. Thomas Aquinas, Bracton, and Hooker. It was precisely for this reason that he was opposed to the eighteenth-century revolutionary "rights of man" which derived from Hobbes, Locke, and the scientific rationalism of the seventeenth century. In presenting a systematic exposition of Burke's acceptance of the Natural Law, I have analyzed the relation between Natural Law and Burke's conception of the law of nations, of human nature, of Church and State, and of his principles of political prudence, prescription, and sovereignty.

Although no full-length study of the Natural Law in Burke's career and philosophy has ever been published before, there is little new in the general thesis of this book. The general argument presented here is based upon Burke's published works, but it will not be altered in essential principles by the extensive manuscript letters to and from Burke recently made available at the Sheffield Library in Yorkshire and the Northampton-shire Record Society in Northamptonshire, England. Sound humanist and Christian scholars have always been aware, however imperfectly, that Burke's political philosophy rested upon a much broader foundation than social utility. In the work of Thomas MacKnight, Sir James Prior, Robert Murray, Irving Babbitt, Sir Lewis Namier, Alfred Cobban, Ernest Barker, Moorhouse F. X. Millar, and others, it is correctly assumed that Burke was essentially a Christian statesman and that his political convictions conformed with the ethical norms of the Natural Law. In one way or another these scholars have contributed to my awareness of the Natural Law in Burke's philosophy. But their references were often limited to a few isolated cursory statements, or were incidental to other considerations, or were muddled by the common failure to distinguish between classical and Scholastic Natural Law and the revolutionary "rights of man" propounded during Burke's time.

More particularly, I am indebted to Professor Ross J. S. Hoffman, who, in his preface to *Burke's Politics* (1949), for the first time pointed out and emphasized the paramount importance of Natural Law throughout Burke's political thought. I have profited greatly not only from Professor Hoffman's many insights into Burke's mind, but also from his critical remarks on my work. I also owe much to Russell Kirk's "Burke and Natural Rights," in *Review of Politics* (October 1951), which was based upon an awareness of the profound differences between Burke's traditional conception of natural rights and the eighteenth-century "rights of man" aberration from tradition in the thought of Rousseau. I am deeply grateful to Dr. Kirk also for personal assistance far beyond our common interest in Burke's political philosophy. Professor Leo Strauss's *Natural Right and History* (1953) also did much to confirm and deepen my original conviction that Burke belonged to the classical and Scholastic tradition of Natural Law. I am pleased to acknowledge my indebtedness to Dr. John C. H. Wu, from whom I have learned much about the Natural Law, particularly of its relation to Christian philosophy and to English common law.

I have benefited greatly from the generous help and wise guidance of Professor Louis I. Bredvold, to whom I am most indebted. Professor Bredvold encouraged me in the summer of 1948 to pursue my first suspicions that the positivists were wrong about Burke and the Natural Law. From my exploration of the negative side of my problem, and after extensive reading in the Natural Law tradition, the essential principles of Burke's political philosophy gradually emerged. I take this occasion, also, to thank Professors Austin Warren, Henry V. S. Ogden, Paul Spurlin, John Arthos, and William Frankena for their many helpful criticisms of each chapter.

I am greatly obliged to Dr. Stanley Pargellis for the award of a Newberry Library Fellowship, which enabled me to do further research for this book. The University of Detroit Faculty Research Committee also helped me with a grant. I am grateful to the Earhart Foundation for financial assistance, giving me free time to revise and rewrite this book and making possible its publication.

PETER J. STANLIS

Contents

Edmund Burke
and the Natural Law

ONE

The Philosophic Content and
Historical Importance of Natural Law

I. Introduction

In the twentieth century the problem of Natural Law as the basic ingredient in moral, legal, and political thought confronts men with a challenge they have not faced for a century and a half. On the surface of events and ideas, there appears to be no scope left in the contemporary world for any widespread belief in Natural Law. The basic philosophies in opposition to Natural Law—the rationalism of the *philosophes,* the sentimental emancipation of Rousseau, the utilitarianism of Bentham, the positivism of Comte, and the materialism of Marx, all of these systems of thought and their derivatives—appear to have swept everything before them and to have demolished completely Natural Law jurisprudence. Yet these philosophies have themselves been overtaken by the disillusionments born of conflicts between "might" and "right." H. G. Wells, who exemplified in his intellectual life many aspects of these philosophies, manifested his despair just before his death in 1946:

If his [Wells's] thinking has been sound, then this world is at the end of its tether. . . . He [Wells] has come to believe that that congruence with mind, which man has attributed to the secular process, is not really there at all. . . . A remarkable queerness has come over life. It is as if the law of gravitation no longer functioned in a physical world. Everything is moving in every direction with increased velocity. Mankind has reached an impasse and there is no way around, or above or through this impasse. It is the end.[1]

Thoughtful men who have given their allegiance to inherited secular belief are dissatisfied with the utter lack of any normative principles and turn once more to the Natural Law. The spiritual perplexity of many contemporary thinkers regarding the Natural Law is well expressed by Alfred Cobban:

> It would seem, then, that we must acquiesce in the abandonment of the law of nature by the modern world, even though to do so is to accept the rule of arbitrary human will in the life of society. Henceforth there can be no ethical standards of social and political, behaviour, because will cannot make right. Even individual ethics will hardly be safe, for how can an individual be conceived as an ethical unit in a completely non-ethical society? Distasteful as the conclusion may be, it must be agreed that the Law of Nature, and with it the possibility of any universal ethical standard, has gone for good, unless an entirely new line of approach can be found. Centuries of thought have led in the end to this. The only way out lies in a radical re-thinking of the whole idea of the Law of Nature, to see if there is any chance of reconstructing it on a foundation free from the flaws that have brought the traditional principles of Western civilization crashing down in ruins.[2]

In this study of the place of Natural Law in Burke's political philosophy, I shall show that what is most needed is not a "radical re-thinking" or reconstruction of the Natural Law, but a correct understanding of it. I shall also show that Burke's political philosophy, which cannot truly be understood without reference to classical and Scholastic Natural Law, supplies a superb solution to the persistent confusions and doubts expressed by Cobban.

There is ample evidence that the yearning of men for belief in Natural Law is not merely an academic sentiment; after a century and a half of slumber the Natural Law is vigorously alive, both in Europe and the United States.[3] Nor can the strong revival of Natural Law concepts be explained away as an emotional reaction to the disillusionments brought about by the two world wars. Roscoe Pound noted in 1911 that "it is not an accident that something very like a resurrection of natural law is going on the world over."[4] As a philosophical concept of great importance, and as one of the most persistent themes in history, the Natural Law has always claimed the serious attention of lawyers, scholars, and politicians. The claim, however, has not always been acknowledged, either in theory or practice.

Even though the Natural Law was a vital reality in judicial practice during the nineteenth century, both in the United States and Britain,[5] as a theory of law or philosophy it was held in contempt by hard-headed politicians and practical lawyers. Positivist scholars such as Buckle, Morley, and Leslie Stephen treated the Natural Law as a dead relic of prescientific ages. The contempt in which the Natural Law was held during the nineteenth century was in part the result of misconceptions concerning "natural rights" which had grown up during the eighteenth century. There was a failure to distinguish between the traditional interpretations of Natural Law and claims made under revolutionary "natural rights." This in turn led positivist scholars to neglect totally the Natural Law tradition in the political thought of Burke, who was well known as an avowed enemy of "natural rights." Indeed, Burke was commonly enlisted as the foremost of modern political thinkers opposed to the Natural Law: "The reaction of the nineteenth century against natural law formulae," wrote Georges Gurvitch in the *Encyclopaedia of the Social Sciences,* "is traceable ultimately to Edmund Burke." After examining the importance of Natural Law in the political thought of Burke, I shall show how much truth there is in this widely held conviction. But before I proceed to the main purpose of this study, I shall summarize briefly the philosophical content and historical importance of Natural Law in Western thought, up to the time of Burke.

II. The Philosophic Content of Natural Law Traditions

It should be understood at the outset that the term "Natural Law" as used throughout this book refers to ethics, law, politics, and human behavior, and has nothing to do with physical science. Even when thus limited the language of Natural Law contains ambiguities, for the words "nature," "natural," "reason," "rational," and so on, are subject to widely varied meanings, and to avoid confusion the linguistic context as well as the historical uses of these terms must be understood. David Hume's rejection of Natural Law undoubtedly resulted in part from his impatience with the ambiguities in the eighteenth-century uses of "nature." "The word *natural*," he wrote, "is commonly taken in so many senses, and is of so loose a significa-tion, that it seems vain to dispute whether justice be natural or not." When we consider the constructive historical functions and the vital agreement of many thinkers concerning the Natu-ral Law, Hume's doubt that meaningful communication is possible about the Natural Law cannot be accepted as anything but a precaution carried to excess. There are other difficulties besides those of language. It would be naïve to assume that because an identical phrase appears in many writings from antiquity to the present each writer meant the same thing and that the phrase is a part of a consistent continuity of Natural Law belief. Definitions, too, are circumscribed by semantic problems; one must get behind similarities in vocabulary and see whether the concepts described are indeed the same. For since Natural Law, like any other vital body of beliefs, was subject to historical development, new materials were added to its philosophic content and it was obliged to operate in various circumstances, so that its practical application to dif-ferent purposes required changes in its method. In its organic development, the Natural Law itself was altered; there were at least three distinct traditions of Natural Law up to Burke's time.

Despite these precautionary remarks, there is evident through-out the various Natural Law traditions a hard core of funda-mental ethical, legal, and political beliefs. These constantly recurring cardinal principles are so deeply ingrained in human thought that, however much they may be ignored or obscured, they have successfully resisted every effort to destroy them, and are as alive in the twentieth century as they were in the fourth century B.C. As Cobban has said, "We could go back century by century, and find in varying terms the same essential belief in the existence of a Natural Law and natural rights." What, then, is the essential content of Natural Law? One way of answering this question would be to examine what various thinkers have said concerning Natural Law, from the dawn of moral reflection to the time of Burke (see Appendix I). Among the ancient and medieval thinkers, the most profound and all-inclusive statements on the Natural Law are probably those of Cicero and St. Thomas Aquinas.[6] Cicero supplied the touchstone for the classical conception of Natural Law; St. Thomas supplied it for the Scholastics. The Roman Stoic thought Natural Law stemmed from God, its "author" and "interpreter," whereas the Christian saint believed that man, as a rational creature created in the spiritual image of God, was capable of fulfilling his moral nature by participating in God's reason and will through the Natural Law. Indeed, until Hobbes's speculations in the middle of the seventeenth century, Natural Law was almost universally assumed to be an emanation of God's reason; the most common principle of Natural Law was that God ruled the universe through an eternal and universal law. Not all adherents of Natural Law believed the same principles, and what was stressed by one writer was often minimized by another. Nevertheless, until the time of Hobbes, the classical and Scholastic conceptions of Natural Law were in agreement upon the following basic principles: Natural Law was an emanation of God's reason and will, revealed to all mankind. Since fundamental moral laws were self-evident, all normal men were capable through unaided "right reason" of perceiving the difference between moral right and wrong. The Natural Law was an eternal, unchangeable, and universal ethical norm or standard, whose validity was independent of man's will; therefore, at all times, in all circumstances and everywhere it bound all individuals, races, nations, and governments. True happiness for man consisted in living according to the Natural Law. Whereas Natural Law came from God and bound all men, various positive laws and customs were the product of man's reason and will and applied only to members of particular political communities. This was the distinction between Natural Law and civil laws. Finally, no positive law or social convention was morally valid if it violated the Natural Law; moral sovereignty and justice, therefore, were intrinsic, and not the product of power exercised by kings or popular legislatures.[7]

These basic principles, variously combined, emphasized, and applied, are the fundamental elements in the ancient and

Scholastic traditions of Natural Law. How well did Burke know these Natural Law traditions? To what extent did he accept or reject them in his practical political activities and thought? Did he distinguish between this traditional theistic conception of Natural Law and later completely secular natural law theories? Before attempting to answer these and other related problems, we shall note how the Natural Law has worked in practice throughout the history of Western civilization.

III. The Historical Importance of Natural Law

The following illustrative sketch briefly summarizes the vital role of Natural Law in the most important religious problems and political events of European history. From the dawn of human speculation to modern times the concept of Natural Law has been prominent in moral, legal, religious, and political philosophy. As Alfred Cobban has said, "Natural Law . . . provided the soil in which the fundamental ideals of Western civilization grew up." [8] As I have noted, the Natural Law was conceived as the final determinant of ethical judgment, the measure of validity in law, the "natural" bridge between God and man, supplementing specific divine revelations. It was the ideal criterion in sanctioning political sovereignty. It was conceived as an ultimate law inherent in the nature of things and centered in man himself. Clearly, belief in Natural Law assumes a noble idea of man, of his unique value both as a free and rational individual and as a social being. Such a conception of man and the universe could not but be cosmic in all human affairs. Indeed, throughout history men of various religious and political beliefs have appealed to the Natural Law, both to defend an established social order and to justify revolution. It has therefore been intimately tied up with the fundamental problems of liberty, equality, order, and justice. As one of the oldest and most persistent themes, Natural Law has retained a tenacious control in the minds of men.

The historical significance of Natural Law is barely suggested in its various manifestations throughout the literature and

philosophy of ancient, medieval, and modern writers. Its continuous application to human affairs evolved into the essential
ideas and events that have dominated man's civil life. The
Natural Law was propounded by Aristotle, Cicero, and Seneca,
men whose writings were among the standard textbooks in
schools throughout Europe during the ancient, medieval, and
Renaissance periods. Natural Law infused an idealistic morality
into Greek and Roman Stoicism. It established Roman honor,
"that unbought grace of life," as Burke called it in 1790, which
created an inspired and selfless public spirit that sustained
the Roman Empire. Natural Law was the unifying force which
gave coherence to the law books and digests of Justinian, the
Corpus juris civilis (534 A.D.). Next to Christianity itself,
probably nothing has had a more profound and extensive effect
on the history of Western civilization than the Justinian compilations of Roman law, which were based completely on Natural Law. The chief Roman jurists who made the Justinian code,
Gaius, Ulpian, and Paulus, differed in their emphasis of particular legal principles, but they agreed in regarding Natural
Law as a system of ideal laws founded in intuition and right
reason. Their agreement established Natural Law as the simple,
just, and universal core of all Roman law. Thus, through the
principle of moral equality in Natural Law, the Romans developed the conception of an organic society of all human beings
(*societas hominum*), a unity of human nature which destroyed
the provincial sense of exclusive tribal superiority, and established for centuries the communal sense of human universality,
of each individual's corporate union with others in common
social institutions.

The Roman traditions of Natural Law were largely absorbed
by St. Ambrose, St. Jerome, St. Augustine, St. Gregory, and
other Church Fathers. Their reconciliation of "nature" and
"right reason" with Christian "revelation" and "grace," established the foundations for the development of the Canon Law
of the Church. This fusion of classical and Christian thought
achieved its artistic supremacy in the *Divine Comedy* of Dante
and reached its theological perfection in the *Summa theologica*
of St. Thomas Aquinas. St. Thomas' aphorism, "Grace does not

abolish Nature but perfects it," is a perfect summary of the harmony of Christianity and Natural Law. The canonists of the
Catholic Church transformed the Natural Law through the spiritual principles of Christianity, and their baptism of Natural Law
gave it an unparalleled clearness, unity, and force. They regarded Natural Law primarily as an emanation of God's reason
and will, and its principles were held to be superior to every
human positive law, being an infusion of the providence of
God into natural justice, the "natural" equivalent of divine
revelation. The morality of Natural Law supplemented, but
never contradicted, the divine ethics of Revelation; [9] it was
perceivable by the unaided "right reason" of all uncorrupted
men. Thus, Natural Law provided a rational basis for faith and
harmonized human and Christian values. It was regarded as a
span between God and man, linking the divine laws of revelation and of man's natural reason with human positive laws and
customs. Natural Law was the means by which a close correlation between godly and worldly wisdom was achieved; without
it, the positive *social* program of medieval Christianity, which
released that characteristic wolfish energy of the period, would
probably have been impossible.[10] St. Thomas Aquinas' Christian
conception of Natural Law, together with the Aristotelian
precept that man is by nature a political animal, and with the
established sense of corporate community life inherited from
both Christianity and Roman law, combined to make the
practical application of Natural Law flexible and adaptable to
various historical circumstances. Despite the strong faith in
human reason assumed in the Thomistic conception of Natural
Law, the rationalist element was not individualistic and autonomous, but corporate and subordinated to religious faith.

Henry de Bracton (d. 1268), who seems not to have read
his contemporary, St. Thomas Aquinas, utilized the Natural
Law to achieve the equivalent synthesis in the civil and common
law of England. In part he inherited the Natural Law from
Canon Law. As Richard O'Sullivan has shown: "From the
beginnings of its formulation in the period after the Conquest,
English law and equity in turn received from canonist sources
the conception of the law of nature." [11] Bracton's *De legibus*

et consuetudinibus angliae (partly published in 1567 and completed in 1569) has been called "the crown and flower of English medieval jurisprudence, which had no competitor in literary style or completeness of treatment till Blackstone composed his *Commentaries* five centuries later." [12] Richard O'Sullivan, in the *Grotius Society Transactions* (1945), has indicated the continuity from Bracton's time of the Natural Law tradition in English common law:

> The validity of a system of natural law and of essential human rights was taught, and even taken for granted, by all the great common lawyers from Bracton, Fortescue and Littleton, through Thomas More and Christopher St. Germain, to Coke and on to Holt. For all these men, law is founded on ethics. . . . This conception of the law of nature or of reason . . . was taught at the Inns of Court in the fifteenth and sixteenth and seventeenth centuries when the Inns of Court were a truly legal university. The tradition survived into the eighteenth and nineteenth centuries and is not absent even in the twentieth century. [13]

Although the Natural Law was the most important single element in the legal thought, practice, and education of Englishmen for over seven centuries, its most vital social influence is to be found in the theological and political conflicts of modern times.

Despite the religious conflicts of the sixteenth and seventeenth centuries, Natural Law retained its hold upon the moral imagination of large bodies of Catholics and Protestants. On the Continent its basic precepts continued to be accepted and taught by such legal thinkers among the Catholics as Vitoria (1480–1546) and Suarez (1548–1617), and by such eminent Protestants as Grotius (1583–1645) and Pufendorf (1632–1694). The growing tendency to favor the Thomist tradition of theology established Natural Law as an accepted branch of Catholic thought. Those branches of Protestantism which interpreted the Augustinian doctrine of grace to mean that man's reason and will were wholly corrupted by original sin were much less receptive to Natural Law. In Britain, however, Anglicanism became the center of Natural Law philosophy, particularly after the publication of Hooker's *Of the Laws of Ecclesiastical Polity,* parts of which appeared in 1594, 1597, and in the seventeenth century. Hooker's argument was Thomism qualified by the common law tradition of Bracton and Reformation nationalism. One of Hooker's modern admirers sees in his legal philosophy of the national sovereign state "the true progenitor of the American Constitution." [14] Hooker's *apologia* for the Church of England, so reminiscent in its defense of prescription of Burke's later arguments in the *Reflections on the Revolution in France,* made excellent use of the Natural Law against the extreme Augustinianism of the Calvinists. In Anglicanism Natural Law continued to operate as a fusion of theological and political thought, subject to various developments, as evidenced in the work of the Cambridge Platonists and Bishop Bramhall (1594–1633), who attacked Hobbes's materialism and cynical antirational conception of man. I shall return to this Anglican tradition of thought when I examine the relationship of Natural Law to Burke's politics.

The common law tradition first propounded by Bracton had far-reaching political effects as well. It established as a principle of political sovereignty that both king and people are subject to the common law, that power to be just must be in accordance with the Natural Law. This tradition of constitutional liberty and justice against the claims of arbitrary royal or popular prerogatives was dramatically illustrated in the opposition of Sir Edward Coke to King James I early in the seventeenth century. Coke became the symbol of civil liberty among the constitutional-minded lawyers who opposed the Stuart claims to divine right from James I until the Revolution of 1688. To justify 1688 and to refute Hobbes's defense of absolute monarchy, Locke wrote his famous *Two Treatises of Government,* in which popular sovereignty, centered in the legislative power of parliament, replaced the Stuart doctrine of divine right. Locke's interpretation of 1688 rests upon his revolutionary and individualistic development of Natural Law and the social contract, whereas Burke rejected both divine right and popular sovereignty. Through Bracton, Coke, Locke, and such later English common law thinkers as Blackstone, the modified traditions of Natural Law and political sovereignty passed over to Colonial America, where they became the ultimate basis for the chief arguments in support of the American Revolution.[15] The French Revolution of 1789 was both condemned and justified by appeals to Natural Law and "natural rights." Much has been written about the similarities and differences in the origins, nature, and effects of these two great revolutions, particularly as revealed in the American Declaration of Independence (1776), and the French National Assembly's *Déclaration des droits de l'homme et du citoyen* (August 1789). However similar or different were the circumstances and ambitions which brought about the English, American, and French revolutions, some form of Natural Law or "natural rights" principles supplied the moral and intellectual framework for defenses of these three most crucial historical events. But with the triumph of the American and French revolutions, the Natural Law at once achieved its greatest practical significance in modern political affairs, and lost its hold upon the minds of men. Since 1789 men have doubted, vilified, and ridiculed the Natural Law for a variety of reasons, yet it has never ceased to affect legal and political thought, and in crises involving political justice men have invariably appealed to it. Because Burke's political philosophy, in its relation to Natural Law, is profoundly involved in the three great revolutions of 1688, 1776, and 1789, before one can understand the importance of Natural Law in Burke's politics one must see what happened to the classical and Scholastic conception of Natural Law during the eighteenth century.

TWO

Natural Law and Revolutionary "Natural Rights"

The bulk of contemporary jurists (particularly those of the positivist school) . . . are really attacking a false idea of natural law, and in exterminating it, exterminate only a man of straw, drawn from the pages of cheap-jack textbooks. . . . The idea of natural law . . . does not go back to the philosophy of the eighteenth century, which more or less deformed it.

Maritain, *The Rights of Man and Natural Law*, p. 59.

In 1789 Jeremy Bentham published his *Introduction to the Principles of Morals and Legislation,* in which he made a famous attack upon the Natural Law: "A great many people are continually talking of the law of nature: and then they go on giving you their sentiments of what is right and what is wrong: and these sentiments, you are to understand, are so many chapters and sections of the law of nature." With so many whimsical and personal projections of moral feelings and aspirations being put forth as the "universal" and "eternal" Natural Law, Bentham concluded, "the expressions *law of nature* and *natural right* are no more than a senseless jargon." Yet four years later, in 1793, Bentham's contempt for Natural Law was wholly contradicted by John Quincy Adams, who in the course of attacking Thomas Paine's *Rights of Man* defended the traditional veneration for Natural Law: "When the glorious Congress of 1774 declared that 'the inhabitants of the English Colonies in North America were entitled to certain rights by the immutable laws of nature' . . . they knew very well what they meant, and were perfectly understood by all mankind." [1] In contrast to Bentham, Adams' assertion is clearly consistent with Aristotle's statement that the Natural Law "does not exist by people's thinking this or that." The differences between Bentham and Adams concerning Natural Law are not so much a matter of belief as of understanding. As a Christian, Adams both understood and believed in the Natural Law, and undoubtedly the utilitarian Bentham would have detested it even if he had understood it. But like secular contemporary sociologists who deny the existence of all moral norms or standards, Bentham could not even distinguish between what Natural Law was in fact, and derivations or violations of Natural Law made in its name. In denying all norms but those of social utility, Bentham was reduced to the absurdity that if men have the power to violate the imperatives of Natural Law, there is no such thing as Natural Law. This common sociological delusion has been well answered by Maritain:

That every sort of error and deviation is possible in the determination of [Natural Law precepts] merely proves that our sight is weak and that innumerable accidents can corrupt our judgment. Montaigne maliciously remarked that, among certain peoples, incest and thievery were considered virtuous acts. Pascal was scandalized by this. We are scandalized by the fact that cruelty, denunciation of parents, the lie for the service of the party, the murder of old or sick people should be considered virtuous actions by young people educated according to Nazi methods. All this proves nothing against natural law, any more than a mistake in addition proves anything against arithmetic, or the mistakes of certain primitive peoples, for whom the stars were holes in the tent which covered the world, proves anything against astronomy.[2]

Bentham's confusion concerning the Natural Law was not merely intellectual; it was inherent in the historical development of utilitarianism itself. Bentham did not know that his utilitarianism, in its English origins and even in its nature, had much in common with the detested "natural rights" championed by Paine, whose revolutionary "rights" were the antithesis of the traditional Natural Law which Adams had defended.

The same contradictions found in Bentham and Adams exist among modern scholars of the eighteenth century. Henry V. S. Ogden in *The State of Nature and the Decline of Lockian Political Theory in England, 1760–1800* (New York, 1940) contended that in the last four decades of the eighteenth century all appeals to "nature" suffered a sharp decline roughly proportional to the growth of utilitarianism. Yet in 1941 Alfred Cobban said: "Up to the end of the eighteenth century . . . it would have been taken for granted that there is a Natural Law, and that positive law is justified in so far as it derives from the basic principles of Natural Law." [3] Like Bentham and Adams, Ogden and Cobban were each right in a particular way. There were indeed many arbitrary and personal claims made in the name of "nature," and the resulting confusions tended to discredit all appeals to "nature" in favor of Benthamite utilitarianism. Nevertheless, the radical pamphlet literature of England from 1760–1800 reveals that this growth in utilitarianism frequently was combined with appeals to "natural rights." If anything, the emphasis is upon "rights." Priestley's later utilitarianism was built upon a "natural rights" foundation, and Paine's *Rights of Man,* Part I, is purely an argument of abstract "rights," whereas Part II is founded upon social utility. Contradictory or not, there was frequently a parallel development of utilitarianism and of "natural rights." In the next chapter I shall show that the greatest single error of modern scholarship on Burke derives largely from the failure to distinguish between eighteenth-century "natural rights," which was a revolutionary doctrine, and the still vital but submerged and partly deformed traditional conception of Natural Law.

To resolve these confusions it is necessary to return to the revolutionary interpretations of Natural Law propounded by Hobbes and Locke. The key to the problem is provided in two admirable books by Leo Strauss, *The Political Philosophy of Hobbes* (1936), and *Natural Right and History* (1953). In the preface to his book on Hobbes, Strauss asks and answers the most crucial question concerning the fate of Natural Law in the last three centuries:

We must raise the . . . question, whether there is not a difference of principle between the modern and the traditional view of natural law. Such a difference does in fact exist. Traditional natural law is primarily and mainly an objective 'rule and measure,' a binding order prior to, and independent of, the human will, while modern natural law is, or tends to be, primarily and mainly a series of 'rights,' of subjective claims, originating in the human will.[4]

The vital differences between the revolutionary "natural rights" and the traditional Natural Law, Strauss points out, is evident in a comparison of Hobbes's political theory with that of Plato and Aristotle. "Essentially the same result is reached," Strauss adds, "if one compares the doctrines of Locke, Montesquieu, and Rousseau with those of, e.g., Hooker, Suarez, and Grotius."[5] Thus, Hobbes's philosophy is the great dividing line between medieval and modern secular thought; his revolutionary break with the past, his destruction of the primacy of "law" or "reason" in favor of "power" or "will" is the fountainhead of revolutionary social thought.

Historically, the foundations of Hobbes's individual "natural rights" are to be found in nominalism. Hobbes is the seventeenth-century heir of William of Occam, whose denial of universals paved the way for the eventual denial of Natural Law. In his personal development Hobbes first used then abused Aristotle and the Schoolmen; by the time he attacked them in *Leviathan* (1651), his gradual emancipation from their most essential principles was complete. Hobbes's attitude toward tradition in human affairs was as revolutionary as that of Bacon in scientific method. Hobbes's addiction in middle age to Euclid led to his conviction that the methods of physical science, particularly of mathematics, could be applied to social and political thought. Much nonscientific thought was enamored of mathematics during the seventeenth century. Grotius had utilized mathematical method in his presentation of Natural Law;[6] Descartes was a mathematician turned philosopher; Spinoza built on Hobbes in his attempt to bring religion and ethics into harmony with mathematical science. Hobbes, therefore, was but one of many writers who prepared the way for the cult of Newton, whose discoveries were taken by materialists as proof that laws of motion, such as Hobbes had predicated, followed mechanical principles. In presenting his political philosophy in mathematical form, Hobbes contributed greatly to the general confusion in the eighteenth century between ethics and physics, between "nature" as a moral norm and "nature" as an orderly process subject to empirical description.[7] This confusion, together with the passion for abstract mathematical reasoning, characterizes much eigtheenth-century radical speculation and obscures the distinction between the classical or Scholastic Natural Law and abstract "natural rights."

Hobbes's part in subverting the traditional understanding of Natural Law is even more clearly evident in his theory of political sovereignty. Ancient and medieval Natural Law thinkers had almost always treated the idea of a "state of nature," a pre-civil state of primitive man, as a hypothetical and ridiculous fiction. Hobbes probably never believed in any historical state of nature,[8] but he posited it as a useful means of illustrating seriously his conception of the social contract as an irrevocable agreement sanctioning the legal sovereignty of established authority. Strauss has noted the important fact that "it is only since Hobbes that the philosophic doctrine of natural law has been essentially a doctrine of the state of nature."[9] Despite Hobbes's personal preference for monarchy, it did not matter in his theory who ruled in his absolute state. As Sabine has said: "Hobbes had been at pains to point out that his views were consistent with any *de facto* government."[10] Hobbes's definition of law in effect denied the existence of Natural Law as understood by his predecessors: "These dictates of Reason [i.e., Natural Law] men use to call by the names of Lawes; but *improperly:* for they are but conclusions, or theorems concerning what conduceth to the conservation and defence of themselves; whereas Law, properly is the word of him, that by right hath command over others."[11] In Hobbes's theory of sovereignty, the absolute will of the sovereign was paramount over right reason and was the only source of law. Clearly, Hobbes's absolutist state left no room for any citizen to appeal to the normative ethical principles of justice which had formerly characterized the Natural Law.

But the greatest blow which Hobbes struck at the classical and Scholastic understanding of Natural Law was in his theory of human nature. Hobbes propounded a mechanistic psychology in which man was conceived as a purely physiological creature whose actions or "motions" were either conditioned responses to sensations, or the spontaneous overflow of infinite and self-generating passions. Hobbes's principles of sensation and of association of ideas anticipated in purer form the better-known empiricism of Locke and later associationalism of Hartley.[12] Hobbes's creature of limitless passions anticipated the Rousseauist man of sensibility. According to Hobbes, man was dominated by the appetites of pride, vanity, and ambition, all of which required "a perpetuall and restlesse desire of power after power, that ceaseth only in death." [13] Such a creature of sensations and passions, without free will or the capability of acting according to "right reason," could not possibly believe in or abide by the traditional Natural Law. Combined with Hobbes's nominalism, state of nature, theory of contract, and conception of sovereignty, this mechanistic view of man made him out to be an asocial individualist whose nature existed prior to the state, and whose membership in society was voluntaristic. Contrary to classical and Scholastic Natural Law teaching, Hobbes's man was not by nature a political animal, born without his consent into an organically developed civil society, and with no civil character apart from his common corporate nature and constitutional inheritance. Although Hobbes stressed the absolute *duty* of each citizen to obey the established power, his theory of sovereignty was totally subordinate as an influence to his theory of human nature, which laid the foundation for modern "natural rights." [14] There had been a traditional "natural rights" doctrine connected with classical and Scholastic Natural Law, but the revolutionary Hobbist theory of "natural rights" was centered in the private will or ego of each individual, and was not limited by the social duties and ethical norms of Natural Law. It remained for Locke and his eighteenth-century disciples to complete the destruction of classical and Scholastic Natural Law by converting it from a bulwark for liberty and justice as an inheritance of constitutional law, to a revolutionary doctrine of liberty and equality as an abstract, inherent, individual "natural right."

Until the extensive work of Strauss, most scholars were so aware that Locke's *Second Treatise* (1690) was meant to refute Hobbes's political theory that they stressed the very obvious party differences between them and ignored or minimized their far more fundamental similarities in principles. Locke's highly favorable reputation as a friend of democracy and Hobbes's defense of absolute monarchy also helped to obscure their great similarities. Indeed, among scholars who make no distinction between the traditional Natural Law and the eighteenth-century development of Hobbes's revolutionary "natural rights," Locke is frequently invoked as an exponent of Natural Law.[15] On the surface there is much to warrant the claim that Locke followed the traditional Natural Law philosophy. He regularly used the vocabulary of Natural Law and natural rights, and all his life he believed ardently and sincerely in some apparently normative "nature." Locke's indebtedness to Hooker and through him to St. Thomas Aquinas and ultimately to Aristotle is a commonplace of scholarship on Locke. Yet it is precisely this commonplace that Strauss has doubted, and his answer to the question whether Locke meant the same thing as his predecessors when he appealed to "nature" is crucial to every scholar who would understand the fate of Natural Law in the eighteenth century:

Hooker's conception of natural right is the Thomistic conception, and the Thomistic conception, in its turn, goes back to the Church Fathers, who, in their turn, were pupils of the Stoics, of the pupils of pupils of Socrates. We are then apparently confronted with an unbroken tradition of perfect respectability that stretches from Socrates to Locke. But the moment we take the trouble to confront Locke's teaching as a whole with Hooker's teaching as a whole, we become aware that, in spite of a certain agreement between Locke and Hooker, Locke's conception of natural right is fundamentally different from Hooker's. The notion of natural right had undergone a fundamental change between Hooker and Locke. . . . The period between Hooker and Locke had witnessed the emergence of modern natural science . . . and therewith the destruction of the basis of traditional natural right. The man who was the first to draw the consequences for natural right from this momentous change was Thomas Hobbes. . . . At first glance Locke seems to reject altogether Hobbes' notion of natural law and to follow the traditional teaching. . . . [But] his teaching seems to endanger the very notion of a law of nature . . . Locke cannot have recognized any law of nature in the proper sense of the term. This conclusion stands in shocking contrast to what is generally thought to be his doctrine, and especially the doctrine of the second *Treatise*. . . . However much Locke may have followed tradition in the *Treatise* . . . a comparison of its teaching with the teachings of Hooker and of Hobbes would show that Locke deviated considerably from the traditional natural law teaching and followed the lead given by Hobbes.[16]

Hobbes's nominalism, his posit of the state of nature and theory of contract, his conception of sovereignty and mechanistic view of human nature, were assumed independently or adopted from Hobbes by Locke, who modified and greatly softened the most pessimistic and cynical elements in Hobbes's philosophy, and popularized throughout the eighteenth century the modern secular theory of "natural rights."

It is ironical that Hobbes, the conscious enemy of traditional Natural Law, provoked by his militant rashness a host of defenders of the Natural Law,[17] so that by his radical opposition he kept vital the philosophy he wished to destroy. Locke, the presumed friend of Natural Law, by his superior "common sense" prudence, his rational simplicity, and moderation, softened and made palatable the basic "natural rights" principles of his professed enemy Hobbes, and popularized them throughout Europe. Whether Locke arrived at his principles independently or in conscious imitation of Hobbes is not relevant here. As Plamenatz has said: "We need not wonder . . . if we find in the political writings of Locke most of the ideas of Hobbes, except those explicitly rejected by the younger philosopher." [18] Both thinkers were nominalists and both felt compelled to seek for universal ethical certainty in the current methods of mathematical science.[19] The result in both philosophers was that love of rational simplicity in all things, that passion for abstract logical speculation so characteristic of eighteenth-century radical thought. But the fundamental similarity between Locke and Hobbes is their common empirical theory of knowledge and mechanistic conception of human nature. Locke's empiricism and denial of innate ideas is indistinguishable from Hobbes's basic principle that all knowledge is derived from sensations of external objects.[20] In this, Locke contradicts both his professed faith in Christian revelation and his declared belief in the innate rights to "life, liberty and estate" of traditional Natural Law. This contradiction between Locke's theory of knowledge and his social thought makes his whole political philosophy endlessly equivocal.

But it is in his mechanistic conception of human nature, with its implicit "greatest happiness" principle, that the utilitarian strain in Locke's thought joins hands with Hobbes's Epicurean ethics. Where Hobbes had made "fear of death" man's dominant passion, the far more optimistic Locke posited the correlative principle of the "pursuit of pleasure." As Strauss has shown, the desire for power is the common denominator of their common hedonism.[21] The similarities in their egocentric conception of man, and of Locke's popularization of their hedonism, are well summarized by Sabine:

> The psychology which in the eighteenth century grew out of Locke's theory of mind was fundamentally egoistic in its explanation of human behavior. It ran in terms of pleasure and pain, and not like Hobbes's in terms of self-preservation—a doubtful improvement—but the calculation of pleasure was exactly as self-centered as the calculation of security. Hobbes's better logic had its way in spite of Locke's better feeling.[22]

In man's desire for self-preservation, Hobbes had practically identified self-interest and the Natural Law; Locke did the same concerning his "greatest happiness" principle. The necessary means of self-preservation and of the pursuit of happiness is the possession of power; as these are identified with "natural rights," the revolutionary "natural rights" are nothing more than a disguised principle of power. In the traditional sense, the "natural rights" of Hobbes and Locke are not rights at all. Hobbes and Locke merely call powers "rights," and then treat them as if they were what Cicero or Hooker would have called rights. Although few writers used the terms "law of nature" and "natural rights" more frequently than Hobbes and Locke, it is clear that their egocentric conception of human nature left no place for the Natural Law of classical and Scholastic tradition.

Compared with these common philosophical principles, the differences between Hobbes and Locke in political theory are superficial and extraneous. Locke's optimistic interpretation of the "state of nature," his greater willingness to treat it as an actual historical phenomenon, is no less destructive to traditional Natural Law than Hobbes's darker and more hypothetical "state of nature." If anything, Locke is more revolutionary than Hobbes; he minimizes civic duties further by making the social contract revocable at will. Also, from the viewpoint of constitutional political sovereignty based upon Natural Law Hobbes and Locke are alike revolutionists. Both exalted private will above normative law: Hobbes upheld the absolute and arbitrary will of the monarch, based upon hereditary or acquired right, and Locke championed the equally absolute and arbitrary will of parliament, based upon popular support.[23] Under Natural Law the "divine right of freeholders" is no more valid than the "divine right of kings." Until the time of Hobbes, the tradition of Natural Law had been essentially theistic. The natural rights introduced by Hobbes and popularized by Locke exalted man's private reason and will above any eternal and unchangeable divine law. Under the added impact of natural science and deistic speculation, as the eighteenth century unfolded the classical and Scholastic Natural Law was ripped completely loose from its divine origin, so that from a law fitted to the spiritual nature of man, as a being of supernatural destiny, it became merely a fancied description of the physical order of nature, or a hedonistic and utilitarian precept for the survival of man as a biological creature in the jungle of nature. Nothing was so instrumental in bringing about this vital change as the development of physical science.

There is a direct connection between the abandonment of the theistic conception of Natural Law and the supremacy of mathematical logic and self-sufficiency of private reason in natural rights. Every philosopher from Aristotle to Hooker had posited as the basis of his faith in Natural Law a belief in God's being and beneficence. Grotius was the first modern to say, for illustrative purposes, that Natural Law would be valid even if God did not exist. A. P. D'Entreves has summarized the historical development of this hypothesis:

Grotius . . . proved that it was possible to build up a theory of laws independent of theological presuppositions. His successors completed the task. The natural law which they elaborated was entirely 'secular.' They sharply divided what the Schoolmen had taken great pains to reconcile. The doctrine of natural law which is set forth in the great treatises of the seventeenth and eighteenth centuries— from Pufendorf's *De Jure naturae et gentium* (1672) to Burlamaqui's *Principes du droit naturel* (1747), and Vattel's *Droit des gens ou principes de la loi naturelle* (1758)—has nothing to do with theology. It is a purely rational construction. . . . God is increasingly withdrawn from immediate contact with men. . . . What Grotius had set forth as a hypothesis has become a thesis. The self-evidence of natural law has made the existence of God perfectly superfluous.[24]

The revolutionary belief that Natural Law was a product of private reason opened the way for arbitrary claims to be made in its name. This belief caused men to regard Natural Law not as a practical but as a purely speculative science, like mathematics. As practical affairs involved a great variety of circumstances, the traditional method of judging men's actions by the Natural Law involved moral prudence rather than mathematical logic. St. Thomas Aquinas had said on this vital point: "Laws are laid down for human acts dealing with singular and contingent matters which have infinite variations. To make a rule fit every case is impossible." [25] Traditional Natural Law left much room for infinite variations of circumstances and was therefore capable of absorbing the constantly changing conditions of civil society. John Wu, an eminent twentieth-century representative of traditional Natural Law, has summarized how "the speculative and rationalistic philosophers of the eighteenth century . . . treated the natural law as if it were geometry":

The modern speculative, rationalistic philosophies of Natural Law are aberrations from the highroad of the scholastic tradition. . . . It is most regrettable that practically all of the seventeenth, eighteenth and nineteenth century philosophers of Natural Law departed from this great tradition. They proceeded *more geometrico;* they wove whole systems of so-called Natural Law just as a spider would weave a net out of its own belly. To mention a few, Hobbes, Spinoza, Locke, Pufendorf, Christian Wolff, Thomasius, Burlamaqui, Kant, Hegel, and even Bentham with his felicific calculus, all belong to the speculative group. Many of the nineteenth century judges in America abused the name of Natural Law by identifying it with their individualistic bias.[26]

Hobbes and Locke were among the earliest and most important "speculative" and "rationalistic" theorists to believe that an ideal system of laws, based upon uniformity in reason and mathematical method, could be established for all men everywhere. Strauss has shown that as a result of this notion, "modern political philosophy in contrast to classical political philosophy . . . claimed unconditional applicability (applicability under any circumstances) for its theories." [27] Ironically, this secular parody of Natural Law, this divergence by Hobbes, Locke, and others from the norms of Natural Law prudence, was taken by later positivist critics as the norm, and whereas Hobbes rejected traditional Natural Law because it was not based upon infallible mathematics, later critics rejected the supposed traditional natural law of Hobbes because it did claim mathematical certainty.

An equivalent fate overtook the traditional Natural Law in France during the eighteenth century.[28] In England, following the lead of Hobbes and Locke, Hume and the utilitarians completed the philosophical revolution begun by the physical sciences and augmented by the mathematical method of Hobbes and Locke's empiricism. The full significance of Hobbes's revolutionary method and "natural rights" was greatly obscured by his use of the traditional vocabulary of Natural Law.[29] For reasons of habit and prudence, and because Natural Law enjoyed such great prestige, Hobbes could not abandon the language of Natural Law, even though he emptied it of all its traditional moral content. Locke and his eighteenth-century disciples also retained the vocabulary, and even the ethical overtones, of traditional Natural Law, though it would have been far better if they had devised a terminology more suitable to their hedonist psychology.[30]

I have noted the profound difference in content between traditional Natural Law and the revolutionary "natural rights." Despite the appeal to "nature" common to the "natural rights" of both Hobbes and Locke,[31] there was in each man a deep strain of utilitarian thought. The later supposed antithesis between "natural rights" and utilitarianism is merely a verbal illusion. Bentham was undoubtedly right to condemn traditional Natural Law as "nonsense on stilts," but in his failure to perceive his own kinship with the radical "natural rights" theory he revealed great ignorance of his philosophical ancestors. As Plamenatz observed, it would "have been as easy to prove that the spiritual ancestor of Bentham was Locke rather than Hobbes." Sir Frederick Pollock was one of the few later critics of utilitarianism to perceive that although Bentham was the first utilitarian to consciously break with the vocabulary of "nature" and of "rights," his principles added up to a pure "natural rights" philosophy.[32] Halévy, perhaps the most eminent scholar to deal with eighteenth-century philosophical radicalism, took Bentham at his own word; he saw that claims of private "natural rights" and social utility were often incompatible, and therefore concluded that their basic principles were historically antithetical. It is no paradox, however, that as the heir of Hobbes and Locke, Bentham was the great enemy of classical and Scholastic Natural Law precisely because he accepted their revolutionary "natural rights." Bentham merely converted Hobbes's and Locke's hedonistic philosophy into the language of social utility. By developing Hutcheson's principle of "the greatest good of the greatest number," Bentham socialized the individual "natural rights" of his predecessors, recast their hedonistic premises into language more suitable to their principles and more acceptable to the taste of the nineteenth century.

The rich pertinence of all that we have noted concerning Natural Law, "natural rights," and utilitarianism will become abundantly clear in the next and succeeding chapters. In retrospect and summary there emerge certain basic facts concerning the fate of the Natural Law in eighteenth-century England. The fundamental change in the meaning of appeals to "nature" is most evident in the revolutionary character of the new doctrine of "natural rights." Under the influence of physical science, the conscious attacks of Hobbes and the inept compromises of Locke, traditional Natural Law as a system of normative ethics centered in God's being and man's "right reason" was replaced by or confounded with a purely materialist view of the universe and a hedonistic conception of individual "natural rights." The external attacks of Hobbes were probably less disastrous to traditional Natural Law than the apparent allegiance of Locke, who hastened its dissolution from within. By employing the traditional language of "nature" in popularizing Hobbes's egocentric philosophy, Locke left standing the shell of traditional Natural Law principles, with their religious imperatives and idealistic connotations, but he unwittingly destroyed the meaning which Natural Law had carried for almost twenty centuries. But the moral norms and imperatives of traditional Natural Law did not perish. The final effect of Hobbes's and Locke's philosophies was not to destroy the Natural Law, but to involve it in hopeless confusion with alien principles and arbitrary claims made in its name. In the last half of the eighteenth century, when various political movements of reform and revolution were justified by frequent appeals to Lockian doctrines of "natural rights," utilitarians such as Bentham, Godwin, and Mill, who often sympathized with radical movements, treated with contempt all appeals to "nature" and individual "rights."

These facts become highly important when it is recalled that the first and most important writers to evaluate Burke's political philosophy, and to establish its most widely accepted meaning, were truebred utilitarians and positivists. With the growth of utilitarian thought, the whole concept of Natural Law assumed an antiquarian character, and even the appreciation of what Natural Law had achieved in history was gradually lost. Often utilitarian and positivist writers no longer even recognized the Natural Law in the thought of their predecessors. The question naturally arises, to what extent did the utilitarians' neglect of Natural Law carry over into their evaluation of Burke's political philosophy? Was Burke himself aware of the Natural Law tradition in Western thought? Did he perceive the vital distinction between traditional Natural Law and the eighteenth-century revolutionary "natural rights"? How important was the Natural Law in Burke's political convictions, and to what extent did he appeal to it in practical affairs during his twenty-nine years in parliament? We are now prepared to see that the failure to ask and answer these and related fundamental questions has been the most serious omission in scholarship on Burke during the past century or more, and has resulted in a badly distorted view of Burke's political philosophy and career. Burke was delivered over to the descendants of his political enemies, who gladly claimed him for themselves.

THREE

Burke and the Natural Law

The pretended rights of these theorists are all extremes: and in proportion as they are metaphysically true, they are morally and politically false. . . . By these theorists the right of the people is almost always sophistically confounded with their power . . . but till power and right are the same, the whole body of them has no right inconsistent with virtue. . . . Far am I from denying in theory, full as far is my heart from withholding in practice (if I were of power to give or to withhold,) the *real* rights of men. In denying their false claims of right, I do not mean to injure those which are real, and are such as their pretended rights would totally destroy.

Burke, *Reflections on the Revolution in France*, II, 331–335.

I. Burke's Supposed Utilitarianism

From at least 1857–1861, when Buckle's *The History of Civilization in England* appeared, until the present, it has been the almost universal conviction of utilitarian and positivist scholars and critics that Burke had a strong contempt for the Natural Law, and that the ultimate basis of his political philosophy was to be found in a conservative utilitarianism. This common conviction is generally based upon the awareness that Burke frequently attacked what he called "metaphysical" or "abstract" rights, and that he generally placed against such "rights" arguments of moral prudence, legal expediency, and practical utility. Buckle was the first important critic to see in Burke's thought a conception of politics "purely empirical," in which "not truth" or "general principles," but "large views of general expediency" prevailed.[1] A decade after Buckle's work, John Morley gave classic expression to what was to become a touchstone of utilitarian criticism on Burke:

The defenders of expediency as the criterion of morals are commonly charged . . . with holding a doctrine that lowers the moral capabilities, and that would ruin society if it were unfortunately to gain general acceptance. The king and the minister in 1774 entertained this view, and scorned to submit their policy to so mean a test as that prescribed by the creed of utility. If they had listened to the voice of the most eloquent and sagacious of the upholders of this test, they would have saved the empire. . . . The actual bearings of circumstances, so visible to anybody who, like Burke, looked upon them from the point of high practical sense, were hidden from the sight of men who surrounded themselves with a hazy medium of abstract and universally applicable ideas. . . . Their opponents, who chose to measure their policy by the standard of convenience, of the interest of the greatest number, of utility and expediency, were guided by it to the loftiest heights of political wisdom and beneficence. The baneful superstition that there is in morals, and in the art of politics, therefore, which is a province of morals, some supernaturally illumined lamp, still survives to make men neglect the intelligible and available tests of public convenience and practical justice, which is no more than expediency in its widest shape. If Burke were among us at this day, enjoining habitual recourse in every political measure to this standard, he would find that men are nearly as disposed as ever to reason downwards from high-sounding ideas of Right, Sovereignty, Property, and so forth; which have in truth no invariable conformity to facts, and which are only treated with reverence because they are absurdly supposed to be ultimate, eternal entities, incapable of further resolution.[2]

Morley was even convinced that the French Revolution "made conformity to general utility . . . the practical standard" of government, and that therefore "Burke . . . must have been much nearer to the best, most vital, and most durable part of the revolution than he knew, and than his successors have supposed."[3] In his second and much better book on Burke, published in 1879, Morley first recognized in Burke's thought some vague force or law or "religious mysticism" which transcended empirical experience and history, but he still spoke of "Burke's utilitarian liberalism" and concluded that "even when resting his case on prudence and expediency" Burke would "appeal to the widest and highest sympathies."[4] Morley once remarked that "as a Burkian and a Benthamite" he was much dismayed by an appeal to nature made by Chamberlain, maintaining that "right must depend not upon nature, but upon the good that the said rights are calculated to bring to the greatest number." [5] As the outstanding disciple of Bentham and Mill, Morley claimed Burke as his master and in two books on Burke he never once mentioned the Natural Law.

Among Morley's contemporaries, Lecky and Sir Leslie Stephen shared his view that Burke was a utilitarian. Lecky noted in 1891 that for Burke Church and State were "based upon expediency" and "defended by purely utilitarian arguments" which "have been rarely stated more skilfully than by Burke." [6] The positivist Stephen, a more perceptive writer, summarized Burke's philosophy as "theological utilitarianism" and noted a close general connection between Burke's supposed utilitarianism and his allusions to metaphysical rights which he opposed:

Passages may be found in Burke's writings where language is used superficially resembling that of his antagonists. He speaks of the 'natural rights of mankind' as 'sacred things,' and even says that all power is 'a derogation from the natural equality of mankind at large.' Elsewhere men have a natural right to the fruits of their industry. . . . These transient deviations into the quasi-metaphysical language, when more closely examined, are easily intelligible. The natural equality of mankind, in Burke's mouth, is simply an expression of the axiom which must necessarily lie at the base of all utilitarian, as well as of all metaphysical, systems.[7]

Stephen concluded that "Burke had not solved the problem of reconciling expediency with morality"; clearly, Stephen saw no more in Burke's "transient deviations" into "natural rights" than an accidental accretion inherent in his supposed utilitarianism.

Charles E. Vaughan, a learned modern political positivist and recognized authority on Burke, applied to the great Whig the usual Benthamite antithesis of "natural right" and "expediency":

From the beginning, Burke recognizes that, in method and principle, the struggle is between expedience and judicial Right. . . . In his view of things, Right is always contrasted with, and opposed to, expediency. . . . In this we shall find the key to the whole discussion . . . the last appeal is not to Rights but to expediency. . . .

He stood side by side with Hume and Bentham in their assault upon abstract ideas of Right, in their constant reference of everything to expediency.[8]

In another book Vaughan qualified his last point considerably by noting a vast difference between the simple expediency of Hume and Bentham and Burke's expediency, qualified by "higher principles" and "a tissue of moral and religious ideals." [9] According to Vaughan, by "expediency" Burke meant "the permanent welfare of the whole nation"; therefore, he made "expediency the ultimate principle of politics." Vaughan thought Burke's expediency "comprises two ideas . . . enlightened self-interest and duty . . . and Burke refuses to mark the bounds between them." Burke merely applied his "expediency" in different ways at various times; in his early work it was interpreted in a generous sense and was an end in itself, but in French affairs it was placed under the sanction of the moral law and religion. "Here," wrote Vaughan, "for the first time, Burke explicitly severs himself from Hume and the utilitarians. Here . . . he deals a deadly blow at those who strive to divorce politics from morals." [10] Vaughan also noted and was deeply troubled by something in Burke's writings on Indian affairs which Leslie Stephen had passed off as "transient deviations into quasi-metaphysical language." Vaughan's explanation is even more glib and unconvincing:

He slips for the moment into an admission—repeated afterwards, it must be confessed, in his assaults on the French Revolution—that there is such a thing as the 'natural rights of mankind,' and that they are 'sacred.' . . . Burke slips almost unconsciously from Right in the distinctly abstract to Right in the strictly legal sense; from the Right inferred out of certain universal principles by the philosophers to the right inferred out of certain particular statutes by the lawyer. . . . Such passages come as a shock to those who have carefully followed the general tenor of Burke's utterances . . . they have the effect of pulling the reader up short, of making him ask how in the world they ever got there. . . . We are probably justified in saying that the 'appeal to abstract Right' is rather a controversial device than an expression of the author's deliberate and reasoned judgement. . . . If we are to hold Burke to the strict consequences of his words—he assumes . . . some kind of moral code to have existed, doubtless in a more or less rudimentary shape, before the state and in total independence of it.[11]

Nothing so reveals the addiction to theory and the limited moral imagination of Burke's utilitarian and positivist critics as this fixed refusal to take him at his own word, and the readiness to pass off his appeals to "natural rights" as mere rhetoric.

Like Leslie Stephen and Vaughan, John MacCunn, one of Burke's best critics, also recognized Burke's appeals to "natural rights," and expressed his great bewilderment: "Manifestly he does not hold, as Bentham did, that these rights have no existence. Why, then, should he cry havoc on the men who made it their business to declare them to the world?" In answering his own question, MacCunn offers yet another explanation of the apparent dilemma: "Burke does not attack the doctrine as a theorist denouncing a theory, but as a politician whose interest is fixed on the application of the doctrine to politics." [12] By "rights" MacCunn assumed Burke meant "civil" rather than "natural" rights,[13] so that he concluded: "To Burke, as to Bentham, all rights, in so far as they are substantial, are not ultimate but derivative." MacCunn's analysis of Burke on natural rights came closer than any predecessor to the truth, yet he too failed to sift the problem beyond Burke's supposed utilitarianism.

Most twentieth-century scholars on Burke, such as Halévy, Whitney, Osborn, and Lester, have simply repeated with variations the contentions of Morley and his successors.[14] It is not surprising, therefore, that practically every popular textbook in which Burke's ideas are discussed contains statements such as the following: "He was primarily a utilitarian, a worshiper of the expedient, who was convinced that the mere fact that any custom or institution had grown up over a long period of time established an overwhelming presumption in its favor. The whole business of appealing from tradition to reason and nature was distasteful to him." [15] Such has been the grand consensus of positivist opinion on Burke for the past century or more. Sabine alone among Burke's modern critics refined upon

the prevailing judgment by drawing out the historical consequences to the Natural Law of Burke's supposed utilitarianism:

> Burke made an important contribution to the nineteenth cen-
> tury proposal to replace the system of natural law. . . . In a sense
> Burke accepted Hume's negations of reason and the law of nature.
> Burke showed precisely . . . the reaction that was to follow upon
> Hume's destruction of the eternal verities of reason and natural
> law. . . . It is true that he never denied the reality of natural rights.
> . . . However, like Hume, he believed that they were purely con-
> ventional . . . they arise not from anything belonging to nature or
> to the human species at large, but solely from civil society. . . . Ac-
> cordingly, Burke not only cleared away, as Hume had done, the
> pretense that social institutions depend on reason or nature but far
> more than Hume he reversed the scheme of values implied by the
> system of natural law.[16]

It is impossible here to analyze in detail the nature and origins
of the various errors of omissions, irrelevant intrusions, false
distinctions, misinterpretations, and contradictions which run
through the evaluations of Burke's utilitarian and positivist
critics. The "sophisters, economists, and calculators" whom
Burke predicted would triumph after his era, garbled his principle of prudence, misunderstood his distrust of abstract metaphysical rights, failed to consider his conception of the law of
nations, and refused to treat seriously his appeals to "nature"
even when they were aware of them, yet they claimed him for
themselves and imposed their claim on the twentieth century.
Not that many individual aspects of the work of Burke's utilitarian critics are not valid. But those who supposed Burke a
utilitarian warped his essential philosophy out of its true orbit.
The failure of a century of scholars to consider whether Burke
adhered to the Natural Law was a fatal omission, because the
true nature of Burke's cardinal political principles cannot be
understood apart from its connection with the Natural Law.

II. Burke's Knowledge of the Natural Law Tradition

Since "very early youth," Burke confessed in 1780 to a gentleman interested in reforming parliament, he had "been conver-
sant in reading and thinking upon the subject of our laws and

constitution, as well as upon those of other times, and other
countries," and a decade before his death he stated in parliament that "he had in the course of his life looked frequently
into law books on different subjects." Burke's interest in the
law began at least as early as 1747, when his father entered his
name at the Middle Temple. Early in 1750 Burke went to London to study law, and although he soon abandoned his studies
to take up first literature and then an active life in politics, his
speeches reveal that he had acquired a profound knowledge and
enduring respect for the law. "No man here," he said in 1770,
"has a greater veneration than I have for the doctors of the law,"
and four years later, in his speech on American taxation, he
voiced his greatest tribute to the law: "The law . . . is, in my
opinion, one of the first and noblest of human sciences; a science which does more to quicken and invigorate the understanding than all other kinds of learning put together; but it
is not apt, except in persons very happily born, to open and to
liberate the mind exactly in the same proportion." Burke always believed that nothing sharpened the mind like the study
of the law; he therefore cautioned his colleagues in March
1775 not to underestimate the resources of the American colonists, who had bought as many copies of Blackstone's *Commentaries* as the British: "This study [law] renders men acute,
inquisitive, dexterous, prompt in attack, ready in defence, full
of resources."

In addition to his frequent remarks in parliament, Burke's
interest in the law is suggested in the volumes of his library,
which included the works of many writers, both ancient and
modern, on Natural Law jurisprudence.[17] Among 664 items in
Burke's library were works containing discussions of the Natural
Law by Aristotle, Cicero, Epictetus, Bacon, Coke, De Lolme,
Prynne, Blackstone, and many others, including Grotius' *On
War and Peace,* two editions of Pufendorf's *Law of Nature and
Nations,* and Vattel's *Droit des gens* and *Law of Nations.* Burke
also possessed, among others, the political writings of Plato,
Aristotle, Machiavelli, Milton, Sidney, Locke, Montesquieu,
Rousseau, Voltaire, and Bolingbroke. Of course Burke also had
access to the great personal libraries of his aristocratic Whig

friends. How many of these writers Burke actually read and whether he accepted or rejected their ideas will appear from time to time throughout this study.

Arthur L. Woehl, in "Burke's Reading," has proved by direct references and quotations from Burke's writings how profoundly he had absorbed almost all of the classical writers on the Natural Law. "Direct evidences of a wide reading in Aristotle . . . are frequent," Woehl noted, and "the *Ethics* and the *Politics* appear directly in quotations and indirectly in Burke's theory on the characters of men and governments." [18] There is universal agreement among scholars about the early and sustained importance of Cicero's influence on Burke, in matters of style, temperament, and beliefs.[19] Burke had read practically everything that Cicero has left us. While at Trinity College he was particularly attracted to Cicero's *De officiis*, which he described as "a blameless piece." In 1761 he made use of Cicero's *De legibus* to controvert the Hobbist theory that laws receive their authority from mere institution. Burke quoted Cicero eleven times in his works and made frequent allusions to him in his speeches. It was largely from Cicero that Burke adopted one of the most important ideas derived from the Natural Law —that the state is an indirect emanation of God's power and goodness and rests on divine law. Burke's insistence that God willed the state seeks authority in Cicero more frequently than in Hooker.[20] Burke's moral intensity in applying the Natural Law is closer in spirit to Cicero than to any other writer. In a parliamentary report Burke once wrote that "much has been written by persons learned in the Roman law, particularly in modern times." [21] Among the jurists who helped to form the Roman law Burke knew the work of Paulus and Calistratus; he was familiar with Gravinia's *Origines juris civilis* and the Justinian compilations.[22] All of these works on Roman jurisprudence breathe the spirit of Cicero and the Roman Stoics, and are based upon the Natural Law.

Among Continental legal philosophers Burke had certainly read Sigonio's *De antiquo jure provinciarum,* Calvin's *Institutes,* Suarez' *Tractatus de legibus* and the works of Grotius and Pufendorf. He made direct use of Montesquieu's *L'esprit des lois* and Vattel's *Le droit des gens;* from the first he learned the historical method of treating ideas, while the second was his most frequently quoted modern authority on the law of nations.[23] Burke also knew the work of the famous Jansenist jurist, Jean Domat, whom he described in his *Reflections* as "one of the greatest lawyers" in the National Assembly. Domat based his *Civil Law in Its Natural Order* on a revolutionary interpretation of St. Thomas Aquinas' principle that legislation ought to be for and by the people.[24] Burke's criticism of this revolutionary theory of popular sovereignty was based upon the Natural Law.

Burke's particular awareness of English legal history and general knowledge of the Natural Law were enormously increased by his role as editor and writer of Dodsley's *Annual Register,* from 1758 to at least 1765. In 1757 Burke had written a fragmentary "Essay Towards an History of the Laws of England," a supplement to his *Abridgment of English History.* This interest in English legal and constitutional thought was strongly reflected in the large number of book reviews on legal works which Burke wrote for the early numbers of the *Annual Register.* As editor and chief contributor, he certainly reviewed all of the following books on law that appeared in Britain from 1758 to 1765: Blackstone's *Discourses on the Study of Law* (1759), Wallace's *Laws of Scotland* (1760), Grey's *Debates of the House of Commons* (1763), and Elly's *Liberty of Subjects in England* (1765). Burke probably severed his connection with the *Annual Register* soon after he entered parliament, yet he is known to have reviewed Blackstone's *Commentaries* (1767–1768), Beccaria's *Essay on Crime and Punishment* (1767), Dalrymple's *Memoirs of Great Britain and Ireland* (1771), and Sullivan's *Lectures on the Feudal and English Laws* (1773).[25] All of these reviews reveal that early in his public life Burke had acquired an encyclopedic knowledge of criminal, civil, constitutional, and Natural law. His review of Wallace's *Laws of Scotland* shows his awareness that the law of Scotland, far more than of England, was founded upon the Roman law, and was therefore more consciously related to Natural Law. But Burke also knew that Coke was the most eminent modern English defender of the Natural Law. In combining these facts in his review of Wallace's book, Burke wrote: "The laws of Scotland are here referred to, and grounded upon, those of nature and of nations; and the author has endeavoured to do, what, if it had been done with regard to the law of England, might be considered as a union of Lord Coke with Grotius and Puffendorf." [26] As Burke well knew, English common law supplied for Coke the bridge which connected statutes with the Natural Law. In this light, Burke's general legal erudition takes on added significance as a measure of his knowledge of Natural Law.

Burke's knowledge of the law is most clearly revealed in his innumerable quotations and references to the ancient records, charters, legal treatises, statutes, procedures, and decisions which comprised the common law of England. Burke's understanding of English common law is pertinent in determining his conception of the Natural Law, because unlike many writers on jurisprudence during the eighteenth century, Burke never treated the Natural Law merely as an abstract code of ethics perceived directly by the naked reason. To Burke the spirit of the Natural Law was embodied in the rules of equity which governed English common law, and was transmitted through legal precedents and prescription. Although Burke by no means identified English common law and the Natural Law, he used his knowledge of both to illuminate their close reciprocal relationship. It is important to know, therefore, how well Burke knew the common law. In 1773 Burke candidly admitted in parliament: "I have studied . . . God knows: hard have I studied, even to the making dog-ears of almost every statute book in the kingdom . . . the letter as well as the spirit of the laws, the liberties, and the constitution of this country." [27] Woehl has shown that Burke's references to the laws of England "begin with Ina of Wessex, and continue with the long line of kings, from Alfred on, who recorded a body of law." The enormous labor that Burke expended in the process of mastering English law is well summarized by Woehl: "Burke evidently ransacked legal and historical documents of all kinds, including the Journals of the Lords and Commons, the Rolls and Laws of Parliament, State Trials, Statutes of Jeofails, Woodfall's Parliamentary Debates, the legal decisions of Chief-Barons and Justices Hardwicke, Willes, Parker, Raymond, Vaughan, Holt, Lee, Mansfield and Wilmot." [28] Burke read widely and used digests of English common law. A specimen of how Burke utilized his vast knowledge of English law in his parliamentary speeches, even when commenting upon the source of authorities in law, will indicate the temper and skill he brought to legal theory and legislative practice:

It is well known, that the elementary treatises of law, and the dogmatical treatises of English jurisprudence, whether they appear under the names of Institutes, Digests, or Commentaries, do not rest on the authority of the supreme power [the monarch], like the books called the Institute, Digest, Code, and authentic collations in the Roman law. With us, doctrinal books of that description have little or no authority, other than as they are supported by the adjudged cases and reasons given at one time or other from the bench; and to these they constantly refer. This appears in Coke's *Institutes,* in Comyn's *Digest,* and in all books of that nature.[29]

Even while debating, Burke frequently made good extemporaneous use of his legal knowledge: "In this part of his speech," the Commons clerk recorded, "Mr. Burke entered into a detail of legal authority, which he traced so far back as the reign of Richard II, and followed up with different instances to the reign of George the First, with much learning and ingenuity." [30] It is no exaggeration to say that Burke knew the chief works on European jurisprudence, and especially on English common law, from the Justinian code to his own time.

Among the great body of writers on English law there were several whom Burke particularly admired. "Bracton," he said in parliament, "is allowed by all to be a good authority," and Hooker was for Burke the great fountainhead of post-Reformation English canon law.[31] Next to Cicero no legal theorist had quite the same authority for Burke as Coke, whom he quotes nine times in his works and to whom he alludes in his speeches more frequently—and in general with unreserved admiration—than to any other writer.[32] In the *Reflections* Burke said he venerated "Sir Edward Coke, that great oracle of our law, and indeed all the great men, who follow him, to Blackstone," because Coke had inspired his seventeenth-century successors in legal theory to give a strong moral basis to English civil liberty under the common law. Among the men who followed Coke was Selden, whom Burke called "a great ornament of the common law." Burke admired also the moderate lawyers of 1688, whose interpretation of that revolution, consonant with the idea that the British state is founded on an inherited constitutional limited monarchy, he defended so skillfully in the first part of the *Reflections* and in *An Appeal from the New to the Old Whigs* (1791). Burke's legal erudition was so well known and respected among his colleagues in the House of Commons, his mastery of English common law was so complete, that he was the fittest man among them to handle the enormous legal problems entailed in the impeachment of Warren Hastings. Nothing but a profound ignorance of Burke's thought and career could have induced Sabine to write that "he was unaware of the relation of his own ideas, or of the system of natural law that he opposed, to the whole intellectual history of modern Europe." Indeed, as an examination of Burke's appeals to the Natural Law will reveal, no British statesman of his time was more aware than Burke of the relationship between his intellectual inheritance and the Natural Law.

III. Burke's Appeals to the Natural Law—1761–1789

To appreciate fully Burke's appeals to the Natural Law in Irish, American, domestic, and Indian affairs, it is necessary to understand the historical conditions and immediate circumstances which called forth his pleas, and to examine the manner in which Burke sought to establish the principles of Natural Law through practical political action. It is generally conceded by historians of all schools of thought that during most of the eighteenth century Ireland was to England as an abject slave to a proud master. Morley has clearly summarized the essential nature of the problem Ireland faced:

> After the suppression of the great rebellion of Tyrconnel by William of Orange, nearly the whole of the land was confiscated, the peasants were made beggars and outlaws, the Penal Laws against

the Catholics were enacted and enforced, and the grand reign of Protestant Ascendancy began in all its vileness and completeness. The Protestants and landlords were supreme; the peasants and the Catholics were prostrate in despair. The Revolution brought about in Ireland just the reverse of what it effected in England. Here it delivered the body of the nation from the attempted supremacy of a small sect. There it made a small sect supreme over the body of the nation.[33]

Even in the last decade of the century, after a series of mild reforms, Burke could lament that sectarian differences kept the people of Ireland as much apart as if they were not only separate nations, but separate species. To complicate and intensify the differences in religion and the tyranny of the penal laws, Ireland, like the American colonies at a later date, was subjected to a commercial policy by which England severely restricted her industry and fettered her economic productivity to enrich Bristol and Manchester merchants. The greater part of the people of Ireland lived out their lives in extreme poverty, often without even the elemental necessities of life. This dual problem of religious and economic tyranny was further intensified in Burke's time by George III's assumption that his arbitrary will was the law of the land.

Since Ireland was much weaker than America and closer to England, the abstract "right" of the king and parliament to rule there by arbitrary will was far more successful and tyrannical, and was intensified by differences in religion. Burke observed that in his coronation oath "the king swears he will maintain . . . 'the laws of God.' I suppose it means the natural moral laws." Burke complained, nevertheless, that under English kings Ireland had suffered "penalties, incapacities, and proscriptions from generation to generation," and was "under a deprivation of all the rights of human nature." [34] Burke summarized the "vicious perfection" of the system by which England deprived her Irish subjects of their natural rights:

It was a complete system, full of coherence and consistency; well digested and well composed in all its parts. It was a machine of wise and elaborate contrivance; and as well fitted for the oppression, impoverishment, and degradation of a people, and the debasement in them of human nature itself, as ever proceeded from the perverted ingenuity of man.[35]

Those in Britain who wished to rule by arbitrary will found that the best means of depriving the Irish of the rights of nature was to exclude them from the protective benefits of the constitution. Burke objected strongly to this policy:

> Our constitution is not made for great, general, and proscriptive exclusions; sooner or later it will destroy them, or they will destroy the constitution. . . . This way of proscribing men by whole nations as it were, from all the benefits of the constitution to which they were born, I never can believe to be politic or expedient, much less necessary for the existence of any state or church in the world.[36]

The long-standing great political pretexts for exercising arbitrary power were that the Irish people were by nature turbulent, and that the authority of the English state had to be maintained. Burke denied the first charge, and said of the second: "The coercive authority of the state is limited to what is necessary for its existence." [37] This did not include the statutes of persecution against Irish liberty, property, trade and manufactures, nor the suppression of their education, professions, and religion. "Nothing can be more absurd and dangerous," wrote Burke, "than to tamper with the natural foundations of society in hopes of keeping it up by certain contrivances," and he appealed to Britain to "restore nature to its just rights and policy to its proper order." [38] Burke agreed with Dr. Johnson in hating England's stern debilitating policy against Ireland, and would have preferred to see the authority of the English government perish rather than be maintained by such iniquity.

Burke knew that the ultimate grounds for persecuting Ireland were religious, and in appealing to the Natural Law against the arbitrary will of rulers he defended the religious rights of Ireland's Catholics on the same grounds that he defended the Protestant Dissenters' claims of conscience in the Relief Bill of 1773. At that time Burke invoked "an author who is more spoken of than read, I mean Aristotle," and he applied the Greek philosopher's distinction between power and moral right: "Yes . . . you have the power; but you have not the

right" because "this bill is contrary to the eternal laws of right
and wrong—laws that ought to bind all men, and above all
men legislative assemblies." [39] Burke's attack on the English
government's failure in Irish affairs to distinguish between its
power and moral right, implies his belief in the Natural Law.
Except in Indian affairs, Burke's belief in the Natural Law is
perhaps nowhere more explicit than in the "Tract on the
Popery Laws," which resulted from his two winters in Dublin,
1761–1762 and 1763–1764. The time is important, because it
shows that the fundamental principles of Burke's political
philosophy were fixed in his mind even before he entered
British public life. In the "Tract on the Popery Laws"
the distinction between political power and moral right, between Hobbes's theory of arbitrary will and Cicero's "right
reason," underscores Burke's strong appeals to the Natural
Law:

It would be hard to point out any error more truly subversive of
all the order and beauty, of all the peace and happiness, of human
society than the position that any body of men have a right to make
what laws they please; or that laws can derive any authority from
their institution merely and independent of the quality of the
subject-matter. No arguments of policy, reason of state, or preservation of the constitution, can be pleaded in favour of such a practice.
They may, indeed, impeach the frame of that constitution; but can
never touch this immovable principle. This seems to be, indeed, the
principle which Hobbes broached in the last century, and which
was then so frequently and so ably refuted. Cicero exclaims with the
utmost indignation and contempt against such a notion; he con-
siders it not only as unworthy of a philosopher, but of an illiterate
peasant; that of all things this was the most truly absurd, to fancy
that the rule of justice was to be taken from the constitutions
of commonwealths, or that laws derived their authority from the
statutes of the people, the edicts of princes, or the decrees of judges.
. . . Everybody is satisfied that a conservation and secure enjoyment
of our natural rights is the great and ultimate purpose of civil society; and that therefore all forms whatsoever of government are
only good as they are subservient to that purpose to which they are
entirely subordinate. Now, to aim at the establishment of any form
of government by sacrificing what is the substance of it; to take
away, or at least to suspend, the rights of nature . . . is preposterous in argument . . . and cruel in its effect.[40]

The Hobbist theory of sovereignty, that the will of the state is the ultimate measurement of law, is nowhere more false, according to Burke, than in religion:

> Religion, to have any force on men's understandings, indeed to exist at all, must be supposed paramount to laws, and independent for its substance upon any human institution. Else it would be the absurdest thing in the world; an acknowledged cheat. Religion, therefore, is not believed because the laws have established it; but it is established because the leading part of the community have previously believed it to be true.[41]

In Ireland more than four-fifths of the people adhered to their inherited Catholicism: "This religion, which is so persecuted in its members, is the old religion of the country, and the once established religion of the state." Compared with a claim based on such historical prescription, wrote Burke, "An opinion at once new and persecuting is a monster." The whole of Burke's objection to such religious persecution, based on the theory that arbitrary legislative will, rather than Natural Law, is the foundation of social justice, is summarized in one sentence in his "Tract on the Popery Laws": "They have no right to make a law prejudicial to the whole community . . . because it would be made against the principle of a superior law, which it is not in the power of any community, or of the whole race of man, to alter.—I mean the will of Him who gave us our nature, and in giving impressed an invariable law upon it." [42] Nothing is more plain than that Burke's defense of religious conscience and freedom in Ireland rests on the Natural Law.

Burke applied the same Natural Law principles in attacking the economic restrictions and civil disabilities imposed upon Ireland. For Burke, the right of holding private property in Ireland, no less than that of following religious conscience, depended not upon the will of any legislators, but was secured "on the solid rock of prescription, the soundest, the most general, and the most recognized title between man and man . . . a title in which not arbitrary institutions, but the eternal order of things gives judgment; a title which is not the creature, but the master, of positive law; a title which . . . is rooted in its principle in the law of nature itself, and is, indeed, the original ground of all known property; for all property in

soil will always be traced to that source, and will rest there." [43]
The Irish penal laws which "disabled three-fourths of the inhabitants from acquiring any estate of inheritance for life," which
excluded Catholics from military service, the legal profession,
and all public offices, which prohibited any private or public
education and proscribed the clergy, were a total "depravation
of society," and Burke's arguments for their repeal are based
throughout on the eternal law of reason and general justice, the
Natural Law.

Had Burke's utilitarian critics read his "Tract on the Popery
Laws" with greater care, they would have found that in this
early work he expressly rejected the principle that utility is
the sole source, test, and ultimate foundation of thought. Although Burke had a principle of utility, he was no utilitarian.
He generally gave prior consideration to equity in law, because
the necessary legal means of achieving any social end had to
be grounded in the moral law before Burke would consider
the social consequences. The following passage proves that
for Burke both equity and utility were derived from "the substance of original justice," the Natural Law:

> In reality there are two, and only two, foundations of law; and
> they are both of them conditions without which nothing can give
> it any force: I mean equity and utility. With respect to the former,
> it grows out of the great rule of equality, which is grounded upon
> our common nature, and which Philo, with propriety and beauty,
> calls the mother of justice. All human laws are, properly speaking,
> only declaratory; they may alter the mode and application, but have
> no power over the substance of original justice. The other founda-
> tion of law, which is utility, must be understood, not of partial or
> limited, but of general and public utility, connected in the same
> manner with, and derived directly from, our rational nature; for any
> other utility may be the utility of a robber.[44]

To reinforce his assertion that "law is a mode of human action
respecting society and must be governed by the same rules of
equity which govern every private action," Burke quoted supporting passages from Cicero, Paulus, and Suarez. Throughout
his argument the primacy of equity to utility, and the subordination of both to Natural Law, is clearly evident.

Burke confessed that among the first thoughts that crossed

his mind on being elected to parliament in 1765 was the hope
that he might achieve some measure of justice for his native
land. His political career bears out his hope. The affairs of
Ireland called forth Burke's powers as a practical statesman on
several important occasions, and vitally influenced his own
career. Throughout his life Burke maintained a correspondence
with Irishmen such as Dr. Leland and Lord Kenmare, whose
major interest was religious emancipation, and he wrote private
and public letters to Edmund Pery, Thomas Burgh, William
Smith, and Sir Hercules Langrishe, all members of the Irish
parliament. Burke and Lord Nugent obtained some small commercial favors for Ireland in 1778, and further concessions
were made in 1779. Burke was instrumental in drawing up the
Savile Act of 1778, which eased restrictions on Catholics in
England and became the model for similar legislation in Ireland. In 1779–1780 the grievous restrictions on the Irish export
trade were repealed, and in 1782 additional economic and
religious disabilities were slightly lifted, and greater legislative
independence was achieved by the Irish parliament. Burke's
part in these reforms was auxiliary to the crisis brought on by
the American war, which compelled the English government
to conciliate Ireland. Burke's active attempt to "fix the principles of free trade in all the parts of these islands, as founded in
justice, and beneficial to the whole," cost him his Bristol con-
stituency in 1780, but he saw his principle fulfilled in 1785 in
Pitt's famous Irish propositions, based on Adam Smith's theory
of free trade. The French Revolution provoked another crisis
in Irish affairs. To the last month of his life Burke labored to
prevent Ireland from resorting to Jacobin principles of revolution. Burke's lifelong struggle to extend the benefits of equal
citizenship to Ireland under the British constitution is an important practical manifestation of his belief that Natural Law
supplied the ethical norms of every just society.

In practically every discussion of Burke's part in American
colonial affairs, it has been the universal opinion of positivist
scholars that against George III's claim of an abstract right to
tax the colonies, Burke took his stand almost completely on the
principle of utilitarian expediency, and that therefore he re-

jected all belief in "natural rights" based on the Natural Law.[45] Burke certainly did attack the metaphysical abstract "right" of taxation assumed by Townshend, Grenville, and Lord North, and his own words reveal precisely how far "expediency" applied in his attack:

I shall not now enquire into the right of Great Britain to tax her colonies; all that is lawful is not expedient, and I believe the inexpediency of taxing our colonies, even supposing it to be lawful, is now evident to every man.[46]

I am resolved this day to have nothing at all to do with the question of the right of taxation. . . . I put it totally out of the question. . . . I do not examine, whether the giving away a man's money be a power excepted and reserved out of the general trust of government; and how far all mankind, in all forms of polity, are entitled to an exercise of that right by the charter of nature. Or whether, on the contrary, a right of taxation is necessarily involved in the general principle of legislation, and inseparable from the ordinary supreme power. These are deep questions, where great names militate against each other; where reason is perplexed; and an appeal to authorities only thickens the confusion. For high and reverend authorities lift up their heads on both sides; and there is no sure footing in the middle. This point is the 'great Serbonian bog, betwixt Damiata and Mount Casius old, where armies whole have sunk.' I do not intend to be overwhelmed in that bog, though in such respectable company.[47]

The first passage reveals that expediency was an important practical element in Burke's attack, while the second shows that Burke believed in the existence of rights under "the charter of nature," but that out of fear of a useless quarrel in metaphysics, he did not wish to discuss the American problem in terms of "rights." Nothing could be more false than the conclusion of Morley and the "respectable company" of critics who have followed him that these passages prove Burke made "expediency" the complete antithesis of "natural rights," that he rested his case on expediency and therefore denied all belief in Natural Law. Later we shall see that Burke's "expediency" is not the expediency of the utilitarian calculator, but a manifestation of moral prudence, which is not contrary to the Natural Law, but an essential part of its practical fulfillment.

Certainly the American colonies never considered it merely "inexpedient" to be taxed without their legislative consent. To them, as to Burke, the abstract "right" of taxation without representation was positively unjust. It was a constant threat to or actual violation of their property rights, and the attempt to enforce unjust taxation resulted in threats to their lives and liberty under the British constitution which they, like Burke, believed was founded on Natural Law:

> It is the glory of the British Prince and the happiness of all his subjects that their constitution hath its foundation in the immutable laws of nature; and as the supreme legislature, as well as the supreme executive, derives its authority from that constitution, it should seem that no laws can be made or executed which are repugnant to any essential law of nature.[48]

This memorable appeal to Natural Law was spoken by James Otis in 1768. Whereas the colonists, in their petitions of grievances, came more and more to appeal directly to the Natural Law, Burke's appeals were almost always indirect, through the British constitution, which was for him merely the practical means of guaranteeing the "rights" of Natural Law throughout the empire: "Our constitution," Burke said in parliament, "was a provident system, formed of several bodies, for securing the rights, the liberties, the persons and the properties of the people." [49] In both domestic and American affairs Burke felt that George III and his ministers, in trying to make the power of the Crown supreme, had placed their arbitrary will above the constitution and therefore had violated the sovereignty of Natural Law: "The same baneful influence," said Burke in 1770, "under which this country is governed, is extended to our fellow sufferers in America; the constitutional rights of Englishmen are invaded . . ." and the "unalienable rights of their constituents" are defeated by "ministerial requisitions that are altogether arbitrary and unjust." [50] In February 1772, Burke said in parliament: "When tyranny is extreme, and abuses of government intolerable, men resort to the rights of nature to shake it off." [51] Burke regretted and opposed the arbitrary principles and policies of the king, and favored the

American cause not because the colonists had an abstract "right" to rebel against British rule, as Tom Paine and Dr. Price had argued, but because Britain had imprudently invoked its sovereign power as an abstract "right" to tax and rule the colonists by arbitrary decrees, and above all, because the king and parliament were themselves in rebellion against rules of prudence in the Natural Law by their denial of the colonists' civil rights under the constitution.

Burke saw that constitutional liberty in England would stand or fall upon the outcome of the struggle with America, that if the British government succeeded in destroying liberty abroad, Englishmen would soon have none at home. In March 1775, he said: "In order to prove that the Americans have no right to their liberties, we are every day endeavouring to subvert the maxims which preserve the whole spirit of our own." [52] Before seeing how the king's "oppressive stretches of power" in America were paralleled in Britain, it will be useful to summarize Burke's reactions to the arbitrary decrees passed against the colonies. In March 1774, the Boston Port Bill was passed, taking away the city's trade and in effect revoking its charter. Burke promptly attacked it: "I call this bill unjust, for is it not fundamentally unjust to prevent the parties who have offended from being heard in their own defence. Justice . . . is not to be measured by geographical lines nor distances." Such an act, he added in private, is "the doctrine of devils"; it is "contrary to the nature of man and the nature of things." "Franchises," he continued, "are for the preservation of men's liberties, properties, and lives. . . . It is bad to take away a charter; it is worse to take away a city." Such a "proscription of whole cities and provinces is to take away from them benefits of nature . . . deprive them of their civil privileges, and . . . strip them of their judicial rights." When the bill was extended to all New England, Burke again objected: "You sentence . . . to famine at least 300,000 people in two provinces, at the mere arbitrary will and pleasure of two men." In short, these acts of parliament toward America "take away the rights of men" and prove that when power becomes arbitrary, when legislative authority is placed above constitutional and Natural law, "a man may be regulated out of his liberty, his property and his life." [53] As with British rule in Ireland, Burke charged that in her American policy Britain was "endeavouring to invert the order of nature," and that her claimed "right" to rule the colonies by arbitrary decrees was totally opposed to the British constitution and Natural Law.

Burke's practical endeavors to restrict the arbitrary powers of the king and to preserve civil liberty in America are among the best-known episodes of his political career. Almost from the moment he entered parliament in 1765 he was absorbed in American affairs, and as the intellectual guide and manager of the Rockingham Whigs he did more than any other man to make his colleagues and the British public aware of the fatal course they were following. The one measure of tax relief enjoyed by America in the decade before the Revolution was passed by the short-lived Rockingham administration of 1766, which repealed Grenville's odious Stamp Act. It was on this occasion that Burke, in his first appearance in the House of Commons, revealed his political greatness. On March 9, 1766, Dr. Johnson wrote of Burke's initial speech: "He has gained more reputation than perhaps any man at his first appearance ever gained before. He made two speeches in the House for repealing the Stamp Act, which were publicly commended by Mr. Pitt, and have filled the town with wonder. Mr. Burke is a great man by nature, and is expected soon to attain civil greatness." [54] From 1766 until the conclusion of hostilities with America Burke continued to fill the political world with wonder. In pamphlets such as his early masterpiece *Thoughts on the Cause of the Present Discontents* (1770), in parliamentary speeches such as his *Speech on Conciliation* (1775), and in public essays such as his *Letter to the Sheriffs of Bristol* (1777), Burke struggled to maintain the natural rights of Americans under English constitutional law. In 1771 Burke became the agent in parliament for the colony of New York. Through this post he acquired a complete mastery of details and knowledge of the civil temper of the colonists, which he utilized throughout his exposition of constitutional and Natural Law principles. Burke's writings on American affairs received Morley's unqualified admiration:

"It is no exaggeration to say that they compose the most perfect manual in our literature, or any literature, for one who approaches the study of public affairs, whether for knowledge or for practice." [55] Despite the eloquence and wisdom of Burke's efforts on America's behalf, he did not succeed in convincing the British public that great empires can best endure when grounded upon the solid foundation of constitutional and Natural law. The principles Burke taught were learned from the bitter lessons of history; afterwards, his words remained as a constant reminder and depository of political wisdom for those who were to rule the British Empire in the nineteenth century.

In the spring of 1768 began the first great domestic constitutional issue to arise after Burke entered parliament—the Wilkes affair. In 1764 John Wilkes had been convicted of publishing an inflammatory pamphlet, the famous *North Briton, Number Forty-five,* but he had fled to France to escape sentence. Wilkes returned to England in 1768 and was elected to the House of Commons for Middlesex, but before he took his seat the court sent him to prison on his old conviction. In November 1768, Wilkes appeared before the House to plead his innocence and to be admitted as a member, but the House voted 219 to 136 to expel him. Wilkes was elected twice more for Middlesex and each time was immediately voted out of the House. When he was elected for the fourth time, the House of Commons, over the opposition of the Middlesex freeholders' petition, ordered that Wilkes's defeated opponent, Colonel Luttrell, be declared elected and seated. In "the rights of election invaded in Middlesex," and in the king's refusal to grant redress to the freeholders' petition, Burke saw a deep threat to free elections under the constitution:

I stand up to . . . bear my testimony to its injustice, as well as to its inexpediency; to support the unquestionable birthright of the British subject, and to defend the sanctity of our laws. . . . They [the London freeholders] could neither prostitute their parts nor their principles to the arbitrary fiat of an all-directing favourite. . . . Till the sacred right of election, wrested from their hands, filled the freeholders of Great Britain with universal apprehension for

their liberties, they never disturbed the royal repose with their com-
plaints. . . . By what rule, then, does the majority of this House
square its conduct, when it acts in direct opposition to the majority
of the people? . . . That the people should not choose their own
representatives, is a saying that shakes the constitution. . . . The
question amounts to this, whether you mean to be a legal tribunal,
or an arbitrary and despotic assembly. . . . The substance of the
question is, to put bounds to your own power by the rules and principles of law.[56]

Burke knew that given good reason the House had the right to
expel a member, but it had no constitutional authority to alter
the election results, nor to seat the defeated candidate. For the
Commons to declare any elected member unworthy at its
arbitrary discretion "is to corrupt judicature into legislature."
Burke drew out the logical implication in the Commons' claim:
"Whatever it decides is *de jure* law." Burke then concluded:
"Nobody will, I hope, assert this, because the direct consequence
would be the entire extinction of the difference between true
and false judgments. For if the judgment makes the law, and
not the law directs the judgment, it is impossible there should
be such a thing as an illegal judgment given." [57] The main
thesis of a theory of sovereignty based on will rather than on
law is that a *de facto* judgment is *de jure* law, and Burke's opposition to the king and Commons in the Wilkes affair proves
that he did not believe a law was good because government
willed it, but that government was morally obliged to will only
that which was good. The ethical code of the Natural Law and
the legal traditions of the English constitution provided Burke
with the normative standards of what government should or
should not will.

The most important domestic constitutional issue during the
last three decades of the eighteenth century was the growing
popular agitation for a shorter duration of parliaments and a
greater extension of the franchise. Nothing so illustrates Burke's
veneration of the British constitution as a prescriptive instrument perfectly suited to fulfill the functions of just government
as his refusal to set aside experience in favor of radical innovation. "The great object of most of these reformers," Burke
declared on May 7, 1782, "is to prepare the destruction of the
constitution, by disgracing and discrediting the House of Com-

mons." Burke noted that by far the largest segment of these reformers made their plea "in the nature of a claim of right, on the supposed rights of man as man." In a highly significant passage, Burke analyzed the claim that personal representation in government is a "natural right":

They who plead an absolute right cannot be satisfied with anything short of personal representation, because all *natural* rights must be the rights of individuals, as by *nature* there is no such thing as politic or corporate personality: all these ideas are mere fictions of law, they are creatures of voluntary institution; men as men are individuals, and nothing else. They, therefore, who reject the principle of natural and personal representation are essentially and eternally at variance with those who claim it. As to the first sort of reformers, it is ridiculous to talk to them of the British constitution upon any or upon all of its bases; for they lay it down that every man ought to govern himself, and that, where he cannot go, himself, he must send his representative; that all other government is usurpation, and in so far from having a claim to our obedience, it is not only our right, but our duty, to resist it. Nine tenths of the reformers argue thus—that is, on the natural right.[58]

In attacking the reformers' claim that personal representation is a "natural right," Burke was not rejecting the natural rights of the classical and Scholastic Natural Law, as so many critics have supposed; he was merely denying one of the many false and arbitrary claims put forth during the eighteenth century in the name of "natural right." Burke also was distinguishing between *civil* and *natural* rights, not in order to reject natural rights, as MacCunn supposed, but to show that the franchise belongs to the civil order. The franchise was a derivative right, not of man as man, but of man as citizen. The conditions under which it was exercised were determined by the constitution and the civil conventions of any given society. Therefore, the reformers' claim of an abstract "right" of representation, paramount to the constitution itself, was a revolutionary innovation. As the English constitution was itself based upon the traditional Natural Law, Burke's attack on the false claims of revolutionary "natural rights" was a direct defense of the prescriptive English constitution and an indirect defense of the traditional Natural Law.

Burke's most cherished belief concerning the British con-

stitution was that it was the largest national moral frame of
reference for judging Englishmen's political behavior, and that
it was derived from and in harmony with the Natural Law.
In Burke's criticism of Pitt's Regency Bill (1790), he asserted
that in the hierarchy of moral and legal values, the constitution
stood just below the Natural Law: "The framers of it [Pitt's
Bill] first proceeded to a violation of precedents, next to a
violation of law, then to a violation of the constitution, and
now they had arrived at a climax of violence; a violation of the
law of nature." The greatest single "right" of nature which
the constitution sought to protect was that of life: "As self-
preservation in the individuals is the first law of nature, the
same will prevail in societies." And again: "Defence is the
natural right of man,—nay, the first of all his rights, and which
comprehends them all." [59] From the absolute natural right to
life Burke derived those civil rights which were necessary and
convenient to men's social existence, particularly liberty and
property, and these in turn were the basis of other lesser civil
rights, such as protection from libel: "Undoubtedly the good
name of every man ought to be under the protection of the
laws, as well as his life, and liberty and property." The highly
whimsical English laws on libel, Burke thought, should be
made to reflect more closely the spirit of the Natural Law:
"It is high time to fix the law in such manner as to resemble,
as it ought, the great Author of all law, in whom there is no
variableness nor shadow of turning." [60] The British constitution
established the basic rights of nature, and all derived civil
rights, by protecting all men equally from the encroachments
of arbitrary power. As Burke said, it set limits to power by
saying to rulers and ruled alike, "Thus far shalt thou go, and
no farther."

Burke's eulogy of the British constitution reveals it as the
great bulwark guarding the traditional rights of man against
arbitrary power:

The constitution . . . says to an encroaching prerogative,—your
sceptre has its length, you cannot add an hair to your head, or a
gem to your crown, but what an eternal law has given to it. Here it
says to an overweening peerage,—your pride finds banks that it

cannot overflow: here to a tumultuous and giddy people,—there is a bound to the raging sea. Our constitution is like our island, which uses and restrains its subject sea; in vain the waves roar. In that constitution I know, and exultingly I feel, both that I am free, and that I am not free dangerously to myself or to others. I know that no power on earth, acting as I ought to do, can touch my life, my liberty, or my property.[61]

The constitution was therefore necessarily opposed to *all* claims to absolute or arbitrary power, whether that of the king against the colonies, that of the Lords against the people, of the Commons against Wilkes, of Pitt against the king in his illness, and of such advocates of popular power as Tom Paine, Dr. Price, and Dr. Priestley against constituted limited monarchy. Nor did it make any difference to Burke that any of these persons or groups claimed such power by an appeal to "rights," as did both George III and Paine. "Strict right," said Burke, "must necessarily be arbitrary, and could admit of no modification." As in Irish and American affairs, Burke sought to limit arbitrary power in England's domestic and constitutional conflicts, so that man's basic natural rights to life, liberty, and property under the Natural Law would be maintained. The whole issue in Burke's objective is contained in one sentence: "Arbitrary power . . . is a subversion of natural justice, a violation of the inherent rights of mankind." [62]

No connection has ever been noted between Burke's views on economics and his belief in the Natural Law. In his *Letter to a Noble Lord* Burke confessed that he had studied "political economy" from early youth to the end of his service in parliament, but as economics was a new subject Burke never acquired a fully developed theory of it. Most scholars, following a strong hint from Adam Smith, have claimed that Burke simply believed in the laissez faire principles of Smith's *Wealth of Nations* (1776),[63] while Halévy and Laski thought they found utilitarianism at the heart of Burke's economic principles.[64] Burke certainly adhered to three vital and closely related principles in Smith's theory—free trade, the "natural identity of interests," and the passive or negative function of the state in individual economic relationships—but it is nonsense to claim from this that Burke was a Benthamite in economics. Bentham was indeed the logical heir of Smith's theory, but Burke's understanding of these three principles, centered in the Natural Law, was vitally different from that of Bentham and even from Smith himself.

In Burke's thought, free trade was not based upon utility but on justice: "But that to which I attached myself the most particularly," Burke declared, "was to fix *the principle* of a free trade in all the ports of these islands, as founded in justice, and beneficial to the whole." To Burke justice was the foundation and social utility was the consequence of free trade, a position the reverse of Bentham's utilitarianism. Burke attacked the "zealots of the sect of regulation" not on utilitarian grounds, nor because he believed in the natural goodness of man in economic affairs, but because natural justice took precedence in economic liberty over any restraints or controls imposed by the state. Burke favored a large measure of personal liberty in economics, a full use of the natural faculties which God has given to all mankind. In Indian affairs Burke came to see the need of state intervention because personal liberty had been converted by the East India Company agents into a limitless avarice. But there was a clear distinction between necessary regulation and arbitrary suppression of trade. The East India Company confounded being controlled with being suppressed, and criticized Burke as an enemy of free trade; Burke's Bristol constituents defended the suppression of Irish trade as necessary control, and rejected Burke's argument for free trade.

To appreciate Burke's position toward India and Ireland, and to see how his economic principles were consistently centered in Natural Law, it is necessary to understand Burke's conception of wealth. Burke rejected totally the Rousseauist theory, shared by Bentham and some of his Bristol constituents, that wealth was limited in quantity, that the enrichment of one man or nation necessarily impoverished others:

I know that it is but too natural for us to see our own *certain* ruin in the *possible* prosperity of other people. It is hard to persuade us that everything which is *got* by another is not *taken* from ourselves. But it is fit that we should get the better of these suggestions, which come from what is not the best and soundest part of our nature, and that we should form to ourselves a way of thinking more rational, more just, and more religious. Trade is not a limited thing: as if the objects of our mutual demand and consumption could not stretch beyond the bounds of our jealousies. God has given the earth to the children of men, and He has undoubtedly, in giving it to them, given them what is abundantly sufficient for all their exigencies: not a scanty, but a most liberal, provision for them all. The Author of our nature has written it strongly in that nature, and has promulgated the same law in His written word, that man shall eat his bread by his labor; and I am persuaded that no man, and no combination of men, for their own ideas of their particular profit, can, without great impiety, undertake to say that he shall not do so—that they have no sort of right either to prevent the labor or to withhold the bread.[65]

In economic affairs Burke posited a faith in God's providential nature toward man; the ultimate foundation of Burke's economic theory rests not in any human contrivances but in the Natural Law.

There is no doubt that Burke believed in a divinely directed "natural" identity of self-interests and social benevolence in economic affairs: "The benign and wise Disposer of all things . . . obliges men, whether they will or not, in pursuing their own selfish interests, to connect the general good with their own individual success." [66] Yet Burke was not an optimistic economic determinist; he was simply more convinced than most men that in economic affairs the power of man's reason and will is strongly circumscribed by both physical and moral natural laws. Because God has established "the nature of things with which we shall in vain contend," in economic self-fulfillment man's institutions play a role secondary to nature:

To provide for us in our necessities is not in the power of government. It would be vain presumption in statesmen to think they can do it. The people maintain them, and not they the people. It is in the power of government to prevent much evil; it can do very little positive good in this, or perhaps in anything else.[67]

Burke certainly knew that political power is very important in regulating human affairs, that it is the final court of practical appeal in disputes, but he also understood that "the nature of things is a sturdy adversary," that fixed created conditions of environment and resources had far more to do with determining man's economic happiness or misery than any human contrivances. As Burke said in the *Reflections*, "I do not like to compliment the contrivances of men with what is due in a great degree to the bounty of Providence." This distinction, habitually ignored by rationalists, was obscured in the economic crisis which struck Britain in 1794 and 1795 and which called forth various "projects" to manipulate the economy. To combat these schemes Burke wrote "Thoughts and Details on Scarcity" (1795), in which he explicitly stated his belief that economics rests upon Natural Law:

> We, the people, ought to be made sensible, that it is not in breaking the laws of commerce, which are the laws of nature, and consequently the laws of God, that we are to place our hope of softening the Divine displeasure to remove any calamity under which we suffer.[68]

God's reason and will, which Burke called "the law of laws and the sovereign of sovereigns," applies in economics as in everything, and Burke believed that man's part in fulfilling a sound economy was clearly subordinated to the Natural Law.

Burke's speeches in Indian affairs reveal his legal erudition at its best and also provide the clearest expression of the Natural Law in his political philosophy. Burke was actively concerned in the affairs of India from at least March 21, 1780, when he spoke on the renewal of the East India Company's charter, until April 23, 1795, when Hastings was acquitted. His first important appeal to the Natural Law occurred on December 1, 1783, in his speech supporting Fox's East India Bill. "This bill," Burke said, was "intended to form the Magna Charta of Hindostan," yet he noted that those who opposed it did so on the grounds "that the bill is an attack on the chartered rights of men." [69] Here, for the first of several times in Indian affairs, he made a vital distinction between what he considered the true "natural rights" derived from the classical and Scholastic Natural Law, and false or arbitrary claims to "rights." Because the word "rights" was an abstraction, and subject to various interpretations, Burke approached his problem semantically. "The phrase of 'the chartered rights of men,' " he noted, "is very unusual in the discussion of privileges conferred by charters of the present description." All previous charters, he continued, such as those of King John and Henry III, "may, without any deceitful ambiguity, be very fitly called *the chartered rights of men*," because they are merely written documents expressly recognizing the sanctity of the Natural Law, to which all public measures should conform:

The rights of men, that is to say, the natural rights of mankind, are, indeed, sacred things; and if any public measure is proved mischievously to affect them, the objection ought to be fatal to that measure, even if no charter at all could be set up against it. If these natural rights are further affirmed and declared by express covenants, if they are clearly defined and secured against chicane, against power and authority, by written instruments and positive engagements, they are in a still better condition: They partake not only of the sanctity of the object so secured, but of that solemn public faith itself, which secures an object of such importance. Indeed, this formal recognition, by the sovereign power, of an original right in the subject, can never be subverted, but by rooting up the holding radical principles of government, and even of society itself.[70]

But, Burke remarked, "the charter of the East India Company" is "formed on principles the *very reverse* of those of the great charter." He elaborates this crucial point:

Magna Charta is a charter to restrain power, and to destroy monopoly. The East India charter is a charter to establish monopoly, and to create power. Political power and commercial monopoly are *not* the rights of men; and the rights of them derived from charters, it is fallacious and sophistical to call 'the chartered rights of men.' These chartered rights . . . do at least suspend the natural rights of mankind at large; and in their very frame and constitution, are liable to fall into a direct violation of them.[71]

If the East India Company had governed in India "under the controul of the sovereign imperial discretion, and with the due observance of the natural and local law," Burke would have opposed revoking its charter. But the company refused to recognize the Natural Law and the local laws of India, which guaranteed the natives' rights; it insisted that the charter

granted by parliament left its officials free to govern India as
they saw fit. The company, Burke concluded, had violated its
"subordinate derivative trust," had "notoriously, grossly abused"
its power; parliament could not stand by in total indifference
to the moral law, nor make a sale of its duties, but should adopt
Fox's bill and "provide a real chartered security for the *rights
of men* cruelly violated under that charter." [72] For Burke the
issue was of conflicting claims to sovereignty, and his choice is
clear: "If I kept faith . . . with the Company," he said, "I
must break the faith, the covenant, the solemn, original, indispensable oath, in which I am bound, by the eternal frame
and constitution of things, to the whole human race." Burke's
eloquent appeal to the "natural rights" of traditional Natural
Law enabled him, in his first great attack on abuses in India,
to transcend the commercial and national powers which sacrificed human rights to a narrow self-interest.

In February 1785, two years after Fox's bill had been rejected
in the House of Lords, Burke made his famous speech exposing
the hoax of the Nabob of Arcot's debts. [73] There is only one
appeal to nature in this long speech, but it is an explicit defense
of the enduring character of Natural Law:

> The benefits of heaven to any community ought never to be con-
> nected with political arrangements, or made to depend on the per-
> sonal conduct of princes. . . . The means of subsistence of man-
> kind should be as immutable as the laws of nature, let power and
> dominion take what course they may. [74]

In a short speech in March 1787 Burke made a general protest
against those in parliament who wished to obstruct Hastings'
impeachment: "I rise in support of the eternal principles of
truth and justice, and those who cannot or dare not support
them are endeavouring to cough them down." Hastings had
a small group of powerful friends, most of whom were skilled
lawyers, and they succeeded in throwing up an endless series
of legal impediments to keep the impeachment from coming
to an issue. "The greatest obstruction of all," Burke lamented,
"proceeded from the body of the law. There was no body of

men for whom he entertained a greater respect . . . for the profession itself he felt a degree of veneration, approaching almost to idolatry." However, when the lawyers among the opposition tried to invalidate the impeachment by dissolving parliament, Burke protested: "These gentlemen of the law, driving us from law to law, would, in the end, leave us no law at all." As Burke wrote to Dundas in December 1787, these obstructions were further complicated because "all the local knowledge of India is in the hands of the person prosecuted by the House of Commons," and Hastings had suppressed or destroyed the main sources of information. Burke secured a large body of detailed evidence on India from Philip Francis, Hastings' mortal enemy and prejudiced accuser, and also from the records of the India House. But as manager of the impeachment Burke took his stand against Hastings mainly on the Natural Law, and Hastings himself supplied Burke with material for his most severe indictments.

Burke made it clear that Hastings' defense ultimately rested on the argument that he had the right to rule India through arbitrary power. Hastings claimed this right on two accounts; first, because parliament, through the East India Company, had granted him unlimited power to rule in India, and second, as Burke summarized him, because "the whole history of Asia is nothing more than precedents to prove the invariable exercise of arbitrary power." [75] Throughout his impeachment speeches Burke frequently reminded his hearers of Hastings' claim:

Mr. Hastings comes before you . . . he says, 'I had arbitrary power to exercise, and I exercised it. Slaves I found the people, slaves they are; they are so by their constitution; I did not make it for them; I was unfortunately bound to exercise it, and I did exercise it. . . .' In India, to use the words of Mr. Hastings, the power of the sovereign was everything, the rights of the people nothing. . . . The prisoner . . . assumes to exercise a power which extended to the property, liberty, and life of the subject. . . . He makes the corrupt practices of mankind the principles of his government; he collects together the vicious examples of all the robbers and plunderers of Asia, forms the mass of their abuses into a code, and calls it the duty of a British governor.[76]

As manager for the prosecution, Burke saw that he was obliged to destroy Hastings' assumption that sovereignty rested solely in a governor's arbitrary will, a principle which totally contradicted the ethical norms of Natural Law.

Burke's most extended and eloquent attack on Hastings' claim of arbitrary power, made on February 16, 1788, derives wholly from his ardent faith in Natural Law:

Will you ever hear the rights of mankind made subservient to the practice of government? It will be your lordships' duty and joy— it will be your pride and triumph, to teach men, that they are to conform their practice to principles, and not to derive their principles from the wicked, corrupt, and abominable practices of any man whatever. Where is the man that ever before dared to mention the practice of all the villains, of all the notorious depredators, as his justification? To gather up, and put it all into one code, and call it the duty of a British governor? I believe so audacious a thing was never before attempted by man. 'He had arbitrary power!' My lords, the East India Company have not arbitrary power to give him. The king has no arbitrary power to give. Neither your lordships, nor the Commons, nor the whole legislature, have arbitrary power to give. Arbitrary power is a thing which no man can give. My lords, no man can govern himself by his own will; much less can he be governed by the will of others. We are all born—high as well as low —governors as well as governed—in subjection to one great, immutable, pre-existing law, a law prior to all our devices and all our conspiracies, paramount to our feelings, by which we are connected in the eternal frame of the universe, and out of which we cannot stir. This great law does not arise from our combinations and compacts; on the contrary, it gives to them all the sanction they can have. Every good and perfect gift is of God: all power is of God; and He who has given the power, and from whom alone it originates, will never suffer it to be corrupted. Therefore, my lords, if this be true—if this great gift of government be the greatest and best that was ever given by God to mankind, will he suffer it to be the plaything of man, who would place his own feeble and ridiculous will on the throne of divine justice? It is not to be overturned by conquest; for by conquest, which is the more immediate designation of the hand of God, the conqueror succeeds to that alone which belonged to the sovereign before him. He cannot have absolute power by succession; he cannot have it by compact; for the people cannot covenant themselves out of their duty to their rights. . . .[77]

The whole of Burke's argument against Hastings' theory of sovereignty is contained in a few aphorisms infused with the Natural Law: "Law and arbitrary power are at eternal hostility. . . . We should be brought back to our original situation; we should be made to know ourselves as men born under law. He that would substitute will in the place of law is a public enemy to the world . . . against law, no power can be set up." "There never was a man who thought he had no law but his own will, who did not also find that he had no ends but his own profit." [78] To Burke, who maintained that since the introduction of the Roman law into Britain "the law of nature and nations (always a part of the law of England) came to be cultivated," nothing could be more destructive of the ethical norm necessary for a just society than Hastings' theory of sovereignty based upon arbitrary will.

Hastings' claim that arbitrary power was the normal mode of rule in Asia implied that there was no universal law of just conduct on essential principles, as taught by the Natural Law. Burke emphatically rejected such a contention:

This gentleman has formed a geographical morality, by which the duties of men in public and private stations are not to be governed by their relation to the great Governor of the universe, and by their relation to one another, but by climates. After you have crossed the equinoxal line, all the virtues die. . . . Against this geographical morality I do protest, and declare therefore, that Mr. Hastings shall not screen himself under it, because . . . the laws of morality are the same everywhere; and actions that are stamped with the character of peculation, extortion, oppression, and barbarity in England, are so in Asia, and the world over. [79]

Burke's great sympathy for the people of India was only exceeded by his fear that Hastings' friends, in defending him, would introduce his "Eastern" principles into England: "The doctrine that in the East there are no laws, no rights, no liberties, is a doctrine which has not only been stated by the prisoner at the bar, but has been disseminated with a wicked activity throughout this country." Burke valued his public services in Indian affairs above anything else in his career, because in

addition to his primary aim of bringing Hastings to justice
and reclaiming national honor, Burke wished to destroy the
corrupting influence against the constitution which the English
nabobs had come to exercise in parliament. Although Hastings
was acquitted and later came to be held in high honor, Burke
purified parliament of Hastings' Eastern morality and raised
the moral level of British colonial policy abroad. These larger
derivative consequences of Hastings' trial were enormously
important in preserving Britain's constitutional liberty and
colonial supremacy.

To disprove Hastings' contention that morality varied in
time and place, Burke read widely in Oriental jurisprudence.
He read the *Koran,* the *Shasta,* and the *Heyada;* he quoted
Tamerlane's *Institutes,* recently translated by Major Davy,
Hastings' former secretary; he used Joseph White's translations
of the *Institutes of Timour* (Oxford, 1783), and Jean Baptiste
Tavernier's *Travels into Persia and the East Indies* (1677).
Burke placed the results of his reading before the House of
Lords: "The morality of the East, my lords, as far as respects
governors, is as pure as our own. . . . Mr. Hastings finds no
authority for his practice, either in the Koran or in the Gentoo
law. . . . The same laws, the same sacredness of principle,
however they may be disobeyed, both in Europe and in Asia,
are held and strictly maintained." Burke finally concluded:

> Mr. Hastings has no refuge—let him run from law to law; let him
> fly from common law, and the sacred institutions of the country in
> which he was born; let him fly from acts of parliament . . . still
> the Mohammedan law condemns him . . . let him fly where he will
> —from law to law—law, thank God, meets him everywhere—arbi-
> trary power cannot secure him against law; and I would as soon
> have him tried on the Koran, or any other eastern code of laws, as
> on the common law of this kingdom.[80]

Against Hastings' theory of geographical morality and arbitrary
power, Burke set the traditional conception of Natural Law,
and like all of his predecessors back to Aristotle he insisted that
its imperative ethical norms are universally valid.

Since Hastings' acts were, in Burke's words, "crimes . . .
against those eternal laws of justice which you [the judges] are

assembled here to assert," it was necessary for his prosecutors to follow "rules drawn from the fountain of justice," and to condemn him in terms of the eternal Natural Law. "I impeach him," said Burke, "in the name and by the virtue of those eternal laws of justice, which ought equally to pervade every age, condition, rank, and situation in the world." Burke believed that the function of courts of law was to reflect through human institutions the spirit of the divine Natural Law: "Courts of justice were links of that great chain of which the first and great link was Divine Justice." Despite the fact that many parts of Burke's speeches were reported in the third person, and give only an approximate idea of his principles and argument, nothing is clearer than that the appeal to Natural Law is at the heart of his impeachment of Hastings:

> Mr. Burke next entered into a disquisition upon the nature of government, of which we lament our inability to give an adequate idea; but we will endeavour . . . to give the general scope of his reasoning. He first laid it down as a general principle, that all law and all sovereignty were derived from Heaven; for if the laws of every nation, from the most simple and social of the most barbarous people, up to the wisest and most salutary laws of the most refined and enlightened societies, from the Divine laws handed down to us in Holy Writ, down to the meanest forms of earthly institution, were attentively examined, they would be found to breathe but one spirit, one principle, equal distributive justice between man and man, and the protection of one individual from the encroachments of the rest. The universality of this principle proved its origin. Out of this principle laws arose, for the execution of which sovereignty was established; and all, viz. that principle, those laws, and that sovereignty, were thus evidently derived from God. . . . If, then, laws and sovereignty were sacred, as being the gift of God for the benefit of the people; and if the laws and sovereignty of India were, as he contended them to be, founded upon the same principle of universal justice, then Mr. Hastings, as a British governor, sent, not to conquer or extirpate, but to preserve and cherish, was bound to protect the people of that country in the use of those laws, and shield that sovereignty from encroachment or usurpation.[81]

Since the East India Company was a state in the disguise of a merchant, Burke's strictures on Hastings' violations of Natural Law principles and sovereignty were doubly significant, because he believed that above all other men legislators stood in the place of God and were accountable to Him in the practical uses of political power, and were therefore most bound by the moral dictates of the Natural Law. To understand the deepest implications to Burke's political philosophy in his lifelong devotion to the Natural Law, one must examine his reaction to the French Revolution.

IV. Burke and the Natural Law in French Affairs—1789–1797

In 1769, exactly two decades before the French Revolution, Burke had predicted in his *Observations on "The Present State of the Nation"* that the chronically desperate financial condition of France would culminate in "some extraordinary convulsion" that would shake the whole system of government and would have a tremendous effect on all Europe. In 1789 Burke was the first public man in Britain to realize that the revolution was far more than an alteration in the government of France. Burke wrote to his son in November 1792 that the revolution was "an event which has nothing to match it, or in the least to resemble it, in history." He felt that the revolution violated "the whole system of policy on which the general state of Europe has hitherto stood," that the revolutionists tried to make themselves "paramount to every known principle of public law in Europe," and that they sought to establish "principles subversive of the whole political, civil, and religious system of Europe." In 1796 Burke summarized his impressions of the strange and powerful effect the revolution had produced on men's imaginations; he found it "a vast, tremendous, unformed spectre" which "subdued the fortitude of man," and went "straight forward to its end, unappaled by peril, unchecked by remorse, despising all common maxims and all common means." For Burke 1789 was "a revolution in dogma"; it was "a total departure . . . from every one of the ideas and usages, religious, legal, moral, or social, of this civilized world." [82] So catastrophic was the French Revolution that it compelled Burke, against his will and temperament, to become a political theorist in defense of the traditional principles of civilized society, among which the Natural Law held a pre-eminent position.

Throughout Burke's writings on French revolutionary affairs, more often than not his belief in the Natural Law was implicitly assumed, and supplied the spirit that permeates all of his references to God and discussions of religion, society, Church, and State, the nature of the social contract, political sovereignty, and the security of private and corporate liberty and property. It is too frequently forgotten that Burke's initial response to the French Revolution, revealed in October 1789 in his "Letter to M. Dupont on the French Revolution," was warm-hearted, cautious, and friendly.[83] In this letter Burke expressed his unwillingness to form a positive opinion upon matters with which he was imperfectly acquainted. He agreed with his young friend's hope that the French deserved liberty, and stated that if, under the new order of things, law is made paramount to will, if prescriptive rights to life, liberty, and property are maintained, if civil liberty is regarded as man's birthright rather than the reward of merit or industry, as something inherent in man rather than a favor granted from the state, or a subject for endless metaphysical speculations about political power and social systems, he would look with favor upon the revolution.[84]

True liberty, Burke cautioned, is "not solitary, unconnected, individual, selfish liberty, as if every man was to regulate the whole of his conduct by his own will." Such "liberty" was but another name for arbitrary power, such as George III had claimed over the colonies or Hastings over India, and Burke knew it could not be reconciled to civil liberty under Natural Law. Like Aristotle, Burke believed man was by nature a political animal, so that true liberty must be "social freedom," a condition which required restriction on raw will and prevented anyone from exercising arbitrary power. Such liberty, said Burke to his young friend, was but another name for justice, and was consonant with the supremacy of Natural Law, of right reason over the "dangerous dominion of will." If in France he found that "the citizen . . . is in a perfect state of legal security with regard to his life, to his property, to the uncontrolled disposal of his person," he would share the general joy in such a revolution.

Burke's hope for France lasted less than four months. By the beginning of 1790 Jacobin doctrinaire radicalism had begun its attacks on religion, private property, and traditional political institutions. Events across the Channel gradually convinced Burke that the revolutionists had no respect for the classical and Scholastic tradition of Natural Law, which was the whole foundation of civil society in all Europe. In place of Natural Law legal principles, such as that prescription formed the best claim to property, the revolutionists invoked egalitarian speculations centered in the abstract "rights of man" to sanction the arbitrary seizure of corporate and private property. When Englishmen professed to admire these French methods of reform, Burke assumed the offensive against the revolution. An occasion presented itself on February 9, 1790, during the debates on estimates for the army, for Burke to attack the violations of property in France:

> They . . . laid the ax to the root of all property, and consequently of all national prosperity, by the principles they established, and the example they set. . . . They made and recorded a sort of *institute* and *digest* of anarchy, called the rights of man, in such a pedantic abuse of elementary principles as would have disgraced boys at school.[85]

As Burke's great object was to warn his countrymen against the principles and example of the French, his speech on the army estimates revealed in miniature the essential argument he was to follow in his struggle to maintain the principles of traditional Natural Law against the revolutionary "natural rights" of France. Although many scholars have failed to grasp this fundamental distinction between traditional Natural Law and revolutionary "natural rights," Burke understood the distinction perfectly and left no doubt that the basis of his attacks on the revolutionists was that they violated the Natural Law: "They are naturally pointed out, not by their having outraged political and civil laws, nor their having rebelled against the state, as a state, but by their having rebelled against the law of nature, and outraged man as man." [86] Burke wrote this sentence in October 1793, and it may be taken as the touchstone in all that he wrote of French affairs, from February 1790 through his posthumous *Fourth Letter on a Regicide Peace* (1797).

Although the Natural Law is most explicitly stated in Burke's writings on Irish and Indian affairs, its tacit assumption and intense moral spirit is clearly evident throughout his most famous work, the *Reflections on the Revolution in France*, which appeared in November 1790. Before considering Burke's subtle appeals to the Natural Law in the *Reflections*, the historical importance of this great work should be understood. Alfred Cobban did not exaggerate in calling the *Reflections* "the greatest and most influential political pamphlet ever written." If we consider only Burke's immediate practical intention, to warn his countrymen and Europe against French revolutionary principles and to exalt a Christian and Natural Law conception of civil society, the *Reflections* was the most successful book of the eighteenth-century "Enlightenment," and it was almost totally opposed to the prevailing spirit of the age.

So clearly and eloquently did Burke analyze the basic issues and social theories raised by the revolution, that the people of Britain were almost immediately divided into two distinct groups for or against it.[87] The first British edition sold 12,000 copies in the first month; in less than a year there were eleven editions, and by 1796 over 30,000 official copies had been sold. For that era, when a book was circulated among many readers and was frequently read to large public groups, this was a phenomenal achievement. So remarkable was the immediate effect of the *Reflections* that it became the focal point for all private and public discussions of the revolution. Wilberforce, the ardent advocate of emancipation for slaves, praised Burke as the man who "had stood between the living and the dead until the plague was stayed." [88] Reynolds and Gibbon greatly admired the *Reflections*, the latter writing of it: "Burke's book is an admirable medicine against the French disease. I admire his eloquence; I approve his politics; I adore his chivalry; and I can almost forgive his reverence for church establishments." [89] Of course the king said in public that it was "a very good book" which "every gentleman ought to read." In November 1796, Earl Fitzwilliam wrote to Burke and estimated the practical effect his *Reflections* and other writings on French affairs had produced in Britain: "You, my dear Burke, by the exertion of your great powers, have carried three-fourths of the public. . . . Your labours . . . have produced an effect in the country beyond expectation." [90] The French translation, reputed to have been done in part by the imprisoned Louis XVI, enjoyed an even greater contemporary triumph throughout Europe.[91] Letters of congratulations were sent to Burke by Catherine the Great of Russia and King Stanislas of Poland. In over a century and a half the *Reflections* has been used extensively in dealing with the French Revolution, and it remains as great a source of political wisdom as when it first appeared.

Among the revolutionists in France, Burke was of course strongly denounced. Mirabeau, who had visited Burke at Beaconsfield, spoke warmly against the *Reflections* in the National Assembly, and Jean Baptiste Cloots, the eccentric Prussian Jacobin, sent Burke an ironic invitation to France: "Quittez votre île, mon cher Burke; venez en France, si vous voulez jouir du plus magnifique spectacle dont l'entendement du philosophe puisse être frappé." [92] As Morley noted, when the fourteenth edition of the *Reflections* appeared, Romilly "wondered whether Burke was not rather ashamed of his success." In Britain the immediate political consequence of Burke's book was a sharp split in the Whig party. Burke assumed the unofficial leadership of the antirevolutionary Whig minority, while Fox and Sheridan, his lifelong political friends, headed the Whig majority. Their differences were hotly debated through many issues on the floor of parliament, and came to a climax on April 21, 1791, when Burke solemnly renounced Fox's friendship.

Within three years Burke's eloquence and the dire events in France which he had predicted with such amazing accuracy had drawn most of the nation and Fox's supporters to Burke's side. But as Edmond Malone noted in May 1794, personal animosities continued unabated: "We are now so distracted by party there [at the Literary Club], in consequence of Burke and Windham, and I might add the whole nation, being on one side, and Fox and his little phalanx on the other, that we in general keep as clear of politics as we can." [93] If such friction existed among Burke's friends, one may well understand the intense revulsion provoked by the *Reflections* among English radical admirers of the revolution. Such well-known reforming zealots as Dr. Price, Dr. Priestley, the Godwins, Mrs. Catherine Macaulay Graham, and Thomas Paine, as well as the more moderate Mackintosh, George Rous, and Earl Stanhope, savagely attacked his work. In addition there were "replies" from many obscure pamphleteers, such as Joel Barlow, William Belsham, Sir Brooke Boothby, Benjamin Bousfield, Thomas Broome, Thomas Cooper, Norman MacLeod, Charles Pigott, Major John Scott, the political agent of Hastings, Thomas Spence, Francis Stone, Joseph Towers, Mark Wilks, David Williams, and Christopher Wyvill. Exclusive of the many anonymous tracts published by the various radical clubs, there were at least forty-eight "replies" and several defenses of the *Reflections*.[94] Burke's book was the center of perhaps the greatest debate ever carried on in English over first principles in politics, and a careful reading of the *Reflections* will reveal that Burke took his stand on the ground of Aristotle, Cicero, St. Thomas Aquinas, and the traditional conception of the Natural Law.

Burke's appeals to the Natural Law in Indian affairs demonstrated his belief that all men are born "in subjection to one great, immutable, pre-existing law, a law . . . paramount to our feelings, by which we are connected in the eternal frame of the universe. . . ." The rest of this passage revealed that implicit in man's connection with this immutable law is a conception of divine contract. "This great law does not arise from our combinations and compacts," Burke wrote, but "on the contrary, it gives to them all the sanction they can have." In effect he said that God contracted with Himself never to be unjust to man. Thus, the Natural Law was the moral standard in all human contracts. This conception of a divine contract and of the ethical norm of Natural Law underscored Burke's statement in Indian affairs that the greatest and best gift of God to man was government, for the state was the necessary means by which man could live according to the Natural Law. In Burke's *Reflections* all of these ideas are to be found more fully developed in his conception of the social contract.

To Burke man's relationship to civil society is a moral necessity; it cannot be voluntaristic, for that would exalt will above right reason; nothing could be more false and wicked than the Lockian theory of a voluntary and revocable social contract based upon a hypothetical state of nature. The moral primacy and binding necessity of the Natural Law, as the true basis of the social contract, has never been more eloquently expressed, even by Cicero, than in the *Reflections:*

Society is indeed a contract. Subordinate contracts for objects of mere occasional interest may be dissolved at pleasure—but the state ought not to be considered as nothing better than a partnership agreement in a trade of pepper and coffee, calico or tobacco . . . to be taken up for a little temporary interest, and to be dissolved by the fancy of the parties. It is to be looked on with other reverence; because it is not a partnership in things subservient only to the gross animal existence of a temporary and perishable nature. It is a partnership in all science; a partnership in all art; a partnership in every virtue, and in all perfection. As the ends of such a partnership cannot be obtained in many generations, it becomes a partnership not only between those who are living, but between those who are living, those who are dead, and those who are to be born. Each contract of each particular state is but a clause in the great primaeval contract of eternal society, linking the lower with the higher natures, connecting the visible and invisible world, according to a fixed compact sanctioned by the inviolable oath which holds all physical and all moral natures, each in their appointed place. This law is not subject to the will of those who by an obligation above them, and infinitely superior, are bound to submit their will to that law. The municipal corporations of that universal kingdom are not morally at liberty at their pleasure, and on their speculation of a contingent improvement, wholly to separate and tear asunder the bands of their subordinate community, and to dissolve it into an unsocial, uncivil, unconnected chaos of elementary principles. It is the first and supreme necessity only, a necessity that is not chosen, but chooses, a necessity paramount to deliberation, that admits no discussion, and demands no evidence, which alone can justify a resort to anarchy. This necessity is no exception to the rule; because this necessity itself is a part of that moral and physical disposition of things, to which man must be obedient by consent or force: but if that which is only submission to necessity should be made the object of choice, the law is broken, nature is disobeyed, and the rebellious are outlawed, cast forth, and exiled, from this world of reason, and order, and peace, and virtue, and fruitful penitence, into the antagonist world of madness, discord, vice, confusion, and unavailing sorrow.[95]

This vital passage contains in essence all that Burke said about the social contract throughout many parts of his *Reflections*. It reveals his belief in a transcendent moral duty beyond all will or power, a duty imposed by the "primaeval contract" of God's "inviolable oath," binding man through the Natural Law to his civil obligations. "The great ruling principle of the moral and natural world," said Burke, is not "a mere invention to keep the vulgar in obedience." He clearly agreed with Pufendorf's principle that "by the observance of *Natural Law,* it must be supposed that God laid an obligation on man to obey this *law,* as a *means* not arising from Human invention or changeable at Human pleasure." [96] Burke regarded the Natural Law as a divinely ordained imperative ethical norm which, without consulting man, fixed forever his moral duties in civil society.

Throughout the *Reflections* the spirit of the Natural Law and Burke's conception of the divine contract which binds all men appears in various forms—in his discussions of the English constitution, in his principle of political sovereignty, in his idea that civil liberty is an inheritance and private property is secured by prescription, and above all, in his conception of the divine and social functions of Church and State. He states that Britain's "constitutional policy" works "after the pattern of nature" and that her "political system is placed in a just correspondence and symmetry with the order of the world" and is held together "by the disposition of a stupendous wisdom, moulding together the great mysterious incorporation of the human race. . . ." By "preserving the method of nature in the conduct of the state," deliberation is made "a matter not of choice, but of necessity," and political justice is thus secured.[97] Even more explicitly than in Indian affairs Burke insists in the *Reflections* on the divine origin of the state: "He who gave our nature to be perfected by our virtue, willed also the necessary means of its perfection.—He willed therefore the state.—He willed its connection with the source and original archetype of all perfection." [98] Indeed, Church and State are for Burke but two aspects of the same thing—God-given instruments to bring man to his highest spiritual and social perfection, through which man becomes united to the Godhead: "Every sort of moral, every sort of civil, every sort of politic institution, aiding the rational and natural ties that connect the human understanding and affections to the divine, are not more than necessary, in order to build up that wonderful structure, Man." Through the Church, Burke continues, the state is consecrated, "that all who administer in the government of men, in which they stand in the person of God himself, should have high and worthy notions of their function and destination." Clearly, his conception of the divine contract in human affairs implies that all power is a divine trust: "All persons possessing any portion of power ought to be strongly and awfully impressed with an idea that they act in trust: and that they are to account for their conduct in that trust to the one great Master, Author, and Founder of society. . . . Power . . . to be legitimate must be according to that eternal, immutable law, in which will and reason are the same." [99] The belief that power is a divine trust is evident in Burke's conception of the function of Church and State; it reappears throughout his extensive discussions of political sovereignty, which I shall examine in another chapter.

In Burke's discussions of Irish affairs, he regarded prescription in property rights as one of the great derived principles of Natural Law. In 1772 he had said in parliament: "If the principle of prescription be not a constitution of positive law, but a principle of natural equity, then to hold it out against any man is not doing him injustice." [100] In the *Reflections* he repeated this principle: "By the laws of nature, the occupant and subduer of the soil is the true proprietor; there is no prescription against nature." [101] But the revolutionists in the National Assembly, through their false conception of "natural rights," declared that all property was usurped which was not held on terms consistent with man's "original" nature. Their contention overturned prescription as the basis of ownership:

> With the National Assembly of France, possession is nothing, law and usage are nothing. I see the National Assembly openly reprobate the doctrine of prescription, which one of the greatest of their own lawyers [Domat] tells us, with great truth, is a part of the law of nature. He tells us, that the positive ascertainment of its limits, and its security from invasion, were among the causes for which civil society itself has been instituted. If prescription be once shaken, no species of property is secure, when it once becomes an object large enough to tempt the cupidity of indigent power. I see a practice perfectly correspondent to their contempt of this great fundamental part of natural law.[102]

The National Assembly, said Burke, left nothing but their own arbitrary pleasure to determine what property was to be protected and what subverted. He admitted that he saw no reason why landed estates could not be held otherwise than by inheritance. In opposing the wholesale confiscations of Church lands in France, Burke warned his countrymen against the example established by the National Assembly in its violation of the Natural Law:

> I hope we shall never be so totally lost to all sense of the duties imposed upon us by the law of social union, as, upon any pretext of public service, to confiscate the goods of a single unoffending citizen. Who but a tyrant . . . could think of seizing on the property of men, unaccused, unheard, untried, by whole descriptions, by hundreds and thousands together? [103]

To Burke one of the great means of fulfilling the Natural Law was through prescription, which maintained the law of social union by protecting the private property of men and institutions.

It is not necessary here to go into the negative side of Burke's appeals to the Natural Law; in the next chapter I shall examine in detail the significance of his attacks on the revolutionary "rights of man." It is sufficient to note that in the *Reflections* he explicitly distinguished between the false revolutionary "rights of man" and the valid "natural rights" of traditional Natural Law: "Far am I from denying in theory, full as far is my heart from withholding in practice (if I were of power to give or to withhold,) the *real* rights of men. In denying their false claims of right, I do not mean to injure those which are real, and are such as their pretended rights would totally destroy." [104] What are the *real* natural rights of man? Burke agreed with his predecessors in the classical and Scholastic Natural Law tradition that the protection of man's life, liberty, and property constituted his most fundamental rights as man. But more than perhaps any other Natural Law thinker Burke insisted upon the concrete realization of man's natural rights in civil society. He therefore rejected totally, even for illustrative purposes, the Hobbist and Lockian hypothesis of a pre-civil "state of nature," maintaining that a veil was thrown over the origins of civil society and that "men cannot enjoy the rights of an uncivil and of a civil state together." He was profoundly skeptical of all logical arguments based upon mathematical reasoning, maintaining that "in politics the most fallacious of all things was geometrical demonstration." [105] Since "government is not made in virtue of natural rights, which may and do exist in total independence of it," Burke believed there was no use of discussing a man's abstract right to food or medicine. The abstract perfection and clarity which could be established through mathematical reasoning concerning such a "right" was its practical defect in civil society, where the farmer and the physician, not the professor of metaphysics, would determine the means of procuring food and administering medicine.

Burke always refused to treat moral and political questions of "rights" as materials for a speculative and theoretical science:

These metaphysical rights entering into common life, like rays of light which pierce into a dense medium, are, *by the laws of nature,* refracted from their straight line. Indeed, in the gross and complicated mass of human passions and concerns, the primitive rights of men undergo such a variety of refractions and reflections, that it becomes absurd to talk of them as if they continued in the simplicity of their original direction.[106]

To Burke the fulfillment of man's natural rights is set by the limits of man's fallible nature and the variety of circumstances found in every civil society; the Natural Law itself decrees that men recognize the variety of conditions under which life exists. Since man in every state is by nature a political animal, the real natural rights of man are a matter of practical political reason, and are to be found only within the objectives and conventions of civil society.

In the *Reflections*, among the natural and derivative rights of man in civil society Burke included all the advantages which accrue to men by virtue of civil society being established. Specifically, he noted the right to justice under law, and the right of all men to the fruits of their industry and to the means of making their industry fruitful. All men were entitled by right "to the acquisitions of their parents; to the nourishment and improvement of their offspring; to instruction in life, and to consolation in death. Whatever each man can separately do, without trespassing upon others, he has a right to do for himself; and he has a right to a fair portion of all which society, with all its combinations of skill and force, can do in his favor." [107] Burke distinguished between equity as the basis of common rights within a range of social conditions, and that fictitious "equality" which would reduce all men to the same status. He refused to separate considerations of "rights" from social circumstances, or to define men's real rights in any abstract terms: "The rights of men are in a sort of *middle,* incapable of definition, but not impossible to be discerned. The rights of men in governments are their advantages; and these are often in balances between differences of good; in compromises sometimes between good and evil, and sometimes between evil and evil." [108] Moral prudence was the principle by which Burke felt the true natural rights of man in civil society could best be realized.

Practically everything that Burke wrote in the *Reflections* about the divine contract, Natural Law, and natural rights, about prescription, civil liberty, political sovereignty, and Church and State, is either assumed or restated with variations throughout his other writings on French affairs. His famous attack on Rousseau's sensibility in *A Letter to a Member of the National Assembly* (January 1791) was prefigured in the

Reflections, and embodies Burke's conviction that unrestrained emotion implies an intuitive and voluntaristic conception of moral duty contrary to the "right reason" of Natural Law. His sequel to the *Reflections,* the *Appeal from the New to the Old Whigs* (July 1791), contains an exposition of his faith in a divine contract, and of the moral duties it imposes upon man, second in importance only to his declaration in the *Reflections:*

> I allow, that if no supreme ruler exists, wise to form, and potent to enforce, the moral law, there is no sanction to any contract, virtual or even actual, against the will of prevalent power. On that hypothesis, let any set of men be strong enough to set their duties at defiance, and they cease to be duties any longer. . . . The awful Author of our being is the Author of our place in the order of existence; and . . . having disposed and marshalled us by a divine tactic, not according to our will, but according to his, he has, in and by that disposition, virtually subjected us to act the part which belongs to the place assigned us. We have obligations to mankind at large, which are not in consequence of any special voluntary pact. They arise from the relation of man to man, and the relation of man to God, which relations are not matters of choice. On the contrary, the force of all the pacts which we enter into with any particular person or numbers of persons amongst mankind, depends upon these prior obligations. In some cases the subordinate relations are voluntary, in others they are necessary—but the duties are all compulsive. . . . Dark and inscrutable are the ways by which we come into the world. The instincts which give rise to this mysterious process of nature are not of our making. But out of physical causes, unknown to us, perhaps unknowable, arise moral duties, which, as we are able perfectly to comprehend, we are bound indispensably to perform.[109]

This important passage reaffirms and extends Burke's belief in the Natural Law principles that God is the ultimate source of all law and duty, and that the validity of every human contract depends upon the divinely established moral law which all men are obliged to obey.

Beginning with his *Thoughts on French Affairs* (December 1791), Burke became more and more concerned with the international relations between revolutionary France and her neighbors, and with the problem of maintaining a balance of power in Europe. Burke's appeals to the law of nations are a vital part of his belief in the Natural Law. But his primary concern continued to be England, and all that he wrote in the last five years of his life reflected his fear that French revolutionary principles would be accepted by Englishmen. When the enormously wealthy Duke of Bedford declared his approval of the French Revolution, with its confiscations of inherited landed estates, Burke immediately perceived the irony and in his *Letter to a Noble Lord* (1796) invoked prescription to save the duke from his own folly:

The Duke of Bedford will stand as long as prescriptive law endures: as long as the great stable laws of property, common to us with all civilized nations, are kept in their integrity. . . . The whole revolutionary system, institutes, digest, code, novels, text, gloss, comment, are not only not the same, but they are the very reverse . . . fundamentally, of all the laws on which civil life has hitherto been upheld in all the governments of the world. The learned professors of the rights of man regard prescription, not as a title to bar all claim, set up against all possession—but they look on prescription as itself a bar against the possessor and proprietor. They hold an immemorial possession to be no more than a long-continued, and therefore an aggravated injustice.[110]

In Burke's *Letters on a Regicide Peace* (1796–1797), the whole revolutionary legal system of the French Jacobins was attacked as a violation of prescription, of the established sovereignty of independent nations, and even of the Natural Law itself:

They made, not laws, not conventions, not late possession, but physical nature, and political convenience, the sole foundation of their claims. . . . With them it is not for the states of Europe to judge of their title: the very reverse. In their eye the title of every other power depends wholly on their pleasure. . . . It is a declaration not made in consequence of any prescription on her side, not on any cession or dereliction . . . of other powers. . . . In other words, their will is the law, not only at home, but as to the concerns of every nation. . . . Without the least ceremony or compliment, they have sent out of the world whole sets of laws and lawgivers. They have swept away the very constitutions under which the legislators acted, and the laws were made. Even the fundamental sacred rights of man they have not scrupled to profane. They have set this holy code at nought with ignominy and scorn. Thus they treat all their domestic laws and constitutions, and even what they had considered as a law of nature; but whatever they have put their seal on for the purpose of their ambition, and the ruin of their neighbours, this alone is invulnerable, impassible, immortal.[111]

Burke's attack on arbitrary power or will as an alternative to the Natural Law forms the dominant theme of his *Letters on a Regicide Peace:* "It appears as if the contract that renovates the world was under no law at all." "As to the right of men to act anywhere according to their pleasure, without any moral tie, no such right exists." "The law of this their empire is anything rather than the public law of Europe." "This strong hand is the law, and the sole law, in their state." [112] When the revolutionists, under the slogan "the rights of man," seized Savoy, Burke remarked ironically in parliament: "This gentle people, in adding the country of their neighbors to their own dominions, only follow the mild laws of nature." [113] In contrast to the new order in France, wrote Burke, the institutions of the Holy Roman Empire had long taught "the great, the rich, and the powerful . . . to submit their necks to the imperial laws, and to those of nature and of nations." [114] The Jacobins exalted arbitrary will above the ethical norms of Natural Law because they would "not acknowledge the existence of God as a moral governor of the world." [115] This is what is behind Burke's extensive and violent attacks on the *philosophes* and the Jacobins' "atheism by establishment." To Burke the Natural Law was so basic to the ancient inherited social order of Europe that its subversion was enough proof that the revolution was the most extensive project ever launched against all religion, law, property, and real civil order and liberty.

Before drawing any conclusion concerning Burke's appeals to the Natural Law, it is worth noting a significant development which occurred in Burke's relationship with James Mackintosh. Among the many "replies" which the *Reflections* had provoked was Mackintosh's *Vindiciae Gallicae,* which had appeared in April 1791. Between the time of his reply and Burke's death in 1797, Mackintosh experienced a slow, reluctant, painful disillusionment in the French Revolution, similar to that which overtook Wordsworth, Coleridge, Southey, and many other ardent youths. Mackintosh's disillusionment was intensified

by the partisan triumph he had enjoyed over Burke with his
Vindiciae Gallicae. William Hazlitt testified in *The Spirit of
the Age* to the popularity and esteem with which Mackintosh's
book was received: "It was cried up by the partisans of the new
school, as a work superior in the charms of composition to its
undoubted rival: in acuteness, depth, and soundness of reasoning, of course there was supposed to be no comparison." Soon
after its publication Burke wrote to his friend Dr. Laurence:
"I have not read, or even seen Mackintosh;—but Richard tells
me that it is Paine at bottom; and that indeed all the writers
against me are, either Paines, with some difference in the way
of stating, or even myself." [116] Richard Burke's report to his
father was not strictly accurate. Mackintosh's work was really
a mixture of Paine's "natural rights" theory and the current
utilitarianism; it was an intelligent and liberal "new" Whig
expression of the glowing optimism and widespread hope which
the revolution had inspired up to April 1791. Burke must have
read Mackintosh some time afterwards, because in December
1792 he complained in the House of Commons that Sheridan,
like "Mr. Mackintosh and other writers of less eminence" garbled him by "taking a detached passage without explaining it
by what followed or went before it." Orally and in print, Burke
and Mackintosh continued their war of words during the three
or four years following the French Revolution.

Even more than Burke's writings, events across the Channel
caused Mackintosh gradually to modify his original enthusiasm
for the revolution. When the first three of Burke's *Letters on
a Regicide Peace* appeared late in 1796, Burke was pleasantly
surprised to note the grave decorum, candor, and moderation
with which the Scotsman criticized his work in letters to the
Monthly Review for November and December 1796. Mackintosh met Dr. Laurence in London and they discussed a possible
meeting between Burke and his young critic. From Beaconsfield Burke wrote to Dr. Laurence early in December and expressed some ambivalent feelings about the apparent change
in Mackintosh's political views:

I forgot to speak to you about Mackintosh's supposed conversion.
I suspect by his letter, that it does not extend beyond the interior

politics of this island, but that, with regard to France and many other countries, he remains as Frank a Jacobin as ever. This conversion is none at all; but we must nurse up these nothings, and think these negatives advantages as we can have them. Such as he is, I shall not be displeased if you bring him down.[117]

Burke arranged through Dr. Laurence to have Mackintosh visit him during Christmas 1796. According to Hazlitt, who had a strong animus against Burke's interpretation of the French Revolution, the Scotsman was drawn wholly into Burke's political orbit and became an obsequious satellite: "He sent an invitation to the writer to see him; and in the course of three days' animated discussion of such subjects, Mr. Mackintosh became a convert not merely to the graces and gravity of Mr. Burke's style, but to the liberality of his views, and the solidity of his opinions.—The Lincoln's Inn Lectures were the fruit of this interview." [118] Hazlitt attributed the "sudden and violent change in Sir James' views and opinions" to his "personal interview" with Burke. Before their meeting Burke's doubts concerning Mackintosh's recantation were centered in the Scotsman's view of international relations. It is therefore significant that the first series of Mackintosh's thirty-nine "Lincoln's Inn Lectures," which resulted from his discussions with Burke, were called *A Discourse on the Law of Nature and Nations* (London, 1799). In this work Mackintosh's original utilitarianism was wholly abated, and he attacked as "fanciful chimeras" the utopian aspirations of the revolutionary doctrines of equality, based upon the "rights of man." At the same time he appealed frequently to Burke and to such ancient proponents of the classical Natural Law as Aristotle and Cicero. In contrast to his *Vindiciae Gallicae,* in which he had praised Hobbes for introducing the method of mathematics in political reasoning, Mackintosh made much of moral prudence in his second book and revealed great skepticism toward abstract speculations. Undoubtedly Burke was not the sole cause of all these important changes in Mackintosh's political principles. But there is incontrovertible evidence that Mackintosh's lectures owed much to Burke; through his *A Discourse on the*

Law of Nature and Nations, Burke's mighty spirit, like Caesar at Philippi, still walked abroad in triumph after death.

The most serious error in the interpretation of Burke's political philosophy and practical career in parliament has been the general failure to perceive his full and lifelong acceptance of the classical and Scholastic conception of the Natural Law. Utilitarian and positivist critics, who made no distinction between the ethical norms of traditional Natural Law and the revolutionary eighteenth-century "rights of man" doctrines derived from a supposed "state of nature," accepted Burke's attacks on abstract "rights" as a rejection of the Natural Law, and claimed him as a conservative utilitarian. Yet Burke had an encyclopedic knowledge of the tradition of Natural Law in Western thought, and of the common law in England, which is saturated with the spirit of Natural Law. In every important political problem he ever faced, in Irish, American, constitutional, economic, Indian, and French affairs, Burke *always* appealed to the Natural Law. What is more, by Natural Law Burke always meant essentially the same thing, and he applied it as the ultimate test of justice and liberty in all human affairs. As a practical statesman he feared abstractions and was reluctant to take his mind from concrete political problems. But to Burke no *moral* problem was ever an *abstract* question; he therefore conceived of statecraft as the practical application in concrete human affairs of primary moral principles, clearly evident to man's right reason. It is in this vital sense that the Natural Law is implicitly affirmed in all of Burke's great parliamentary concerns. Generally, Burke was content to fulfill the Natural Law indirectly, through the concrete constitutional, legal, and political instruments of the state. But when the state itself was corrupted from its true function, and became the instrument of arbitrary tyranny and injustice, as in the penal code against Ireland, the rule of Hastings in India, and of the revolutionists in France, Burke's appeals to the Natural Law became explicit. In its relative simplicity as a code of ethical principles, and in its enormous complexity in practical application, the Natural Law absorbed Burke's whole intellectual and emotional nature. It was so deeply rooted in him, so refined through his sensitive temperament, that even when it was not explicitly mentioned it appeared as his basic instinct and conviction. The Natural Law was his moral anchor, securing him to the most vital and enduring religious and political traditions of Europe.

Burke's faith in the Natural Law supplied the religious spirit which infuses his entire political philosophy. He was the foremost modern Christian humanist in politics because he saw the world and the nature of man through the revelations of Christianity and the right reason of Natural Law. His world of right reason and Nature was the Stoical world of Aristotle and Cicero and the Christian world of St. Thomas Aquinas and Hooker, and not the rationalistic world of eighteenth-century "nature," based upon mathematical science and empirical philosophy and systematized into an optimistic deism or pantheism. Burke's vision of reality was not centered in the natural sciences, in the cosmos or in the visible world of physical things, but in the divinely created and humanly developed world of man, the transfigured and complex world of civil institutions, with its laws and customs, its art and corporate wisdom, its invisible tissue of loyalties and prejudices, all of which gave cohesion and concreteness to the divine contract, which connected man in the eternal frame of the universe. Man was essentially a religious and political being, born in subjection to one great, immutable pre-existent law; his primary duty as citizen and statesman was to determine, obey, and promote in civil society the divine law ordained by God for his spiritual and temporal benefit. Only by accepting the supernatural or natural laws of God, and the divinely given instruments of civil society, could man flourish and bring himself to that degree of perfection which gave him an exalted yet subordinate place in the creation.

FOUR

The Law of Nations

It is generally agreed that the modern origins of the law of
nations are to be found in two great early seventeenth-century
works, Suarez' *Tractatus de legibus ac Deo legislatore* (1612),
and Grotius' *De jure belli et pacis* (1625). Among their contemporaries, Suarez and Grotius were moderate and mediating
men, and they were therefore particularly aware that the basic
problems of international diplomacy—the just causes and conduct of war, treatment of prisoners, acquisition of sovereignty
and booty through conquest, neutrality, or intervention, mari-
time law, treaties, and so on—had become profoundly complicated by the growth of a conscious and extreme political
nationalism. Their main problem was to determine to what
extent international law was derived respectively from the
universal *jus naturale* and also from the various prescriptive
jus gentium of each particular nation. It was generally taken
for granted that Natural Law, as a universal and eternal ethical
norm, applied equally and simultaneously to all *inter*-national
and *intra*-national relations.[1] Suarez pointed out that when
men became separated into corporate nations, Natural Law as
the moral basis of international justice never could be applied
directly and in the abstract, but always indirectly, through the
just claims of the supplementary and various civil laws, customs, conventions, institutions, and historical circumstances of
each nation.[2] Natural Law was thus conceived as the perpetual
arbitrator between international and constitutional law. Unfortunately, in their attempt to make nationalism and international relations harmonize with Natural Law, Suarez and
Grotius were ambiguous in using the term "law of nations."
Sometimes it meant the particular adaptation of Natural Law
to the internal government of particular states, that is, con-

stitutional law. But since one nation has no legal or moral right to legislate for any other, and every nation has the moral obligation to protect its citizens against any nation which would destroy their corporate sovereignty, there must be a law beyond national constitutional laws to which all nations may appeal in safeguarding their moral right to independent existence. Properly speaking, this is the Natural Law, the normative moral code to which all nations, like all individuals, should adhere. But the application of the moral law to the external legal and political relations between nations, that is, international law, was also called the "law of nations." [3] From Suarez and Grotius to Burke, in varying degrees all thinkers on international law continued to use "law of nations" in this loose and ambiguous manner.

Blackstone and Bolingbroke reveal, respectively, that the international and constitutional conceptions of law, as logical derivatives of Natural Law, were fully understood and accepted during Burke's time:

> As it is impossible for the whole race of mankind to be united in one great society, they must necessarily divide into many, and form separate states, commonwealths, and nations, entirely independent of each other, and yet liable to a mutual intercourse. Hence arises a law to regulate this mutual intercourse, called 'the law of nations,' which, as none of these states will acknowledge a superiority in the other, cannot be dictated by any, but depends entirely upon the rules of natural law. [4]

> As supreme Lord over all His works, His general Providence regards immediately the great commonwealth of mankind, but then, as supreme Lord likewise, His authority gives a sanction to the particular bodies of law which are made under it. The law of nature is the law of all His subjects: the constitutions of particular governments are like the by-laws of cities, or the appropriated customs of provinces. It follows, therefore, that he who breaks the law of his country resists the ordinance of God, that is, the law of his nature. [5]

Burke's predecessors and contemporaries not only distinguished clearly between an *international* and *constitutional* conception of the law of nations, but like Burke himself, they regarded both conceptions not as contrary to, but as necessary derivative parts of the Natural Law.[6] This distinction is of the very greatest importance, and must be kept in mind constantly in order to avoid the common misconceptions concerning Burke's attack on abstract metaphysical "rights," and his appeals to "prudence." Later, in the light of his appeals to the law of nations, I shall examine the significance of his attacks on abstract theory, and determine the connection between his principle of prudence and the Natural Law. The law of nations was for Burke the first qualification of the Natural Law, in the process of applying its eternal and universal moral imperatives to the concrete, practical political affairs of men and nations. Burke assumed the two traditional conceptions of the law of nations as part of his philosophy of history and politics, and he applied them to the great international conflicts brought on by the American and French revolutions.

I. The International Conception of the Law of Nations

One of the greatest omissions in scholarship on Burke has been the failure to consider the vital position of the law of nations in his political philosophy. This law explains why he accepted so completely the principle of man's diversity resulting from historical growth, why he always gave paramount consideration to the infinite circumstances of men, yet based his political philosophy upon Natural Law. The cardinal importance Burke gave to various national circumstances is best revealed in his principle of prudence; since he considered nations not as physical or geographical arrangements but as moral essences, for him historical diversity was not something merely empirical, but a vital moral fact which required that the universal Natural Law should be applied through various social institutions and forms of government. He never regarded Natural Law merely as an abstract moral code, immediately perceived by private reason, but as the most imperative law of the spiritual side of man's common nature, permeating every good act of individuals, civil institutions, races, and nations. Even more than Montesquieu, his master and teacher on this point, Burke realized that man's common nature is infinitely modified by climate, geography, history, religion, nationality, and race, by institutions, customs, manners, and habits, by all the civil circumstances of times, places, and occasions, which cut across and qualify but do not impair the different means by which the Natural Law is best fulfilled. With all their differences, men in any given nation had their citizenship in common, and all were bound in their civil capacity to obey the moral law, so that *as citizens* (not as men in the abstract), they could best live according to the spirit of Natural Law *indirectly,* by acknowledging the intermediary *de jure* sovereignty of their own civil state, and each state in turn, in its intercourse with other states, was obliged to subordinate its self-interest to the superior reason in the moral law. Thus the individual finds his proper place in his nation, much as his nation fulfills its destiny in the evolving life of civilized humanity, so that individuals and nations are mutually bound to each other, reflecting at every point the spirit of the God-given moral law; and this arrangement is repeated, under a great diversity of forms, throughout the order of the civil universe.

Burke is certainly in the tradition of Suarez and Grotius, and of all political philosophers who had said that the law of nations, in both senses, is derived from Natural Law. On international law, however, Burke assumed a new, hypothetical, transitional law between the universal Natural Law and the particular constitutions of particular states—a law of nations which applies distinctly to what he called "the Commonwealth of Europe." He certainly believed that the Natural Law applied equally in India and in England; he admitted that Hastings had brought disgrace upon Britain's honor by violating the law of nations in Asia,[7] and he stated that Cheyt Sing, in refusing to pay tribute to Hastings, "was justifiable upon every principle of the laws of nations, nature, and morality." [8] But in dealing with international European politics, the laws and fate of the whole civilized world were sometimes too grand and hypothetical an object for Burke's practical consideration; he willfully restricted himself, in using the term "law of nations," to the chief elements in the laws common to Europe, the "similitude throughout Europe of religion, laws and manners," to which all European nations were bound. According to Burke the religion, laws, and manners of Europe consisted respectively of three closely fused elements—Christianity, the modified remnants of Roman civil law, and the customs of the Germanic tribes that overran the Roman Empire:✗

The writers on public law have often called this aggregate of nations a commonwealth. They had reason. It is virtually one great state having the same basis of general law, with some diversity of provincial customs and local establishments. The nations of Europe have had the very same Christian religion, agreeing in the fundamental parts, varying a little in the ceremonies and in the subordinate doctrines. The whole of the polity and economy of every country in Europe has been derived from the same sources. It was drawn from the old Germanic or Gothic customary, from the feudal institutions which must be considered as an emanation from that customary; and the whole has been improved and digested into system and discipline by the Roman law. From hence arose the several orders . . . which are called states . . . in every European country.[9]

In considering the individual differences and circumstances of mankind at large, India excepted, this common law of the European commonwealth is the broadest frame of reference Burke ever made. It is the first qualification of Natural Law that leads finally to his principle of political prudence. It is to this vast and complicated ancient Roman-Christian-Germanic civilization, whose "common inheritance" transcends the claims of any of its national or religious parts, that Burke refers, even more than to Natural Law itself, when he attacks European nations that violate the international law of nations.

During the intense nationalism of the Renaissance it became obvious that national self-interest and colonial ambition could lead legislators to justify violations of Natural Law by appeals to the constitutional law of nations. According to Sir James Mackintosh, this inversion of the moral law by political self-interest continued until late in the seventeenth century: "Puffendorf . . . restored natural law to that superiority which belonged to it, and with great propriety treated the law of nations as only one main branch of the parent stock." [10] It is probable that before reading Pufendorf, Mackintosh had learned the "proper" relationship of the law of nations to Natural Law from Burke, who converted him in 1796 from his revolutionary interpretation of international law. All of Burke's previous discussions of the law of nations in American and French affairs show clearly that he regarded it as derivative from Natural Law.

With Burke no political claim could transcend the imperative and normative ethics of Natural Law, and his impartiality in applying this rule in judging man's behavior is proved by the fact that until 1790 he was more severely critical of the arbitrary acts of his own country than of those of any other. In 1777, while discussing the American rebellion, Burke pointed out that traditionally only nations which are recognized as already legally established have any moral claim, under the broadest conception of the law of nations, to make international treaties and declare war. He lamented that the king's treating the colonists as outlaws and rebels, rather than as citizens dissenting from arbitrary rule, made it impossible to settle differences under the British constitution, and in effect put the colonists in possession of the law of nations: "Whenever a rebellion really and truly exists . . . government has not entered into . . . military conventions; but has ever declined all intermediate treaty which should put rebels in possession of the law of nations with regard to war." [11] In February 1778, Burke told parliament that Britain's plan to use Indians and to excite rebellion among the Negro slaves in America violated international law: "He [Burke] insisted that the proclamation for that purpose was directly contrary to the common statute law of this country, as well as to the general law of nations." [12] In December 1779, Burke contended that both the American colonies and France were within their moral and legal rights in forming a political and military alliance:

Mr. Burke entered into an ample investigation of the propriety of America joining with France, and contended, that in all ages and in all countries, it was perfectly natural for revolted subjects to form an alliance with that power known to be most inimical to the state, from whose supremacy they had withdrawn, and to whom the destruction of the interest of the former parent state was obviously a matter of desirable advantage.[13]

In this passage, reported as indirect discourse, it is noteworthy that Burke's contention that the alliance was "natural" rested on an appeal to legal precedents among nations, and that the utility or "desirable advantage" to the allies of destroying Britain's power in America was not the basis for determining political policies, as so many of Burke's utilitarian critics have claimed, but rather a political by-product of following a legitimate self-interest under the moral law.

Burke's most severe attack on Britain's violations of the law of nations occurred in a speech on May 14, 1781, in his "Inquiry into the Seizure of Private Property in St. Eustatius." At a time when Holland and Britain were not officially at war, and Holland, as a member of the League of Armed Neutrality, followed Grotius' principle that neutral ships have free access to world trade, this tiny West Indies Dutch island was seized by Britain's Admiral Rodney and General Vaughan, and in the name of the Crown all the private property of every Dutch, American, Jewish, and even British resident and merchant was confiscated. Burke attacked this confiscation as "a most unjustifiable, outrageous, and unprincipled violation of the law of nations." [14] He considered the confiscation of the property of the Jews particularly unjust, because they had no nation to which they could look for material compensation or moral redress. In the course of his speech, as reported by the Commons' clerk, Burke contended that the rules of war and conquest among civilized nations rest on the law of nations, which is derived from the Natural Law:

Mr. Burke entered largely into the investigation of that right which a conqueror attains to the property of the vanquished by the law of nations. . . . He declared that the general confiscation of the private property found upon the island was contrary to the law of nations, and to that system of war which civilized states . . . by their consent and practice, thought proper to introduce. Perhaps it might be said, there was no positive law of nations, no general established laws framed and settled by acts in which every nation had a voice. There was not indeed any law of nations established like the laws of Britain in black letter, by statute and record; but there was a law of nations as firm, as clear, as manifest, as obligatory, as indispensable. . . . There were certain limited and defined rights of war recognized by civilized states, and practiced in enlightened

Europe. . . . They were established by reason, in which they had
their origin . . . by the convention of parties . . . by the authorities of writers, who took the laws and maxims . . . from the consent and sense of ages; and lastly, from the evidence of precedent.
Mr. Burke . . . said 'that a king conquered to acquire dominion,
not plunder; that a state does not go to war with individuals, but
with a state; and in conquest, does not take possession of private
property.' . . . By this maxim the calamities of war are mitigated.
. . . This law, therefore, directs that the property of individuals, in
a territory surrendering at discretion, is not only to be spared, but
to be secured. . . . When men surrender, they are entitled to protection. There is a virtual compact in conquest, by which protection
arises out of, and accompanies, allegiance. Can the King of Great
Britain seize upon the property of his subjects at his will and pleasure? No; nor can he in the instant of conquest seize on the goods
and effects of the conquered. . . . Every monarch, however despotic,
is bound by the very essence of his tenure, to observe this obligation. . . . The king who should receive the surrender of a people,
thereby admitting them within the pale of his government, and
afterwards strip them of their property, must, in so doing, forfeit
his royal authority, and be considered only as a robber. . . . This
is a principle inspired by the Divine Author of all good; it is felt
in the heart; it is recognized by reason; it is established by consent.
. . . By the convention of parties, this law of nations was established
and confirmed.[15]

Nations as well as individuals are entitled to justice when, as
corporate bodies, they contend unsuccessfully for survival
through war. Burke stated that it was "a first principle in the
law of nations" that in war it must be assumed that each nation
conceives it has justice on its side; therefore, everything before
the beginning of hostilities and after the fighting ceases must
be forgotten in the restoration of justice.[16] The recorder of
his speech does not supply the rich details of his argument, but
states categorically that "Mr. Burke . . . in a variety of most
beautiful and forcible arguments, enforced the doctrine of the
law of nations." [17] Indirect and general as the recorded evidence
is, it nevertheless proves that during the decade before France
burst into flame Burke derived his principles of the law of
nations from Natural Law.

In May 1791, during his speech on the Quebec government
bill, Burke raised the question of how the law of nations is re-

lated to political sovereignty. He denied that Britain had any right to rule French Canada on the radical English reformers' theory of "the rights of man," which was an abstract slogan subversive of the traditional conception of sovereignty based on Natural Law. The radicals' hypothetical, primitive, pre-civil "rights of man" could do nothing to determine any political sovereignty, or even any corporate and national allegiance. Burke then asked:

> On what, then, was this House to found its competence? There was another code on which mankind in all ages had acted—the law of nations; and on this alone he conceived the competence of the House to rest. This country had acquired the power of legislating for Canada by right of conquest. . . . The law of nations enabled us to legislate for the people of Canada, and bound us to afford them an equitable government, and them to allegiance.[18]

He conceived conquest in time of war as an act securing not merely physical power over an enemy, but also dictating a profound moral responsibility upon the victorious state, compelling it, under threat of forfeiting its acquired sovereignty, to grant the defeated people "an equitable government" based on Natural Law.

After 1789 the turn of events in France afforded Burke many occasions to discuss politics in terms of the law of nations. In December 1792, he observed that the French revolutionary leaders confused terms badly; they invoked Natural Law itself against all existing treaties between nations established under the law of nations:

> If a treaty opposed their ambition, they immediately affirmed that it was contrary to the laws of nature; and reduced every moral obligation to the same levelling principle. . . . Thus the [revolutionists'] laws of nature superseded the laws of nations; and Great Britain, in her turn, would be left to the mercy of the honest and innocent republicans of France! [19]

The Jacobin revolutionists, said Burke, simply pronounced all established monarchs usurpers of the Natural Law. "By this means they got rid of the law of nations and the obligation of treaties." [20] The voiding of all treaties was a legalistic preliminary to the contemplated Jacobin conquest of Europe: "They had violated the law of nations by a decree, declaring war against all governments, and forcing those countries, into which their armies should enter, to form a constitution similar to their own." [21] The desire to impose their theory of the state upon Europe was the logical consequence of the Jacobin principle of equality, of abstract uniformity in human affairs, and in February 1793 Burke warned that Britain was included in this leveling process:

> France . . . in order to overturn the fabric of our laws and government . . . invented a new law of nations. . . . She had directed the principal operations of that law to Great Britain. Their minister Cambon . . . had declared that the limits of their empire should be those that nature had set. [22]

The Jacobin conception of "nature" as it applied to civil society was far more geographical and physical than moral and political; their substitution of the empirical-scientific-utilitarian view of "nature" for the traditional ethical normative view caused them, Burke noted, to advance a theoretical social benevolence which disregarded all national and local "artificial" civil loyalties: "France has endeavoured, under the specious pretext of an enlarged benevolence, to sow the seeds of enmity among nations, and destroy all local attachments, calling them narrow and illiberal." [23]

To Burke one of the most monstrous errors of the Jacobins was their reference of all political theory to the touchstone of a hypothetical, abstract state of physical nature, man's supposed "original" state. [24] This desire to remodel civil society from the carte blanche of man's supposed simple and uniform original state led the Abbé Sieyès, whom Lord Acton called "the most perfect representative of the Revolution," to ignore all individual differences, preferences, and local loyalties of Frenchmen, developed historically in civil society under natural and constitutional law, and to wish to establish upon a priori laws of mathematical reasoning a national constitution centered in an abstract social equality.

In February 1793, Burke began a series of debates with

Charles J. Fox concerning the possibility of having diplomatic relations with revolutionary France and the propriety of British intervention in French internal affairs. Fox had derided Burke's appeals to the law of nations, and Burke rejoined by asking on what other basis nations could negotiate prescriptive treaties:

> The right honourable gentleman [Fox] had, with much flippancy, talked of the law of nations. He [Burke] wished to know on what law the French could be expected to treat; they had made a new law of nations of their own, and had pronounced all treaties between kings . . . void.[25]

In June 1793, Burke again pointed out that the revolutionary principles made treaties between nations impossible, and he repeated his usual attack on uniformity in governments:

> He read a long extract of a report by Brissot from the diplomatic committee, wherein it is stated as disgraceful to a free people to have any treaties whatever, especially with sovereigns. . . . It had been said [by Fox], shall we interfere for the purpose of obtruding on the French whatever form of government we shall think fitting for them? He was of opinion, that no country could force a particular form of government upon another, but that all received such a one as was under all . . . circumstances most adapted to their situation.[26]

Burke acknowledged that "it surely was not the business of this country to set up for a general arbiter of the law of nations," but this did not mean, as Fox and his followers claimed, that Britain had no concern with French internal affairs and ambitions. It was not to force an abstract theory of government on France, but to keep revolutionary France from reducing the states of Europe to her theory, that Britain was justifiably concerned. In August 1791, Burke had said of the legality of intervention: "By the law of nations, when any country is divided, the other powers are free to take which side they please. For this consult a very republican writer, Vattel." [27] In June 1793, Burke applied and extended this argument against Fox:

> He insisted that it was a delusion, that nations were not to interfere with each other; for if any nation endeavoured to confuse, to trample upon, violate, or despise the rights of others, the interests

of human society required that all should join against them. If, by
the subversion of all law and religion, a nation adopts a malignant
spirit to produce anarchy and mischief in other countries, it is the
right of nations to go to war with them. In support of this doctrine,
he quoted the authority of Vattel, who lays it down, that if one nation adopt principles injurious to all government and order, such a
nation is to be opposed from principles of common safety.[28]

Burke observed in March 1794 that events had dissipated Fox's
appeals to universal benevolence, and that parliament had
returned to the traditional interpretation of the law of nations:
"He was glad to remark . . . that they were now convinced
of the danger of those principles of universal but fictitious
benevolence which forbade any interference in the affairs of
a foreign state." [29] Although finally the British government
and Continental Powers went to war with France for reasons
of self-interest, Burke alone believed, and in the end helped
to convince Pitt and other leaders, that the new French international doctrines were subversive of the law of nations on
which the established political order of Europe stood.

After Burke accepted the Chiltern Hundreds on June 20,
1794, and retired from parliament, he continued to attack the
revolutionists for their violations of the law of nations. As
usual, the Jacobins were his special target. He attacked their
confusion of descriptive and normative "nature" by reminding
them that "individuals are physical beings subject to laws
universal and invariable," that "commonwealths are not physical but moral essences." [30] He again attacked them for their
"rejection of every principle upon which treaties could be
made." [31] Although Burke seldom distinguished between the
important organized revolutionary groups—Feuillants, Giron-
dists, and Jacobins—he always distinguished clearly between
the Jacobins as a political sect and France as a nation, and
argued that the other Powers of Europe warred only against
Jacobinism, which on principle had renounced the law of
nations:

France since her revolution is under the sway of a sect, whose
leaders have deliberately, at one stroke, demolished the whole body
of that jurisprudence which France had pretty nearly in common

with other civilized countries. In that jurisprudence were contained the elements and principles of the law of nations, the great ligament of mankind. . . . It is a war between the partisans of the ancient, civil, moral, and political order of Europe, against a sect of fanatical and ambitious atheists which means to change them all. It is not France extending a foreign empire over other nations; it is a sect aiming at universal empire, and beginning with the conquest of France.[32]

Through his appeals to the law of nations, Burke justified his call for a total European war against the French Revolution; but these appeals reveal only the negative side and application of his principle. Through the same law of nations Burke always sought to reconcile the legitimate interests of each state in the great "Commonwealth of Europe," and to have every nation live at peace with its neighbors in the spirit of the Natural Law.

II. The Constitutional Conception of the Law of Nations

Burke was in the tradition of Suarez and Grotius in conceiving the law of nations as not only international, but also constitutional. He noted in 1796 that *by analogy* international law was generally derived logically from constitutional laws of nations:

It has ever been the method of public jurists to draw a great part of the analogies, on which they form the law of nations, from the principles of law which prevail in civil community. Civil laws are not all of them merely positive. Those which are rather conclusions of legal reason than matters of statutable provision, belong to universal equity, and are universally applicable.[33]

Thus the constitutional law of individual states is related to the European law of nations as the latter is to the Natural Law. For Burke constitutional law is at once a qualification of the Natural Law and a practical means of its fulfillment on the national level. The close reciprocal relationship between the constitutional laws of nations and the Natural Law is indicated by Burke's belief that "the universal law of almost every nation . . . is a kind of secondary law of nature" and that "constitutions furnish the civil means of getting at the natural." [34]

He felt that the British constitution in particular was so in harmony with the Natural Law that its method of operation was analogous to "nature." "By a constitutional policy, working after the pattern of nature, we receive, we hold, we transmit our government and our privileges, in the same manner in which we enjoy and transmit our property and our lives." [35] Because of "this happy effect of following nature," Burke always felt that any unjust statute passed under the British constitution would immediately reveal itself as a violation of Natural Law. [36] On this vital point he acknowledged that he was in the tradition of Sir Edward Coke, "that great oracle of our law, and . . . all the great men who follow him, to Blackstone," who held that the common law of England regarding life, liberty, and property was far more binding than any statute of king or parliament: "We entertain a high opinion of the legislative authority; but we never dreamt that parliaments had any right whatever to violate property, to overrule prescription, or to force a currency of their own fiction in place of that which is real, and recognized by the law of nations. [37] National constitutional laws derive their power and validity from the Natural Law, and as constitutional law is the basic law of a nation through many generations of men, its sovereignty is in turn superior to that of any statute passed by any particular administration. By virtue of His contract with the original goodness and wisdom of His creation, God cannot by arbitrary will be unjust to any of His creatures, and by analogy, rulers who hold their power in trust under Natural and constitutional law, whether monarchical, oligarchical, or democratic, have no moral right to violate these laws by arbitrary acts against the people's lives, liberty, or property. Britain, said Burke in 1790, "had kept alive the ancient principles and models of the old common law of Europe meliorated and adapted to its present state." [38] Thus Britain's constitutional law is connected through "the common law of Europe" to the Natural Law, and it is also the law within which all Englishmen may fulfill their individual political differences in harmony with the moral law.

Burke's belief in Natural Law and also in a constitutional law of nations enabled him, as he said in 1784, to look at "man's nature in general" and "man's nature as modified by his habits." It was the great glory of the English constitution, Burke said throughout his writings, that it considered both what men have in common and their individual differences. "The foundation of government is there [in the constitution] laid . . . in political convenience and in human nature; either as that nature is universal, or as it is modified by local habits." [39] If the ideas and phrases in the following passages are compared, the first written in 1774 and the second in 1790, it should be clear why the two great principles of man's natural moral unity and civil political diversity appear over and over again in Burke's conception of the English constitution:

Nothing is more beautiful in the theory of parliaments, than that principle of renovation, and union of permanence and change, that are happily mixed in their constitution:—That in all our changes we are never either wholly old or wholly new:—that there are enough of the old to preserve unbroken the traditionary chain of the maxims and policy of our ancestors, and the law and custom of parliament; and enough of the new to invigorate us and bring us to our true character, by being taken fresh from the mass of the people; and the whole, though mostly composed of old members, have, notwithstanding, a new character and may have the advantage of change without the imputation of inconstancy.[40]

Our political system is placed in a just correspondence and symmetry with the order of the world . . . wherein, by the disposition of a stupendous wisdom, moulding together the great mysterious incorporation of the human race, the whole, at one time, is never old, or middleaged, or young, but, in a condition of unchangeable constancy, moves on through the varied tenor of perpetual decay, fall, renovation, and progression. Thus, by preserving the method of nature in the conduct of the state, in what we improve, we are never wholly new; in what we retain, we are never wholly obsolete.[41]

For Burke civil society is organic, a creation of man's corporate wisdom and power, working analogically through precedents and historical continuity to fulfill the unchangeable spirit of the Natural Law. Civil society, patterned upon nature, man, and historical continuity, has therefore at least as rich and vast a variety of conditions and circumstances to shape its character as physical nature, and therefore nations are governed not by any abstract universal and eternal principles derived directly from Natural Law, but indirectly, through man's corporate reason and free will, through the conditional forms of government which, at their best, are an emanation of eternal moral principles, through all the circumstances of time, place, climate, race, and inherited customs and civil institutions. God, Natural Law, and man's development through history, have placed men in various national states, where they are able to fulfill "that action and counteraction, which, in the natural and in the political world, from the reciprocal struggle of discordant powers, draws out the harmony of the universe." [42] Burke felt that "the diversity of interests, that must exist, and must contend, in all complex society," no matter how varied, is always reconcilable to an all-inclusive and just social welfare. This reconciliation is possible by what men have in common under "nature" as an ethical norm; national constitutions modify the method of application, but they do not extinguish or even weaken the power of Natural Law.

From the harmony of Natural and constitutional law Burke derived his principle that "the love of the whole is not extinguished by . . . subordinate partiality." The proper order of progression in arriving at the love of all mankind was also indirect, from love of kin to love of kind:

To be attached to the sub-division, to love the little platoon we belong to in society, is the first principle (the germ as it were) of public affections. It is the first link in the series by which we proceed towards a love of our country, and to mankind.[43]

He believed the germ of public affection began in the family. In November 1793, writing to the Comte d'Artois to comfort him on his brother's death, Burke said: "The ties of nature, which are the laws of God, are much better, surer, safer, and pleasanter, than any which we make for ourselves, politically, as members of parties or states, or in the intercourse of common life as friendships." [44]

His conviction that general public affection should be embodied in a specific object or institution underlies his attacks on abstract "rights" and on that hypothetical "universal benevolence" or sensibility which tended to extinguish local and national feelings. This was his main objection against the French disciples of Rousseau, such as the Abbé Sieyès and Baron Cloots, and their English equivalents, Dr. Priestley and Dr. Price. Burke believed that Price's sermon, "A Discourse on the Love of Our Country" (1790), taught men to hate their country because they loved mankind, and this "red rag that drew Burke into the arena" was thoroughly castigated in the *Reflections*. Burke's attack on Dr. Price's theory of public affection forms an important theme in his criticism of the radical and revolutionary "universal benevolence," which tended to destroy both the international and constitutional conceptions of the law of nations. Windham recorded that shortly before Burke died he "spoke with horror" of Voltaire's *Pucelle d'Orleans*, as a work which tended to destroy "all love of country, and blamed himself for having polluted his imagination by reading it." [45] To Burke a man morally in tune with the spirit of Natural Law venerated his country and its constitution and respected all the differences in man's nature, both within and between all nations.

So profound was Burke's regard for the various circumstances in a nation's life, that although he said the French National Assembly had "in everything . . . strayed out of the high road of nature," even here, where an abstract statement concerning the political course of action to be pursued might have seemed safe, he refused to meet a Paris friend's request to submit a plan of government for France: "Sir, the proposition of plans, without an attention to circumstances, is the very cause of all your misfortunes; and never shall you find me aggravating, by the infusion of any speculation of mine, the evils which have arisen from the speculations of others." [46] Burke required an intimate knowledge of details, amounting to empirical verification, before he would say anything of political plans or constitutional arrangements: "I must see with my own eyes, I must, in a manner, touch with my own hands, not only the fixed but the momentary circumstances, before I could venture to suggest any political project whatsoever." In any constitution, he insisted, "plans must be made for men," not men fitted into plans: "We cannot think of making men and binding nature to our designs." Burke's profound self-skepticism and distrust of abstract rational speculation, his veneration of national differences and strict regard for various local circumstances, are not ultimate principles in opposition to the Natural Law, as his positivist critics have assumed, but follow from his full acceptance of the constitutional law of nations as a necessary part of the Natural Law itself. The law of nations supplied the concrete means of fulfilling the Natural Law in every civil society. The international and constitutional law of nations provides the key to two vital aspects of Burke's political thought; his attacks upon abstract speculation or rationalistic theory, and his exaltation of moral prudence as the first of political virtues.

III. The Principle of Prudence

Burke's deep distrust and lifelong aversion to abstract "metaphysical" speculations about the origins of government and the nature of liberty, and his contempt for appeals to undefined "equality" and the "rights of man," are so well known that it might be supposed no problem could exist on this point.[47] Yet it is precisely in this matter that Morley, Leslie Stephen, Lecky, and other positivist scholars have gone furthest astray. They have identified the revolutionary abstract "rights of man" with the classical Natural Law, and knowing Burke's intense distaste for abstract "rights," have concluded that he rejected the Natural Law for the expediency of utilitarianism. Burke's attacks on the revolutionary "rights of man" and false "natural rights" have invariably been discussed in the abstract, without asking—how "natural" in any moral normative sense were the "rights" he attacked? Were these "rights" derived from the traditional principles of Natural Law? Or were they false claims to "rights" which would destroy, rather than fulfill, the ethical norms of Natural Law? Conversely, were Burke's own appeals to "expediency," "circumstances," "diversity," "moderation," "practical results," and "prudence," a thing apart from or a part of his faith in the traditional principles of Natural Law? The clearest answer to these and related questions depends upon a firm understanding of what Burke meant by abstract speculation and by political and moral prudence, and of how they are related to each other and to the Natural Law. In all of Burke's speeches and political works the explicit or assumed direct antithesis to abstract speculative thought is political prudence. It was impossible to indulge in abstract speculation without violating the principle of prudence; no truly prudent statesman would in any instance be guilty of speculating in abstractions. Thus, abstract speculation and prudence form respectively the negative and positive side of Burke's practical political thought.

Burke's attacks on the abstract theories of his radical contemporaries did not imply a blanket rejection of reasonable generalizations about principles, but a rejection of erroneous theory:

I do not vilify theory and speculation—no, because that would be to vilify reason itself. . . . No, whenever I speak against theory, I mean always a weak, erroneous, fallacious, unfounded, or imperfect theory; and one of the ways of discovering that it is a false theory is by comparing it with practice. This is the true touchstone of all theories, which regard man and the affairs of men—does it suit his nature in general? does it suit his nature as modified by his habits? [48]

Burke's objections to false theory in politics generally included one of several points: an attack on a priori methods of arriving at a theory, a rejection of false claims to "rights" and "equality" and of hypothetical conceptions of a "state of nature," and a passionate disdain of applying theory directly to human affairs without any consideration of the historical processes which have shaped individual differences among men, and without the strictest regard to the moral consequences of political actions. These objections occur over and over again. Yet implicit throughout Burke's criticism there is almost always an attempt to show that true theory is embodied in practice, that although moral principles may be stated in abstract terms they become meaningful only when applied in specific situations, and that in applying the moral law statesmen must respect the particular and changing circumstances of men which constitute their historical inheritance.

Burke's first important criticism of abstract speculative theory occurred in 1769, in his attack on Grenville's *The Present State of the Nation.* According to Burke, Grenville's defense of George III's plan for governing the American colonies contained "many new, dangerous and visionary projects." In his method of American finance, said Burke, Grenville "mows down, without giving quarter, or assigning reason, army, navy, ordnance, ordinary, extraordinaries . . . he pours out with an inexhaustible bounty, taxes, duties, loans, and revenues, without uneasiness to himself, or burthen to the public." In the past, Burke continued, such speculative projects have shown no regard for the circumstances, opinions, habits, and customs of the colonies, and are the chief cause of their alienation from Britain. The mere abstract "right" of parliament to tax the colonies was nothing, compared with the feelings of those who were to be affected by the taxes. Grenville's plan of a compulsory equality in taxes was for Burke "the most dangerous and chimerical of all enterprises," since it ignored completely the differences in economic condition among the colonies. This project provoked one of Burke's earliest attacks on uniformity and abstract equality:

> Among all the great men of antiquity, Procrustes shall never be my hero of legislation; with his iron bed, the allegory of his government, and the type of some modern policy, by which the long limb was to be cut short, and the short tortured into length. Such was the state-bed of uniformity! He would, I conceive, be a very indifferent farmer, who complained that his sheep did not plough, or his horses yield him wool, though it would be an idea full of equality. . . . Such vexatious questions . . . rather belong to metaphysics than politics, and can never be moved without shaking the foundations of the best governments that have ever been constituted by human wisdom. . . . Politics ought to be adjusted, not to human reasonings, but to human nature; of which the reason is but a part, and by no means the greatest part. . . .[49]

Grenville's passion for projects and power was not an isolated disease. George III's later ministers, as well as the king himself, were quite as infected with metaphysical speculations about the "rights" of sovereignty.[50]

Throughout the period of the American Revolution Burke continued to condemn abstract theoretical reasoning in politics, and to oppose it with his principle of prudence. In 1774 he urged that the spirit of practicality and moderation, rather than "geometrical exactness," supplied the best means of arbitrating an amicable settlement with America. He refused to go into distinctions of "rights," or to mark their boundaries, and confessed he hated the very sound of such theoretical discourse. In his famous speech on conciliation with the colonies Burke attacked "refined policy" as the eternal "parent of confusion." He held, too, that "abstract liberty, like other mere abstractions, is not to be found. Liberty inheres in some sensible object." [51] Burke's *Letter to the Sheriffs of Bristol* (1777) contains a candid self-portrait of his love of prudence and distrust of speculative political reasoning:

I do not pretend to be an antiquary, a lawyer, or qualified for the chair of professor in metaphysics. I never ventured to put your solid interests upon speculative grounds. My having constantly declined to do so has been attributed to my incapacity for such disquisitions; and I am inclined to believe it is partly the cause. . . . So truly has prudence (constituted as the god of this lower world) the entire dominion over every exercise of power committed into its hands; and yet I have lived to see prudence and conformity to circumstances wholly set at nought in our late controversies, and treated as if they were the most contemptible and irrational of all things. . . . Instead of troubling our understandings with speculations concerning the unity of empire . . . it was our duty . . . to conform our government to the character and circumstances of the several people who composed this mighty and strangely diversified mass. I never was wild enough to conceive that one method would serve for the whole; that the natives of Hindostan and those of Virginia could be ordered in the same manner. . . . I was persuaded that government was a practical thing, made for the happiness of mankind, and not to furnish out a spectacle of uniformity, to gratify the schemes of visionary politicians. Our business was to rule, not to wrangle; and it would have been a poor compensation that we had triumphed in a dispute, whilst we lost an empire.[52]

Among the "visionary politicians" whom Burke castigated was Dr. Price, whose speculations about government were even more malignant than those of the king's ministers, since they involved not merely practical administration, but the very structure of Britain's government. Burke's extensive criticism of Dr. Price in the *Reflections* was anticipated in 1777 in the following significant passage:

> There are people, who have split and anatomised the doctrine of free government, as if it were an abstract question concerning metaphysical liberty and necessity; and not a matter of moral prudence and natural feeling. . . . Civil freedom is not an abstract speculation. . . . Far from any resemblance to those propositions in geometry and metaphysics, which admit no medium, but must be true or false in all their latitude; social and civil freedom, like all other things in common life, are variously mixed and modified, enjoyed in very different degrees, and shaped into an infinite diversity of forms, according to the temper and circumstances of every community. The extreme of liberty (which is *its abstract perfection, but its real fault*) obtains nowhere, nor ought to obtain anywhere. . . . Liberty too must be limited in order to be possessed.[53]

Even more than the king's Tory friends, whom Dr. Price detested on partisan grounds, this Dissenting minister was addicted to "speculations . . . destructive to all authority." The practical application of such perverted philosophy, Burke contended in 1777, would "tear up, along with practical liberty, all the foundations of human society, all equity and justice, religion and order." This criticism is wholly consistent with Burke's attack on Price's "Old Jewry" sermon thirteen years later, when it appeared that Britain might follow the example of France in launching a project in speculative political reform.

Burke frequently lamented the failure of parliament to treat the discontents of Ireland through a consideration of her circumstances, rather than as a metaphysical question.[54] But it was the French Revolution that provoked Burke's most severe attacks on abstract thought. In 1790 he stated in parliament that he never loved an abstract question, and that he believed many of the political vices of his time were owing to an abstract way of thinking. In his *Reflections* Burke again stressed, in almost identical phrases, the antithesis between circumstances and abstractions which he had made concerning civil liberty and "rights" in his *Letter to the Sheriffs of Bristol:*

I cannot give praise or blame to anything which relates to human actions, and human concerns, on a simple view of the object, as it stands stripped of every relation, in all the nakedness and solitude of metaphysical abstraction. Circumstances (which with some gentlemen pass for nothing) give in reality to every political principle its distinguishing color and discriminating effect. The circumstances are what render every civil and political scheme beneficial or noxious to mankind. . . . Government is not made in virtue of natural rights, which may and do exist in total independence of it; and exist in much greater clearness, and in a much greater degree of abstract perfection: but *their abstract perfection is their practical defect.* . . . In a sense the restraints on men, as well as their liberties, are to be reckoned among their rights. But as the liberties and the restrictions vary with times and circumstances, and admit of infinite modifications, they cannot be settled upon any abstract rule; and nothing is so foolish as to discuss them upon that principle.[55]

Burke submitted the egalitarian principles of the French Jacobins to the test of his touchstone of all political theory— whether it suited man's nature in general, and also man's nature as modified by his civil inheritance and habits. In condemning the Jacobins he utilized and greatly extended the same argument he had made concerning Grenville's policy of uniformity in 1769:

The legislators who framed the ancient republics knew that their business was too arduous to be accomplished with no better apparatus than the metaphysics of an undergraduate. . . . They had to do with men, and they were obliged to study human nature. They had to do with citizens, and they were obliged to study the effects of those habits which are communicated by the circumstances of civil life. They were sensible that the operation of this second nature on the first produced a new combination; and thence arose many diversities amongst men, according to their birth, their education, their professions, the period of their lives, their residence in towns or in the country, their several ways of acquiring and of fixing property . . . all of which rendered them as it were so many different species of animals. . . . The [ancient] legislator would have been ashamed, that the coarse husbandman should well know how to assort and to use his sheep, horses, and oxen, and should have enough of common sense, not to abstract and equalize them all into animals, without providing for each kind an appropriate food, care, and employment; whilst he, the economist, disposer, and shepherd of his own kindred, subliming himself into an airy metaphysician, was resolved to know nothing of his flocks but as men in general. . . . As the first sort of legislators attended to the different kinds of citizens, and combined them into one commonwealth, the others, the metaphysical and alchemistical legislators, have taken the direct contrary course. They have attempted to confound all sorts of citizens as well as they could, into one homogeneous mass; and then they divided this their amalgama into a number of incoherent republics.[56]

Burke believed that among many of the French Jacobins, such as the constitution manufacturer the Abbé Sieyès, metaphysical speculations about abstract liberty, equality, and "rights" raged like an epidemic. Burke was using no literary trope when he compared the Jacobins to the mad scientists and philosophers of Laputa and Balnibari in Swift's *Gulliver's Travels*. He pictured the Jacobin metaphysicians descending from their airy speculations, and listed among the follies which baffle argument their project for coining into money the bells of the suppressed churches. Even Burke's vocabulary suggests his conviction of their insanity; they are "speculators," "visionaries," "enthusiastic projectors," "empiric theorists," and "alchemists," whose political zeal and unbounded confidence in their own rationality and enlightenment and worship of mathematical reason and logic entangles them in the mazes of metaphysical sophistry. For Burke the Jacobins symbolized the ultimate evil in his lifelong struggle against the application of abstract speculation to practical politics.

Burke's greatest fear during the last eight years of his life was that this epidemic distemper, this "contagion of project and system," would gain the upper hand in Britain through the writings of such men as Priestley, Price, and Paine and the political activities of the various radical clubs and societies. In 1792 he lamented that the English radical reformers propagated abstract principles and exalted the realization of them in France. As sublime speculators they never considered the good or evil consequences produced by their theories, but asked only whether their propositions were true. In attacking their love of abstract thought, Burke wrote a significant passage in which he distinguished between abstractions and principles, and indicated the necessity of combining sound principles and circumstances:

I never govern myself, no rational man ever did govern himself, by abstractions and universals. I do not put abstract ideas wholly out of any question, because I know well that under that name I should dismiss principles; and that without the guide and light of sound well-understood principles, all reasoning in politics, as in everything else, would be only a confused jumble of particular facts and details, without a means of drawing out any sort of theoretical or practical conclusion. A statesman differs from a professor in a university; the latter has only the general view of society; the former, the statesman, has a number of circumstances to combine with those general ideas. . . . Circumstances are infinite, are infinitely combined; are variable and transient; he who does not take them into consideration is not erroneous, but stark mad—*dat operam ut cum ratione insaniat*—he is metaphysically mad. A statesman, never losing sight of principles, is to be guided by circumstances; and judging contrary to the exigencies of the moment he may ruin his country for ever.[57]

I have shown that Burke believed in the principles of the classical and Scholastic conception of Natural Law. In distinguishing between abstractions and principles it is clear that he was not rejecting the Natural Law, as his positivist critics supposed, but was attacking the current nominalist conception of reality, the faith in mathematical reasoning and the speculative mania of philosophers who treated politics as a purely theoretical science. Behind all of these errors was the vast intellectual pride of the *philosophes,* the Encyclopedists, and the entire eighteenth-century "Enlightenment." To Burke the Cartesian rationalists and theorists of the Enlightenment, who confidently examined the results of God's reason and will as though it were their own creation, were vain and deluded sophists, guilty of a Faustian pride, consumed in endless and futile speculations about the structure of the universe, the meaning of history, the origin and nature of civil society, liberty, justice, and the abstract "rights of man." It is no paradox, therefore, that he always opposed the revolutionary "rights of man" doctrines precisely because he made the classical and Scholastic Natural Law the whole basis of his political philosophy.

Historically, Burke's opposition to abstract thought condemns the entire revolutionary tradition of "natural rights" introduced by Hobbes and popularized by Locke and his disciples. In his conviction that politics was a practical and not a theoretical science, and that abstract mathematically logical truths were morally and politically false, Burke consciously took his stand in the Natural Law tradition of Aristotle, and his repugnance to the use of mathematical methods in political reasoning is no less intense than Aristotle's. In 1775 Burke invoked the ancient philosopher in maintaining that neither a priori reasoning nor inductive empirical experience could ever attain the certainty of geometry in moral and political affairs: "Man acts from adequate motives relative to his interests; and not on metaphysical speculations. Aristotle . . . cautions us against this species of delusive geometrical accuracy in moral arguments, as the most fallacious of all sophistry." [58] One of the great themes of the *Reflections* was that "in politics the most fallacious of all things [is] geometrical demonstration." [59] According to Burke the chief strength of mathematics and of logical disquisitions consisted in considering one thing at a time, but the best judgments and results in moral and political problems came from having in one view the greatest number and variety of circumstances. The essence of his profound concern with concrete circumstances is found in his principle of political prudence.

The first great qualification of the Natural Law, which assured man the means of its practical fulfillment in civil society, was the law of nations. Men did not behave toward each other simply as men in the abstract, as men in a state of nature, but as citizens of a world political commonwealth. The constitutional law of individual nations forms in Burke's political philosophy the second broadest qualification of the Natural Law. This national basis of law, which provides the political frame of reference within which the fixed and changing circum-

stances of each state are arranged, and which under the Natural
Law regulates the individual differences of people within various nations, culminates in Burke's most fundamental practical
political doctrine—his moral and political prudence. Almost
every page that Burke ever wrote on matters of state breathes
the spirit of his principle of prudence. To understand what he
meant by prudence it is essential to note its intimate connection
through the constitutional law of nations to the Natural Law.
This is precisely what all of Burke's positivist critics have failed
to do; their disregard of his appeals to the Natural Law and
the law of nations led them to make a false antithesis between
Nature and prudence. The spirit of constitutional law is infused with prudence, which in its most general meaning is
simply the ultimate and constant consideration which every
statesman is morally obliged to give, under the Natural Law,
to the national and local circumstances which distinguish men
from one another. But as circumstances are varied, and infinitely variable, they cannot be settled by any abstract rule; the
close reciprocal relationship between prudence and the Natural
Law cannot be understood apart from Burke's convictions concerning the law of change.

It would be impossible for the Natural Law to be applicable
in the practical political order, to exercise a normative function in the various contingencies of man's social existence, without some principle of change inherent in the Natural Law itself.
Otherwise the principles of Natural Law would be like
theorems in geometry, and the Natural Law would be merely
a purely theoretical body of moral propositions applicable to
political problems by a literal-minded, rule-of-thumb process
of mathematical demonstration, without equity or legal temperance. This is precisely how Pufendorf and other seventeenth-
and eighteenth-century legal thinkers conceived the Natural
Law, and it is among the most important differences which
separate them from the classical and Scholastic Natural Law of
Cicero and Hooker, to which Burke adhered. As he observed,
God in His original creation decreed there should be many
natural differences among mankind, according to climate, race,
civil customs, religion, and infinite other circumstances which

set men apart. "Those who think themselves wiser than Providence, and stronger than the course of nature, may complain of all this variation." [60] Burke recognized that these divinely established differences, inherent in the nature of civil society, make the principle of change a vital element in the Natural Law: "We must all obey the great law of change. It is the most powerful law of nature, and the means perhaps of its conservation." [61] All that men can do through politics, he believed, is to provide the means of change that will bring society into harmony with the moral law.

The means of change cannot be found in metaphysical "rights" aimed at establishing a dead uniformity in society; the Natural Law itself, as the ultimate source of prudence, invalidates the uniformity of all metaphysical abstractions: "These metaphysical rights entering into common life, like rays of light which pierce into a dense medium, *are by the laws of nature,* refracted from their straight line." [62] This simile from the *Reflections* was repeated three years later in parliament: "Laws, he said, were bending to occasions while they followed principles, as the rays of light acting under a general law are refracted by a particular modification of glass through which they would, under the same laws, otherwise pass in a direct line." [63] The excellence of Natural Law to Burke was not in its logical consistency, but in its eternal capability to absorb, adapt, and renew the organic changes in man's civilization. The principle of growth was part of the principle of social order under the Natural Law. Like St. Thomas Aquinas and Coke before him, and to a degree Rudolf Stammler in the twentieth century, Burke conceived of Natural Law with a changing content and dynamic method, guided by the principle of prudence, subject to growth by the recognition of new values emerging from the historical development of civilization.

The constitution of each nation provided the practical instruments of achieving changes within the state according to the Natural Law. Constitutional laws also had to include a principle of change which recognized differences between men, or the state could not survive: "A state without the means of some change is without the means of its conservation." [64] Permanent political arrangements are meaningful only as they sustain and are sustained by the changing needs and circumstances of men; transformations in society are necessary and good, and wholly in keeping with the spirit of Natural Law. However, Burke was also convinced that alterations in civil society should not be made by virtue of abstract speculative reason, but by the slow growth, the bland assimilation through history of the corporate will and reason of a whole people. It was the business of man's right reason to recognize and accept necessary organic developments in a nation's constitution. But nothing was more delusive and pernicious, nor more in violation of prudence and the fulfillment of Natural Law through historical prescription, than a radical attempt to reconstruct the social order on any abstract rational theory. To consciously innovate was not to reform according to prudence and right reason. Burke always maintained that the British constitution was prescriptive, and based on the total corporate experience of the nation. Those who thought commonwealths could be constructed or renovated on a priori rational theories, Burke complained, frequently inverted the natural order between prescription and theory:

A prescriptive government, such as ours, never was the work of any legislator, never was made upon any foregone theory. It seems to me a preposterous way of reasoning, and a perfect confusion of ideas, to take the theories which learned and speculative men have made from that government, and then, supposing it made on those theories, which were made from it, to accuse government as not corresponding with them.[65]

Since individual differences between men and eras under the constitutional law of nations made prudence the cardinal principle of practical politics, it was impossible to devise any abstract, absolute political theory of any practical validity. That is why those who have looked for a rationally systematic philosophy in Burke's politics have looked in vain and have even been led through frustration to deny that he had a political philosophy. Faith in the classical and Scholastic conception of Natural Law is Burke's ultimate political principle. But prudence prevented him from seeking to apply the normative ethical principles of Natural Law as though they were mathematical theorems. Prudence made his theory thoroughly and profoundly temperate in its application to society, and this too was a vital part of his political philosophy.

The distinction of Aristotle and St. Thomas Aquinas between speculative and practical reason is fundamental to Burke's principle of prudence. According to this distinction, natural science and mathematics utilize speculative reason, while ethics, law, and politics employ practical reason. Speculative reason does not involve man's free will but is concerned with things fixed in the physical order of the universe and connected closely to this order by its universal principles and its logically derived conclusions. Practical reason involves the nature and actions of men, which are under general laws of moral necessity; but because the will of man is free and his circumstances are infinitely varied, in contingent matters and details there can be no general or necessary laws. St. Thomas put the matter this way: "The obligation of observing justice is indeed perpetual. But the determination of those things that are just, according to human or Divine institution, must needs be different, according to the different states of mankind." [66] "Laws are laid down for human acts dealing with singular and contingent matters which have infinite variations. To make a rule fit every case is impossible." [67] The kinship between Burke's conception of the Natural Law and his principle of prudence, and that of the medieval Scholastics, is most evident in his belief that the Natural Law was a part of practical reason. Burke rejected totally the eighteenth-century theories of "natural law" or "natural rights," which sought to provide for all contingencies by utilizing speculative reason and a mathematical foundation and method.

For Burke political theory could never be an exact mathematical science because matters requiring moral prudence could never be settled a priori or through mere empirical experience: "The progressive sagacity that keeps company with times and occasions, and decides upon things in their existing position, is that alone which can give true propriety, grace, and effect to a man's conduct. It is very hard to anticipate the occasion, and to live by a rule more general." [68] Since to Burke "no moral questions are ever abstract questions," and ethical decisions require man's free will and right reason at every point and on each new occasion, prudence, the spirit of Natural Law in practice, was always his positive alternative to metaphysical abstractions:

Nothing universal can be rationally affirmed on any moral or political subject. Pure metaphysical abstraction does not belong to these matters. The lines of morality are not like ideal lines of mathematics. They are broad and deep as well as long. They admit of exceptions; they demand modifications. These exceptions and modifications are not made by the process of logic, but by the rules of prudence. Prudence is not only the first in rank of the virtues political and moral, but she is the director, the regulator, the standard of them all.[69]

Burke always maintained that "the exercise of competent jurisdiction is a matter of moral prudence," because "moral necessity is not like metaphysical, or even physical." Tyranny was a more common abuse in government than usurpation, Burke believed, because it was not so much by the assumption of unlawful powers as by the unwise use of those which are most legal that governments violate their true ends:

You can hardly state to me a case, to which legislature is the most confessedly competent, in which, if the rules of benignity and prudence are not observed, the most mischievous and oppressive things may not be done. So that after all, it is a moral and virtuous discretion, and not any abstract theory of right, which keeps governments faithful to their ends. Crude unconnected truths are in the world of practice what falsehoods are in theory.[70]

He opposed George III's and Warren Hastings' abstract appeals to the "rights" of sovereignty because they violated prudence and their actions resulted in tyranny. He opposed the aspirations of the English radical reformers and French Jacobins because they wished, under an appeal to the "rights of man," to usurp legally established sovereignty and to reform the whole structure of government upon abstract speculative theories.

It is significant that in the greatest reform of abuses in government attempted by Burke, his mild economical reform of 1780, he apologized for his departure from his habitual course of action by appealing to a "humanity" beyond prudence, and sharply distinguished between his own principle of prudence and moral weakness or equivocation:

I feel that I engage in a business . . . totally wide of the course of prudent conduct; and I really think, the most completely adverse that can be imagined, to the natural turn and temper of my own mind. . . . It is much more easy to reconcile this measure to humanity, than to bring it to any agreement with prudence. I do not mean that little, selfish, pitiful, bastard thing, which sometimes goes by the name of a family in which it is not legitimate, and to which it is a disgrace—I mean that public and enlarged prudence, which, apprehensive of being disabled from rendering acceptable service to the world, withholds itself from those that are invidious.[71]

In his reform bill Burke insisted that moral prudence should regulate every change and he governed his reforms by reference to tradition and fundamental justice. His remark, "If I cannot reform with equity I will not reform at all," and his appeals to "frugality," "probity," and "candour," were attacked by Jeremy Bentham as so many pretexts to preserve the corrupt court system. To Burke's "I am not possessed of an exact measure between real service and its reward," Bentham replied: "Except Edmund Burke, no man is thus ignorant." [72] Bentham's willingness to compute the ratio between service and reward illustrates one of the great differences between Burke's principle of prudence and the utilitarian idea of "expediency." To appreciate how completely all of Burke's utilitarian critics garbled his conception of prudence we must first determine more minutely what it meant for Burke.

In Burke's political philosophy prudence is the general regulator of social changes according to Natural and constitutional law. As such, it is the cardinal virtue which supplies the practical means by which Natural Law principles are fulfilled and harmonized with the concrete circumstances of man's social life. But since prudence is necessary not only to reform equitably, but also to prevent changes contrary to the Natural Law, it has both a negative and positive character, found respectively in "temperance" and "right reason." Even the negative side of prudence is conceived by Burke as a divine virtue made evident to man throughout the creation:

> His [God's] hand, in every page of his book, has written the lesson of moderation. Our physical well-being, our moral worth, our social happiness, our political tranquillity, all depend on that control of our appetites and passions, which the ancients designated by the cardinal virtue of Temperance.[73]

According to Burke, in reforming abuses in society a temperate man will be moderate in his expectations and actions. Such moderation is not to be confused with cowardly equivocation; quite the contrary, it takes bold moral courage to be temperate in the face of popular pressure to be extreme:

> Prudence (in all things a virtue, in politics the first of virtues,) will lead us rather to acquiesce in some qualified plan that does not come up to the full perfection of the abstract idea, than to push for the more perfect, which cannot be attained without tearing to pieces the whole contexture of the commonwealth. . . . In all changes in the state, moderation is a virtue, not only amiable, but powerful. It is a disposing, arranging, conciliating, cementing virtue. . . . Moderation (which times and situations will clearly distinguish from the counterfeits of pusillanimity and indecision) is the virtue only of superior minds. It requires a deep courage, and full of reflection, to be temperate when the voice of multitudes (the specious mimic of fame and reputation) passes judgment against you. The impetuous desire of an unthinking public will endure no course, but what conducts to splendid and perilous extremes. Then to dare to be fearful, when all about you are full of presumption and confidence, and when those who are bold at the hazard of others would punish your caution and disaffection, is to show a mind prepared for its trial; it discovers, in the midst of general levity, a self-possessing and collected character, which, sooner or later, bids to attract every thing to it, as to a centre.[74]

If this passage were not enough to acquit Burke of being through prudence a scrupulous calculator, conniver, or moral coward, as Lord Acton charged,[75] Burke's whole practical political career is the best answer to such a misrepresentation. His persistent loyalty to Rockingham and moral guidance of Whig policies for three decades is a sufficient monument to his high personal integrity. He gave up his seat for Bristol rather than support an iniquitous economic and religious policy against Ireland. For years after most of his colleagues would have liked to have quietly dropped Hastings' trial, Burke made himself unpopular for the moral zeal with which he pursued a just decision. He broke lifelong friendships and stood alone for several years rather than give approval of the French Revolution. Goldsmith's line is literally true; Burke was "too fond of the right to pursue the expedient." Because of his refusal to be corrupted by the Crown, Burke spent most of his political career with the loyal opposition. In 1769 when the elder Pitt left his retirement and returned briefly to politics to secure justice for the colonists and the Middlesex electors, the condition under which he was willing to assume power is an eternal tribute to Burke and his party:

> For my part, I am grown old, and unable to fill any office of business; but this I am resolved on, that I will not even sit at council but to meet Lord Rockingham. He, and he alone, has a knot of spotless friends such as ought to govern this kingdom.[76]

In practice the negative side of Burke's principle of prudence did not result in calculated self-interest or an ossified moral will, but reflected that temperance with which the Natural Law should be applied to human affairs.

Since moral prudence is indirectly connected to the Natural Law and partakes of its character, the rules of prudence are clearly perceptible and self-evident to man's unaided right reason. It is therefore no paradox that although political problems involving concrete circumstances cannot be settled on any abstract rule, "all the rules of prudence are as sure as the laws of material nature." [77] To Burke moral insight could come to man through divine revelation, or more commonly through natural right reason. History also was for him a preceptor of prudence, the concrete embodiment of moral revelation in temporal human affairs. Within history, Burke maintained, "the rules of prudence . . . are formed upon the known march of the ordinary province of God";[78] prudence is the spirit of God's moral law fulfilling itself throughout history. Not only through divine revelation, but also through prudence in history and civil society as perceived by natural right reason, God has made clear the whole duty of man toward man. In short, prudence is God's "divine tactic" fulfilled in man's moral and political tact. Understood in this profoundly Aristotelian sense, Burke's principle of prudence is nothing less than the universal, eternal, and unchangeable Natural Law applied in practice through politics to each particular man, at every moment and in all circumstances, under the derived sovereignty of various nations. This is the vital implication in Burke's union of the laws of nature and of nations; in his political theory they are always so interfused that each particular element of each law pervades every fiber of the other in a complex, subtle, and unsystematic whole.

The essential spirit of Burke's moral prudence is perhaps best shown in the many short phrases in which he mentions it incidentally. In partisan disputes "prudence would be neuter," but since practical affairs require choices and firm decisions, the job of a prudent statesman is to "reconcile," "compensate," and "balance" human affairs in a manner "suitable to the local and habitual circumstances of their people." Such words and phrases as "mediation," "equipoise," "wisdom and temper," "the spirit of moderation," and "the amiable and conciliatory virtues of lenity, moderation and tenderness," fill all of Burke's discussions of Natural and constitutional law and practical policy. Everywhere he advises that rulers should "conform to the nature and circumstances of things," that "matters of prudence are under the dominion of circumstances, and not of logical analogies." His speeches are filled with such phrases as "not infallibility but prudence," and "ideas of prudence and accommodation to circumstances." Prudence was for Burke the first object of a statesman; he considered government the exercise of all the great qualities of the human mind, "with the mother virtues of prudence and providence at their head." Since all mankind must bend to circumstances, so much depends upon the state in which men are found that "the situation of man is the preceptor of his duty." Prudence tells us when we should "abate our demand in favor of moderation and justice, and tenderness to individuals." Only after the spirit of the law has failed in its purpose are statesmen justified in applying the letter of the law: "When the maxims of public councils are not steady, it is necessary that law should supply the want of prudence." [79] It is essential to keep in mind that in all these appeals or uses of prudence Burke meant not an intellectual but a moral discretion. Prudence was that part of man's temperament and right reason which enabled him to live by the spirit of the Natural Law.

In Burke's moral philosophy primary principles are self-evident to right reason, and practical expediency is not contrary to the Natural Law. He believed that the Natural Law belongs to practical reason, and conclusions derived from it or particular determinations of it, having to do with contingencies and circumstances, cannot in the nature of things be as certain as laws in physical science and mathematics. Moral prudence, not fixed logical consistency, must determine how the Natural Law is to be fulfilled. This process requires the legislator to master details, because in ruling justly he is involved in a perpetual series of organic adaptations of the law, which must be renewed every day. In contrast to utilitarian expediency, Burke's principle of prudence is more an ethical than an intellectual virtue; it is not the utilitarian computation of empirical observations, nor the calculating, rational analysis of shrewd prophesy concerning circumstances that determine how far power might be utilized without provoking a revolution. Nor is prudence merely the social virtue of tact, which also varies with changes in circumstances. Prudence was for him the *spirit* of practical morality, requiring the intellect both for understanding and action, but being itself a part of the moral law. In contrast to utilitarian expediency, Burke's principle of prudence is the moral fear of injuring unjustly those who are most affected by decisions involving the uses of power. Prudence is therefore the moral virtue of temperance; it supplements courage and makes both moral restraint and action a practical necessity.

The claim of utilitarian critics that Burke belongs to their camp has obscured the absolute contrast between his principle of prudence and their conception of expediency. Though Burke did have a principle of utility, he was no utilitarian. He clearly indicated in the "Tracts on the Popery Laws" that he derived utility from Cicero's principle of moral equity, which was based upon "original justice." It was a utility "connected with and derived directly from our rational nature; for any other utility may be the utility of a robber." In his attack on Warren Hastings' "system of corruption" Burke noted the governor's "attempts to justify it on the score of utility," and added, significantly: "God forbid that prudence, which is the supreme guide, and indeed stands the first of all virtues, should ever be the guide of vices." Burke distinguished carefully between a true and false adherent of moral prudence: "Our love to the occasionalist, but not server of occasions." In any conflict between merely utilitarian convenience and law, his stand was clear: "What the law respects shall be sacred to me. If the barriers of law should be broken down upon ideas of convenience, even of public convenience, we shall have no longer any thing certain among us." [80] When rulers follow true moral prudence they are perfectly in accord with Natural and constitutional law, from which men's true natural and civil rights are derived. Burke believed that when claims to individual "rights" conflicted with moral expediency or prudence they were not really "rights," and not, as Morley and other utilitarian critics have said, that they were rights but had to yield to public expediency.

Burke's moral equity, the foundation of his conception of prudence, has nothing to do with the utilitarians' physical and intellectual "equality" of man, which was derived from modern empirical and rational philosophy, from Hobbes and Locke and not from Cicero. Moral "equity" led Burke to his principle of man's diversity within a political unity under the law of nations and Natural Law, just as the love of "equality" led the Enlightenment utilitarians to the contrary theory of political uniformity under majority will. Burke's refusal to reform parliament on "a representation [based] on the principle of numbers" clearly proves that his view of expediency had nothing to do with the utilitarian "greatest good of the greatest number." The utilitarians transposed this slogan to mean that the greatest number should determine the moral criterion of the greatest good. Burke rejected popular sovereignty as the ultimate moral basis of politics; on such a principle the individual citizen counted for nothing and the state, as the expression of the "general will," became a popular absolute tyranny. Against the utilitarian principle of numerical equality, Burke placed his faith in moral equality: "It is not an arithmetical inequality with which we ought to trouble ourselves. If there be a moral, a political equality, this is the *desideratum* in our constitution, and in every constitution in the world." [81] Neither "abstract right" nor metaphysical "truth" nor "general will" nor "utility," nor anything else could replace or justify transgressions against the ethical norms of the Natural Law.

He believed the reverse of Lecky's statement that "all morals spring from and depend on utility." To Burke a law or action was not good because it was useful, but utility was merely one of several positive social consequences of morality. Since there could be nothing normative or obligatory in the pleasure or profit of utility, it could never be the final principle by which to judge men's actions. To have each individual decide for himself what was useful would be to build utility on the radicals' "natural rights." Utility could easily be rationalized to include a callous personal, class, sectarian, or national self-interest in violation of the Natural Law. The utilitarians believed in a prudent or convenient morality; Burke in a moral prudence. Burke's positivist critics have erred by ignoring the most important fact in his conception of "nature"; as a believing Christian he never separated politics, in theory or practice, from normative ethics, and "nature" was for him the ethical norm of every man's right reason. To Burke the only thing more useless than the utilitarianism of Hume, Godwin, and Bentham, was the unnaturalness of Dr. Price's and Paine's fictitious "natural rights." Utilitarianism, like the radicals' individual natural rights to which in one sense it was strongly opposed, was in the main stream of the revolutionary tradition. Indeed, scholars who have examined the revolutionary period in terms of "natural rights" versus utilitarianism have assumed too narrow a frame of reference to understand either Burke or the revolution. Vaughan admitted that "natural rights," which was a convenient theory on which to launch the revolution, was a dead issue by 1793-1794; it was replaced mainly by utilitarianism, a more useful theory on which to consolidate the revolution. Yet Burke opposed this second phase of the revolution no less ardently than the first, because his theory of sovereignty, his reconciliation of self-interest and social benevolence, and his principle of moral prudence were all based on the Natural Law and not on any principle of utility.

In summary, the Natural Law and the law of nations, culminating in prudence, form the largest and most fruitful frame of reference for an understanding of Burke's political philosophy. The ancient conception of the Natural Law, inherited from Aristotle, Cicero, Justinian, Bracton, St. Thomas Aquinas, Hooker, Suarez, Grotius, and all the English jurists from Coke to Blackstone, was modified by the modern law of nations and Burke's own unique addition of moral prudence. Burke's close affinity with all of his predecessors, but particularly with Cicero, is most evident in his view of "nature" as an imperative ethical norm, rather than as an empirical descriptive process of the physical order. Burke's acceptance of men's differences under the law of nations, and his application of moral prudence to practical affairs, supplied the chief means of living by the spirit of the Natural Law. Thus, his principle of prudence was not contrary to the Natural Law, as his utilitarian critics have maintained, but the indispensable means of its practical fulfillment.

Through the Natural Law and prudence Burke combined his eloquent religious mysticism and stark concrete practicality. Nature and prudence gave Burke his conviction that society is of divine institution but that its various forms, and those who administer them, originate from the people. As a normative code of ethics, the Natural Law was the basis of his conservatism; it taught him that man and society were organically immortal, and were bound through precedents and conventions beyond history to God. The principle of prudence underlay Burke's liberalism, his sensitive regard for men's differences, his veneration of local loyalties and prejudices, his intense dislike of arbitrary absolutism, and his skepticism of ideal, simple, universal, and uniform plans of government. Burke's acceptance of the Natural Law and principle of prudence made his political philosophy thoroughly consistent, yet almost wholly unsystematic. They enabled him to fuse to the limit of their valence the most sublime moral precepts and the most concrete empirical facts, details, and situations, so that political theory and practice were one.

In all of Burke's appeals to Natural, constitutional, and statutory laws, he revealed their rich reciprocal relationships as theory, and also their practical application to the case in point. As Matthew Arnold said, Burke "saturated politics with thought." Because he favored that harmony of discordant powers which tested ideas through an incessant and vigorous opposition, Burke was by temperament a man who would not regard the ultimate test of a philosophy that it was a totally unified system. Life was for him too filled with complexities, far too heterogeneous, varied, and mysterious, for anyone to reduce man's multifarious social and political affairs to a rational and autonomous system. The unity of Natural Law and the law of nations in Burke's political philosophy was like that delicate equipoise or harmony of opposites which he considered so essential in a just state. His political genius was essentially eclectic, and consisted of an extraordinary ability to comprehend the complex relationships between basic political principles and the materials furnished by practical social affairs. In his unique ability to apply the most exalted moral principles to the concrete facts of life Burke fused his principle of prudence and his faith in the Natural Law.

FIVE

Revolutionary "Natural Rights"

I. Burke's Rejection of the State of Nature

It is remarkably prophetic that Burke's first important work in political thought, his satirical attack on Bolingbroke's deism, *A Vindication of Natural Society* (1756), was directed against the same doctrines of a state of nature which called forth his dying protests. With characteristic insight, even at age twenty-seven Burke perceived the revolutionary tendency of the state of nature theory, which in his last years was to help to destroy the established order. Just as Bishop Butler had shown in *The Analogy of Religion* (1736) that the deist objections to revealed Christianity applied as well to "natural" religion, Burke argued through an ironical *reductio ad absurdum* that Bolingbroke's attacks on artificial religion applied equally to political laws and to all civil society:

> Show me an absurdity in religion, and I will undertake to show you an hundred for one in political laws and institutions. . . . If after all, you should confess all these things, yet plead the necessity of political institutions, weak and wicked as they are, I can argue with equal, perhaps superior, force, concerning the necessity of artificial religion; and every step you advance in your argument, you add a strength to mine.[1]

Burke made it clear that Bolingbroke, in celebrating the virtues of a simple natural society, was not merely attacking abuses of power in civil society: "In vain you tell me that artificial government is good, but that I fall out with the abuse. The thing! the thing itself is the abuse!" There are many passages in Burke's satire which indicate that his argument was directed against any antithesis of "nature" and "art" which might lead men to attack artificial institutions as "unnatural."

Burke was aware that satirical irony and intellectual paradox are dangerous weapons with which to combat theories of primitive or natural society. As Morley said, he soon found it necessary to make clear his real intention: "It is significant that in 1765, when Burke saw his chance of a seat in Parliament, he thought it worthwhile to print a second edition of his *Vindication,* with a preface to assure his readers that the design of it was ironical." [2] In this important preface, which actually first appeared in 1757,[3] Burke condemned Bolingbroke's clever use of the antithesis of nature and art in attacking civil society, because such "pleasing impressions on the imagination subsist and produce their effect, even after the understanding has been satisfied of their unsubstantial nature." [4] Burke was convinced that words continue to influence men psychologically, even after they have rejected any belief in a historical state of nature.

Burke's point is well proved in the comments of various writers on his satire. William Godwin even advanced the proposition that Burke's satire had demonstrated what was literally true: "In Burke's *Vindication of Natural Society* . . . the evils of the existing political institutions are displayed with incomparable force of reasoning and lustre of eloquence." [5] Halévy, in commenting upon Godwin's indictment of civil society, seems not even to have been aware that Burke's *Vindication* was a satire: "Godwin perhaps drew his inspiration from Burke, who, in a youthful work, a curious essay devoted to the defense of natural society, had contrasted the state of nature . . . with the state of 'artificial' society." [6] An implicit faith in the superiority of a state of nature to civil society is contained in J. B. Bury's comparison of Rousseau's *Discourse on Inequality* and Burke's satire:

In truth, a more powerful and comprehensive case against civilized society was drawn up about the same time, by one whose thought represented all that was opposed to Rousseau's teaching. Burke's early work, *A Vindication of Natural Society,* worked out in detail a historical picture of the evils of civilization which is far more telling than Rousseau's generalities.[7]

Woodrow Wilson's comments on the *Vindication* reveal a more profound appreciation of Burke's ironic method and position toward his subject: "Much that Burke urges against civil society he could urge in good faith, and his mind works soberly upon it. It is only the main thesis that he does not seriously mean." [8] The main thesis of Burke's satire was the Rousseauist paradox that a simple society, close to "nature," was morally superior to the complex and refined "artificial" civil society of eighteenth-century Europe. Burke did not believe that man was intrinsically morally sound and became corrupted by the external refinements and demands of his civil institutions. Quite the reverse. To Burke the worst possible civil society was superior to any hypothetical simple "state of nature." Burke's satire merely proved that he understood and could present the argument of his philosophical opponents better than they could themselves, and that he rejected totally all serious consideration of the state of nature.

His *Vindication* supplies another source for the much-debated question of his political consistency. The author of *Pearls Cast Before Swine* (London, 1793), one of Burke's many unknown critics, tried to prove by contrasting quotations from his early satire and his later works that after 1790 Burke was inconsistent. The pamphleteers who replied to Burke's *Reflections* put forth in perfect seriousness many things that Burke had argued ironically thirty-five years earlier. In his early satire Burke pretended to believe that "truth" in religion, government, and law, as revealed by mathematical logic systematically extended, was always simple, plain, direct, uniform, and universal, that anything complex was a fraud, that metaphysical speculation was preferable to "vulgar experience," that local or national loyalties indicated a "prejudiced" or "superstitious" mind, and above all, that "artificial" institutions were usurpers of man's "natural rights" corrupting him and preventing him from living in civil society with the same freedom he had enjoyed in a state of nature. All of these ideas and arguments, and even Burke's diction and phrases in the *Vindication*, appeared in various combinations as serious replies to his *Reflections*.

In his early satire, after describing the "artificial division of

mankind into separate societies," and the evils that developed
because men left simple "nature" and lived under complex
artificial institutions, Burke wrote with mock indignation:
"But no wonder, that what is set up in opposition to the state
of nature should preserve itself by trampling upon the law of
nature." [9] For Burke a state of civil society was the absolutely
necessary means of fulfilling the law of nature, and nothing
could be more foolish than to confuse a state of nature with
the moral law of nature. In this he was at one with Cicero and
the Roman Stoics and jurists. Bryce has shown that the Romans'
"law of nature had nothing to do with any so-called state of
nature, [because they] never troubled themselves about primitive man." [10] Burke always refused to consider the nature of
man or the origins of government in terms of any non-civil,
pre-institutional or prehistorical "state of nature." As man was
for him by nature a political animal, not even for hypothetical
purposes would he admit of a "state of nature." In February
1788, while speaking on Indian affairs, Burke said: "There is a
sacred veil to be thrown over the beginning of all government." [11] Burke rejected the state of nature because it had no
historical existence in fact, because politics was a practical and
not a speculative science, and because he doubted that man's
unaided reason could penetrate the divine mystery at the core
of civilized life. God had willed society and the state as the
necessary means of perfecting human nature; Burke therefore
accepted and venerated civil society, with all its imperfections,
in a spirit of piety and reverence.

If no other differences existed, Burke's total rejection of the
state of nature should have taught his critics how far removed
he was from the political thought and tradition of Hobbes and
Locke and their revolutionary conceptions of "natural rights."
Yet J. A. Lester contends that "the Lockian tradition was strong
and respected by all political thinkers of Burke's age, [and that]
Burke was not one to make a conscious break with that tradition." [12] Arthur Goodhart also believed that "from Locke it
is only a short step to Edmund Burke," [13] while Leo Gershoy
claimed that Burke "helped modernize Locke." [14] Vaughan
and Morley, despite their failure to perceive the Natural Law

in Burke's political philosophy, knew better than to connect him with the tradition of Locke. Wrote Vaughan: "He speaks as though he were contending not against practical statesmen, but against abstract theorists, such as Hobbes or Locke." [15] "In the *Reflections*," said Morley, "we have the first great sign that the ideas on government and philosophy which Locke had been the chief agent in setting into European circulation, and which had carried all triumphantly before them throughout the century, did not comprehend the whole truth nor the deepest truth about human character—the relations of men and the union of men in society." [16] Burke rejected the political tradition of Locke mainly because he did not believe in any antithesis between art and nature; he could not accept any "natural rights" based on an imaginary state of nature.

Burke's differences with his Lockian "natural rights" opponents are evident throughout his life, but especially in his resistance during the 1780's to their attempts to reform parliament, and in the debate over the French Revolution. Burke always regarded the English constitution as the practical means through which civil rights were secured under the Natural Law. During the 1780's Priestley, Price, and other reformers of parliament came more and more to look upon the constitution as an artificial barrier, an impediment infringing upon the abstract "rights" which man had enjoyed in a state of nature. Burke's most important attack upon this view of the English constitution occurred on June 16, 1789, in his speech on the "Reform of the Representation of the Commons" in parliament. For what it reveals of his dislike of "natural rights" based on a hypothetical state of nature, this brief speech is one of the most important Burke ever delivered. In another speech in 1790 Burke pointed out the incompatibility between such fictitious "natural rights" and civil society:

Abstract principles . . . he disliked, and never could bear; he detested them when a boy, and he liked them no better now he had silver hairs. . . . But, of all abstract principles, abstract principles of natural right—which the Dissenters rested on, as their strong hold—were the most idle, because the most useless and the most dangerous to resort to. They superceded society, and broke asunder all those bonds which had formed the happiness of mankind for ages. He would venture to say, that if they were to go back abstractedly to original rights, there would be an end of all society.[17]

To Burke civil society, not a state of nature, was man's natural state. Burke drew all his political norms and standards from the classical conception of the Natural Law as embodied in a nation's civil constitution.

The culmination of Lockian or Rousseauist "natural rights" was the Declaration of the Rights of Man, drafted by Sieyès and adopted by the National Assembly on August 26, 1789. In attacking this declaration Burke consistently opposed the state of nature with the norms of civil society:

> A body of rights, commonly called the Rights of Man . . . had been lately set up by some persons . . . as paramount to all other rights. A principal article in this new code was, 'that all men are by nature free, are equal in respect of rights, and continue so in society.' . . . What were the rights of man previous to his entering into a state of society? Whether they were paramount to, or inferior to social rights, he neither knew nor cared. Man he had found in society, and that man he looked at—he knew nothing of any other man—nor could he argue on any of his rights.[18]

Burke believed that as man's nature was essentially civil, his "rights" as a citizen were determined by the conventions of his society. The revolutionary desire to enjoy in civil society the hypothetical "rights" of an original state of nature would end by destroying men's real civil rights:

> Far am I from denying in theory . . . or from withholding in practice . . . the *real* rights of men. In denying their false claims of right, I do not mean to injure those which are real, and such as their pretended rights would totally destroy. . . . As to the share of power, authority, and direction which each individual ought to have in the management of the state, that I must deny to be amongst the direct original rights of man in civil society, for I have in my contemplation the civil social man, and no other. It is a thing to be settled by convention. . . . Men cannot enjoy the rights of an uncivil and of a civil state together.[19]

> The pretended *rights of man* . . . cannot be the rights of the people. For to be a people, and to have these rights, are things incompatible. The one supposes the presence, the other the absence, of a state of civil society.[20]

So completely did Burke reject any antithesis between the "natural" and the "artificial" that he even applied the phrase "state of nature" to describe man in *civil* society. "The state of civil society," he wrote, "is a state of nature" ruled by "the laws of God . . . the natural moral laws." [21] Burke believed that "commonwealths are artificial combinations" in which political "ministers are our natural rulers . . . and natural guides." As man was born without his own consent into a historically developed civil society, his "artificial" or "positive" institutions were as "natural" to him as forests and prairies were to wild animals. Burke's epigram, "Art is man's nature," summarized his whole objection to the primitivism or simplicity of the Lockian state of nature.

Burke was ever conscious of the miraculous power of artificial institutions to subdue and mold the violent passions of men, to order civil virtues through manners, morals, and laws, and without violating individual differences, to bring all men into as natural a moral harmony with each other as the planets and stars. Through artificial institutions the "stupendous wisdom" behind all phenomena was capable of "moulding together the great mysterious incorporation of the human race" in civil society, in all the sanctity of obedience to laws, contracts, charters, treaties, manners, customs, and obligations that sheltered man from a raw and brutal barbarism. Indeed, the true "natural rights" of man, contained in the principles of the moral law, could be achieved in practice *only* in civil society:

> Abstract principles of natural right had been long since given up for the advantage of having, what was much better, society, which substituted wisdom and justice, in the room of original right. It annihilated all those natural rights, and drew to its mass all the component parts of which those rights were made up. . . . It gave alms to the indigent, defence to the weak, instruction to the ignorant, employment to the industrious, consolation to those who wanted it, nurture to the helpless, support to the aged, faith to the doubtful, hope to those in despair, and charity to all the human race. . . . Such were the advantages attributable to society.[22]

The true natural rights of man, founded on Natural Law and embodied in civil institutions, were best preserved and realized in England: "Let me say, for the honour of human nature and for the glory of England, that we have better institutions for the preservation of the rights of man than any other country in the world." [23] England's civil institutions, like those of all nations, clothed her citizens in moral drapery and civil virtues and enabled them to fulfill the moral law.

He feared that the English and French "rights of man" theorists, in their desire to live according to "nature" by seeing not how much of civilization they could accept, but how much they could reject, would strip man down, sans-culotte fashion, to something less than Swift's "single man in his shirt":

> But now all is to be changed. All the pleasing illusions which made power gentle and obedience liberal, which harmonized the different shades of life, and which, by a bland assimilation, incorporated into politics the sentiments which beautify and soften private society, are to be dissolved by this new conquering empire of light and reason. All the decent drapery of life is to be rudely torn off. All the super-added ideas, furnished from the wardrobe of a moral imagination, which the heart owns, and the understanding ratifies, as necessary to cover the defects of our naked, shivering nature, and to raise it to dignity in our estimation, are to be exploded as a ridiculous, absurd, and antiquated fashion.[24]

This implicit argument against primitive or unpolished society clearly exalts the civilizing function of artificial institutions. Throughout his life Burke believed that without civil society man could not by any possibility arrive at the perfection of which his nature was capable. Burke's faith in civil institutions, his belief that man was by nature a political animal, are proof that his conception of Natural Law had nothing to do with any state of nature. Men cannot live in civil society by any *direct* appeal to primitive or pre-civil "natural rights." Through the law of nations and all the necessary intervening laws, customs, and institutions of civil society, men learn to subdue their savage passions and live in harmony with the Natural Law.

Burke knew that his conception of civil society, and therefore of Church and State, was far more complex than that of his "rights of man" contemporaries. He felt that above all other civil institutions the Church served "the natural human means of estimation." Since he believed "the arts beautify and polish life," Burke always objected strongly to antiaesthetic theories,[25] and felt that a rich liturgy in worship, which utilized man's sensory equipment to inculcate soft manners, taught men to love God with their whole nature, and not merely through reason. To make civil law more conscious of its divine origin and function, Burke would even have the Church "exalt her mitred front in courts and parliaments." The state of nature itself would "uncover our nakedness, by throwing off that Christian religion which has hitherto been our boast and comfort, and one great source of civilization amongst us." To Burke even the idea of returning to "primitive" Christianity was a revolutionary delusion. Most of the English people, he said, saw through "the cant and jibberish of hypocrisy" through which the National Assembly "affect to carry back the clergy to that primitive, evangelic poverty, which, *in the spirit,* ought always to exist in them." [26] Nothing proved the hypocrisy of primitivism in practice so much as that the French Assembly's Church policies should be issued by Mirabeau, an avowed atheist: "Your Assembly addresses a manifesto to France, in which they tell the people, with insulting irony, that they have brought the Church to its primitive condition. In one respect their declaration is undoubtedly true; for they have brought it to a state of poverty and persecution." [27] In defending the spiritual and civil function of the Church against primitivist doctrines, Burke reaffirmed his belief in an aesthetic liturgy and in the complex historical continuity and apostolic succession of his High Church Anglican faith.

He also opposed the primitive simplicity which the "rights of man" theorists advocated as the norm in the constitutional structure of the state. This point is illustrated more fully in Burke's conception of the state; it is enough here to note his general criticism of simple political constitutions:

In the gross and complicated mass of human passions and concerns, the primitive rights of men undergo such a variety of refractions and reflections, that it becomes absurd to talk of them as if they continued in the simplicity of their original direction. The nature of man is intricate; the objects of society are of the greatest possible complexity: and therefore no simple disposition or direction of power can be suitable either to man's nature, or to the quality of his affairs. When I hear the simplicity of contrivance aimed at and boasted of in any new political constitutions, I am at no loss to decide that the artificers are grossly ignorant of their trade, or totally negligent of their duty. Simple governments are fundamentally defective, to say no worse of them.[28]

The gradual development of man in civil society reduced the primitive or simple society of the "rights of man" theorists to a purely hypothetical concept:

All these things are . . . sufficient to show of what a visionary nature those systems are, which would settle the ancient constitution in the most remote times exactly in the same form in which we enjoy it at this day; not considering that such mighty changes in manners, during so many ages, always must produce a considerable change in laws, and in the forms as well as the powers of all government.[29]

The closer man approached a simple or primitive state of nature, Burke believed, the more absolute would be his individual liberty: "In all very uncultivated countries, as society is not close or intricate, nor property very valuable, liberty subsists with very few restraints." [30] But such a simple state is most undesirable for *civilized* man, because "a life of absolute licence tends to turn men into savages." The chief negative function of civil institutions is to control man's natural passions, and to stand between him and the raw barbarism of a primitive or simple state, with its destructive absolute individual liberty.

Burke was fully aware of the destructive consequences to civilization of any attempt to put primitivist doctrines into practice. His constant antipathy toward the French Revolution cannot be appreciated apart from his conviction that the radical innovations in government were based upon primitivist theory or the desire to re-establish society on a simple foundation. Burke pointed out in the *Reflections* that a leading member of the French Assembly, M. Rabaud de St. Étienne, expressed the principle of their proceedings as clearly as possible, and that nothing could be more simple:

Tous les établissements en France couronnent le malheur du peuple: pour le rendre heureux il faut le rénouveler; changer ses idées; changer ses loix; changer ses moeurs . . . changer les hommes; changer les choses; changer les mots . . . tout détruire; oui, tout détruire; puisque tout est à recréer.[31]

To St. Étienne civilization as it actually existed was a kind of hell, and man could be redeemed socially only by destroying civilization and reconstructing it on a simple rational basis. To Burke, the opposite of Utopia was not hell but civilization. With all its admitted imperfections, Burke was unwilling to have the real achievements of civil society destroyed or radically modified on the speculative hope that a theoretically perfect primitive or simple civilization might be established. He believed that man should venerate, use, and improve rather than deny, destroy, and recast his social inheritance. The French Revolution, which appeared to many eighteenth-century philosophers as a beatific vision of expanding vistas of hope and progress, seemed to Burke more like a horrible illusion reflected from the fires of hell. Against the revolutionists' boast of an excellence in simplicity in political constitutions, he offered a "far superior excellence in composition," centered in the complex structure of a historically developed civil society.

Because Burke conceived civil society as tremendously complex, he felt that the finite and fallible reason of man could not possibly comprehend the universe, physical or social, but that men "ought to understand it according to our measure; and to venerate where we are not able presently to comprehend." To Burke there was always something mystical at the core of life, something which no amount of science or philosophy, however brilliant or systematically logical, could ever penetrate, and which finally required "a faith that is not contrary to reason, but above it." Burke's religion taught him that God's revelation was often shrouded in mystery, that man's finite mind could not fully comprehend God's infinite wisdom. His religious faith began at that point where man's natural or unaided reason was baffled by the complexities of life. In contrast to Burke's acceptance of a revelation beyond reason, the deists based their faith on natural reason. Burke attacked this principle through irony in *A Vindication of Natural Society*: "A good parson once said . . . where mystery begins, religion ends." Yet this was the literal belief of Burke's critics who based their appeal to the "rights of man" on the simple rights enjoyed in a state of nature.

Burke's rational critics frequently complained that his political thought was too "complex" and "mystical," and charged that institutions which could not be understood by simple common sense were fraudulent and corrupt. He knew that complexity could be pretended by those in power to obscure real corruption and prevent badly needed reforms, but this was an abuse which did not invalidate his principle that a just political constitution was necessarily complex. Burke flatly denied the most cherished belief held in common by deists and "rights of man" political philosophers: "The world would fall to ruins if the practice of all moral duties, and the foundation of society, rested upon having their reasons made clear and demonstrative to every individual." [32] The great principles of the moral law might be simple and self-evident, but in practice they were always involved in complexities. To appreciate the importance of the principle of simplicity and of the consequent antithesis of "art" and "nature" in the thought of Burke's "rights of man" opponents, one must examine some of the replies provoked by his *Reflections*. But first it will be necessary to establish briefly the historical connection between Burke's opponents after 1789 and the revolutionary "natural rights" tradition of Hobbes and Locke.

II. Revolutionary "Natural Rights": The Antithesis of Art and Nature

"The principles of Mr. Locke . . . would have reduced society almost to a state of nature; would have levelled all distinctions of honour, rank, offices, and property; would have annihilated the sovereign power, and in consequence repealed all positive laws; and would have left the people at liberty to have erected a new system of state upon a new foundation of polity."

Blackstone, *Commentaries*, I, 213.

In Chapter Two I noted the vital differences between the classical and Scholastic conception of Natural Law, centered in a theistic view of creation and an objective ethical norm, and the revolutionary "natural rights" theories propounded by Hobbes and Locke, centered in subjective claims to "rights" originating in the human will. We have also examined Burke's consistent appeals to the traditional Natural Law, and noted his objections to false claims to abstract "rights." We have now to see that Burke's pamphleteer political opponents during the 1790's were fully in accord with the "natural rights" principles of Hobbes and Locke. These principles are combined variously among the forty-eight or more writers who "replied" to Burke during the French Revolution. Only the more learned of Burke's numerous opponents, such as Mackintosh and Boothby, were aware that Hobbes and Rousseau, as well as Locke, had contributed to the formation of their political thought. Nevertheless, all of Burke's later critics were speculative and rationalistic theorists, deeply imbued with the Hobbist faith in mathematical method and logic, and with the Rousseauistic belief in intuitive personal morality based on natural feeling or "sensibility." In one way or another they accepted Locke's optimistic state of nature, his common-sense simplicity, his theory of a revocable contract, of the sovereignty of will over reason, and his mechanistic psychology of human nature. They were nominalists in their philosophy and generally held a voluntaristic conception of man's relation to civil society. All of these ideas appear over and over again in the forty-eight or more replies written to Burke's *Reflections* and other writings on French affairs. Locke was the chief source for the "natural rights" theories of Burke's pamphleteer opponents. To appreciate the enormous difference between Burke's philosophy of Natural Law and the revolutionary "natural rights" of his enemies, it is necessary to first summarize Locke's belief concerning the state of nature.

It has frequently been assumed that Locke, as well as Hobbes, posited the state of nature not as an actual historical state but as a hypothetical idea which he used merely for illustrative purposes. Yet Locke's own words in his *Second Treatise* stand in sharp contradiction to such an assumption:

If we may not suppose men ever to have been in the state of nature, because we hear not much of them in such a state, we may as well suppose the armies of Salmanasser or Xerxes were never children, because we hear little of them till they were men and embodied in armies. . . . Those [accounts] that we have of the beginning of any politics in the world . . . are all either plain instances of such a beginning as I have mentioned, or at least have manifest footsteps of it.[33]

This passage gives point to Strauss's claim that "Locke is more definite than Hobbes in asserting that men actually lived in the state of nature or that the state of nature is not merely a hypothetical assumption." [34] Willmoore Kendall agrees with Strauss: "Locke . . . insists upon depicting even the state of nature as a community." [35] Ernest Barker makes the same point, and notes the matter of "rights" in a state of nature: "Locke's state of nature, with its régime of recognized rights, is already a political society." [36] The most important point, however, is not whether the state of nature is historical or hypothetical, but how the supposed "rights" of man in this state antecedent to civil society apply to man in his actual civil state. On this vital point Locke's doctrine of inherent "natural rights" was totally contradicted by the utilitarian strain in his political thought. On the one hand Locke maintained as a general principle that men entered into civil society to protect the "rights" they enjoyed in the state of nature. Among these "rights" was the protection of private property. But despite Locke's reputed defense of inherent property rights, he argued out of his utilitarianism that "every man when he first incorporates himself into any commonwealth . . . submits to the community those possessions which he has, or shall acquire. . . . They become subject to the government and dominion of that commonwealth as long as it hath a being." [37] Locke's contradiction is purely verbal because, as I noted in Chapter Two, his principle of "rights" is but a disguised form of power or will. Locke's "natural rights" in a fictitious state of nature had little or nothing to do with man's natural rights according to the Natural Law. As Strauss said: "Locke's teaching on property, and . . . whole political philosophy, are revolutionary not only with regard to the Biblical tradition but with regard to the philosophic tradition." [38] Locke's theory of the revocable contract is even more revolutionary than his teaching on property.

The drift of Locke's political philosophy is most evident in those parts of his *Second Treatise* which defend the right of revolution. Locke exalted his idealistic state of nature as the norm by which any existing civil society was to be measured. Late in the eighteenth century the followers of Locke refined his revolutionary principles; Burke's contemporary radicals assumed a necessary antithesis between the "rights of man" in a state of nature and the established laws, customs, and arts of civil society. I shall limit this discussion to that part of the revolutionary conception of "nature" which is the antithesis of art.

During the crucial years 1790–1797, those of Burke's opponents who attacked him from the assumption of revolutionary "natural rights" were generally well aware that they were in the political tradition of Locke. In 1793 the Constitutional Society of Sheffield printed an abstract of Locke's *Treatise on Civil Government,* the preface of which stated: "Edmund Burke, the Knight Errant of Feudality, declared in the House of Commons, that 'Locke's Treatise on Civil Government, was the worst book ever written.' We are certain it needs no farther recommendation." [39] There is no record that Burke ever said these words, but it is significant that his "rights of man" enemies considered him a foe to the Lockian tradition, which they revered. Of course Locke was not the only thinker from whom Burke's opponents might have drawn the antithesis of nature and art. The passion for simplicity was an important part of the whole Nonconformist religious tradition, and practically all of Burke's pamphleteer enemies were Dissenters. Also, Rousseau in his *Contrat social* (1762) had made nature so antithetical to art, and the "state of nature" so opposed to artificial society, that many of his British readers, such as William Kenrick, John Gordon, John Brown, and Adam Ferguson, who believed civil society was man's "natural" state, interpreted Rousseau as a primitivist who urged a return to nature. [40] In criticizing the antithesis of nature and art, Burke's contemporary Soame Jenyns attributed a general primitivism to his natural rights opponents. Some Lockian natural rights theorists, such as Dr. Price, disclaimed any antithesis between nature and art. But in general there was a tendency toward simplicity and primitivism among natural rights theorists, particularly after 1789 among English defenders of the French Revolution.[41] Almost all of those who attacked Burke's *Reflections* were in the most radical Nonconformist religious and "natural rights" political traditions. Both in religion and politics Burke's opponents assumed in varying degrees the antithesis between nature and art, and from this antithesis they derived the principles which made their conception of "nature" the opposite of Burke's classical or Scholastic Natural Law.

As there are at least forty-eight pamphlet "replies" to Burke's *Reflections* and other writings on French affairs, it is necessary to limit consideration to the essential themes of the most representative ones. I need not discuss here the element most common in all these pamphlets, the charge that Burke was inconsistent in behavior and principle. Also, although the French Revolution revealed many vital differences in political principles between Burke and his opponents, the debate over the Revolution is not my immediate concern. In the replies to Burke the significance of the revolutionary "natural rights," as embodied in the antithesis of nature and art, becomes clear when one examines the effect of civil society, and of such institutions as Church and State, upon the moral and intellectual nature of man. The antithesis of nature and art involves three great points: (1) An attack on polished and sophisticated "artificial" society. This vital antiaesthetic and anti-intellectual element in the thought of Burke's "rights of man" opponents is revealed in their abhorrence, as a sign of depravity, of any conscious refinement in dress and speech and in the customs, manners, and education of man in civil society. (2) An attack on the historical traditions, structure, doctrines, and liturgy of Roman Catholicism and High Church Anglicanism. Burke's Nonconformist critics attacked "established" churches as contrary to Scripture and primitive Christianity. His deist opponents held that institutional Christianity, and the whole supernatural teaching of the Church, violated common sense and natural reason. Both Dissenters and deists charged that "popery," and its remnants in Anglicanism, fostered "corrupt," "mystical," and "superstitious" practices, encouraged parochial and national loyalties and "prejudices," and prevented the spread of rational enlightenment. The Church would be purified when it did not intervene between man and his Maker, and when pastors were elected by the people. (3) An attack on hereditary monarchy, or on any organically developed and complex form of government. Among the pamphleteer enemies of Burke, legitimacy and tyranny were often conceived as synonymous terms. Their general attitude toward monarchs in government paralleled their suspicions toward priests in religion. Kings were considered impediments to the fulfillment of natural liberty and justice. Like mystery in religion, complexity in government was held to be a fraud perpetrated by unscrupulous rulers to keep the people in servitude and ignorance, and to deprive them of their self-evident "natural rights." Against artificial society and its complex institutions, most of Burke's opponents advanced in various degrees the virtues of plain, simple, uncultivated common sense, centered in the pure reason or instinctive feeling of each individual, and the "rights" enjoyed by man in a state of nature.

Mary Wollstonecraft's *A Vindication of the Rights of Man* (1790) was among the first and most representative replies to Burke's *Reflections*. The antithesis between nature and art underlay her whole argument on the "rights of man" in religion and politics, and was explicitly stated as a general principle and applied specifically to Burke. According to her, "man has been changed into an artificial monster by the station into which he was born," and in particular the strong, rich, and well-established "have been so warped by education, that it may require some ages to bring them back to nature." To Burke she said: "It might be difficult to bring back your sophisticated heart to nature, and make you feel like a man." Throughout her work it is clear that "nature" is simple, clear, and uniform, and spontaneously apprehended by instinct or reason, whereas the "artificial" customs and institutions of civil society are complex and obscure, and are adhered to only by "superstitious" or "prejudiced" men. When men follow nature, "A few fundamental truths meet the first inquiry of reason, and appear . . .

clear to an unwarped mind." This primitivist idea applied to
the whole course of civilization: "The genuine enthusiasm of
genius . . . seldom appears but in the infancy of civilization;
for as this advances reason clips the wings of fancy—the youth
becomes a man." She regarded the cultivation of knowledge
as an impediment to moral and political truth, and "natural"
instinct as an infallible guide: "A kind of mysterious instinct
is *supposed* to reside in the soul, that instantaneously discerns
truth, without the tedious labour of ratiocination. This instinct . . . [is] an authority from which there is no appeal."
On this theory Burke, with his great learning and skepticism
toward infallible private instincts, was hopelessly corrupt. Burke
doubted private reason, but he had not defined the origin of
man's rights: "Will Mr. Burke . . . inform us, how far we are
to go back to discover the rights of man, since the light of
reason is such a fallacious guide that none but fools trust to its
cold investigation?" In history, she continued, the dawn of
reason occurred in religion: "Wickliffe opened a vista for reason
by attacking some of the most pernicious tenets of the Church
of Rome." Unfortunately, the English constitution "was settled
in the dark days of ignorance, when the minds of men were
shackled by the grossest prejudices and most immoral superstition." Since Burke venerated prescription and precedent, Mary
Wollstonecraft asked: "On what principle you, Sir, can justify
the Reformation, which tore up by the roots an old establishment, I cannot guess." The religious and political "rights of
man" are received directly from God, and are not subject to
man-made laws. The antithesis between nature and art finally
led Mary Wollstonecraft to make "natural rights" antithetical
to civil society; to fulfill her "rights" she ignored all precedents,
prescription, historical continuity, and existing artificial institutions.[42]

Mrs. Catherine Macaulay Graham's *Observations on the
Reflections of Burke* (1791) paralleled Mary Wollstonecraft's
attack in many points. She too appealed for "plain thinking"
and scoffed at Burke's "ingenious reasoning" and "refined distinctions between natural and social rights." Mrs. Graham's
antithesis between nature and art took the form of an attack

on artificial manners and dress. She ridiculed as foppery Burke's defense of chivalry. She quoted his statement that artificial institutions were necessary to cover man's naked, shivering nature, and replied:

It is not according to these ideas, recommended by Mr. Burke, that the Scripture teaches us to respect ourselves! Neither in a *moral* view of things, can I perceive how the *ornaments* of artificial greatness, which are found to answer all the purposes of *human pride,* should assist us in acquiring that *true* dignity of character which alone ought to constitute distinction. . . . In a very elaborate defence of all the artificial modes of greatness . . . Mr. Burke has used all the powers of eloquence and subtlety to prove, that the crimes which have been committed by our species, have not arisen from the imperfections of institutions, but from the vices of individuals.[43]

Since man was by nature morally sound, Mrs. Graham explained the origin of evil wholly by external forces and circumstances. Artificial institutions gave "the *opportunity* of committing crimes" and encouraged "that very *depravity* of sentiment" from which crimes proceed. To destroy the sources and occasions of man's corruption, society had to be reformed as in France upon its original natural basis: "The French legislature have . . . adhered to the rights of men in the *strictest sense,* even as they exist in their *abstract* perfection in a state of nature." Mrs. Graham believed that the European system of artificial institutions had to be radically altered or destroyed if men were to enjoy the same liberty and "rights" in civil society that they had known in the state of nature.

In the reply to Burke by an anonymous "W. C." called *A Short Essay on Whigs and Tories* (1791), Locke's state of nature was defended as an actual historical state:

The best way to discover the natural rights of man is to refer to him in a state of nature. There certainly was a time when he existed in such a state, unless we suppose that a government dropped upon him from the clouds. I presume this position is so plain, that no one will be inclined to dispute it; if they are, they must resist every evidence of history, and every presumption of common sense; in that case, it would be needless to reason with them at all, for upon them all reasoning would be thrown away.[44]

Burke's refusal to entertain a state of nature even for hypothetical purposes placed him beyond the pale of "W. C." 's logic. But for those who could reason, "W. C." asked and answered a few plain questions: "If, then, all men were once in a state of nature, I will ask, what right any one man had in such a state to controul another? If any man had such a right, he must have founded it upon some charter derived from heaven." Could rulers produce proof of having such a God-given chartered right? If not, each man in civil society would be free to decide for himself whether he was bound by civil laws. "Where a man is not bound by the laws of his country, he is as free at this moment, as ever he was in a state of nature." No man should ever rebel without good cause, "W. C." admitted, but all men should realize that "the best criterion of natural rights [is] that the invasion of them always produces a revolution." "W. C." concluded that Burke, by his attack on the "rights of man" in a state of nature, had proved himself a Tory and an enemy to mankind.

Joseph Towers, a staunch member of both the Society for Constitutional Information and the London Corresponding Society, invoked Locke in defending natural rights against Burke's attacks. In his *Thoughts on the Commencement of a New Parliament, with Remarks on the Letter of the Rt. Hon. Edmund Burke, on the Revolution in France* (Dublin, 1791), Towers praised the French for their wisdom in adopting the "rights of man" doctrines taught by Locke and Sydney. To spread a similar enlightenment among the English, the two societies to which he belonged "printed and distributed gratis . . . constitutional tracts, and essays and extracts from various authors, such as Sydney, Locke, Trenchard, Lord Somers, and many others." In opposition to Burke's contention that revolution was the last resort against tyranny, and that a just government was necessarily complex, Towers justified the principles of revolution and simplicity by quoting two passages from Locke's *Treatise on Civil Government*. Much of this pamphlet is a defense of abstract natural liberty against the despotism of the French monarchy. Towers attacked Burke's eulogy of chivalry and defense of the Queen of France, and justified the abolition of monarchy and confiscation of Church lands on the grounds of public utility. Towers was baffled by Burke's concern for the suppressed monastic orders in France, and concluded: "Mr. Burke's ideas of religion, in several respects, seem much better adapted to the Church of Rome, than to the principles of any Protestant church in Europe." The usual antithesis of nature and art is best revealed in those parts of Towers' pamphlet in which he condemned the doctrines and liturgy of the Catholic Church.[45]

Charles Pigott's antithesis between simple nature and complex art is an important theme in his *Strictures on the New Political Tenets of Edmund Burke* (1791), in which Burke is charged with laboring to conceal government in a pretense of mystery. "In following him through his political mazes we are absolutely bewildered in a labyrinth of confusion." Voltaire had shown that "to keep the people in ignorance has been the invariable rule of priests and tyrants of every description," and with true "Jesuitical evasion" Burke as the great "advocate of prejudice labours with infinite pains to cherish and keep up these abuses." Had men been truly enlightened, Pigott observed, "no person would . . . have dared to insinuate that 'natural and civil rights are incompatible with each other.'" But Burke's real weakness lay in his total lack of sensibility toward the unnatural suffering inflicted upon innocent men by vicious governments:

> The generality of mankind feel not for afflictions with which they . . . are unacquainted, and human nature would be shockingly depraved indeed, if there was no collateral cause whereby to account for such apparent barbarity; but the origin is obvious; it exists in the vicious formation of governments, which, losing sight of the primary object, have degenerated into the opposite extreme, and by habituating us to such scenes, harden us against them. . . . Rousseau traces up the greatest part of the disasters that afflict mankind to the above source.[46]

Pigott clearly accepted the flattering theory put forth by Locke and Rousseau that man is by nature morally good and that the evils in civil society are caused not by flaws in man's character, but by the bad effects of civil institutions. Pigott concluded that

Burke had become so corrupted from "nature" by his respect for artificial institutions, that scenes in London which "harrow up the soul of sensibility" left Burke wholly untouched.

The antithesis between nature and art also forms an important theme in Paine's *Rights of Man*, Part I (1791) and Part II (1792). It underlies all of Paine's attacks on nobility, monarchy, and complex government, and is the basis of his picture of Burke:

> It is painful to behold a man employing his talents to corrupt himself. Nature has been kinder to Mr. Burke than he is to her. . . . He degenerates into a composition of art, and the genuine soul of nature forsakes him. . . . The artificial noble shrinks into a dwarf before the noble of Nature. . . . The example [of American frontier life] shews to the artificial world, that man must go back to nature for information. . . . Monarchy . . . is a mode of government that counteracts nature . . . the representative system is always parallel with the order and immutable laws of nature. . . . Government is a plain thing, and fitted to the capacity of many heads. . . . The affectation of mystery [in government] with all the artificial sorcery by which they [kings and priests] imposed upon mankind, is on the decline.[47]

Paine's antithesis between nature and art led him to deny that historical continuity and social precedents connected the generations of men. It led him to assert that historical precedents could be skipped entirely, and that government is not a steppingstone to man's social self-realization according to the moral law, but an impediment coming between man and God and preventing men from living according to their original equality in a state of nature:

> The error of those who reason by precedents drawn from antiquity, respecting the rights of man, is, that they do not go far enough into antiquity. . . . But if we proceed on . . . we shall come to the time when man came from the hand of his Maker. . . . Why not trace the rights of man to the creation of man? I will answer the question. Because there have been upstart governments thrusting themselves between, and presumptuously working to unmake man. . . . All men are born equal, and with equal natural right. . . . It is not among the least evils of the present existing governments in all parts of Europe, that man . . . is thrown back to a vast distance

from his Maker and the artificial chasm filled up by a succession of barriers.[48]

According to Paine, in civil society "a man by natural right has a right to judge in his own cause." Paine's application to civil society of "rights" enjoyed in the state of nature implies that he accepted literally Locke's revolutionary conception of the revocable contract. Paine made Locke's social contract the whole test of any legitimate origin and continuation of government:

As man must have existed before governments existed, there necessarily was a time when governments did not exist, and consequently there could originally exist no governors to form a compact with. The fact therefore must be, that the individuals themselves, each in his own personal and sovereign right, entered into a compact with each other to produce a government: and this is the only mode in which governments have a right to arise, and the only principle on which they have a right to exist.[49]

Paine's belief in a historical state of nature led him in *Rights of Man*, Part II, to assert that society could best exist with practically no government at all.

Joseph Priestley's *Letters to Edmund Burke Occasioned by His Reflections* (1791) repeats with variations many of Paine's arguments, but with a greater awareness of the "natural rights" tradition in politics, and of Nonconformity in religion. Priestley justified the French Revolution on the "plain principle laid down as a maxim" by Locke and others, "that all power . . . is derived from the people." To the question—which rights should society respect?—Priestley answered: "those which man had *from nature,* without societies or artificial combinations of men." If men feel they are not enjoying in civil society the same rights they knew in a state of nature, they are free to revolt: "They then revert to a state of nature, and may enter into a new state of society, and adopt a new form of government, in which they may make better terms for themselves." [50] The last fifty pages of Priestley's criticism consists of an application of the principles laid down in his *History of the Corruptions of Christianity* (1782), in answer to Burke's defense of the established Church in France and England.

Priestley's appeal that men should return in religion to the "original" simplicity and purity of the primitive Church of the first four centuries after Christ parallels his appeal to a simple or primitive state of nature as a political norm. Nowhere in Priestley's thought is the antithesis of nature and art more evident, however, than where he holds that established churches necessarily violate men's consciences, and that the use of liturgy, drama, and aesthetic appeals in worship are "unnatural" corruptions of Christianity.

A Dissenting minister, Mark Wilks, answered Burke's *Reflections* by printing a sermon called *The Origin and Stability of the French Revolution* (1791), in which the usual parallel arguments concerning Church and State, or religion and politics, are clearly stated:

> As it respects the Church, to hear him [Burke] boast of her estates, her majesty, her splendour, her orders, her gradations and her full efficiency, is enough to drive a wise man mad. To hear him talk of the balances and counterpoises that fix the State, which furnish sure correctives to any violent spirit, is to hear him talk at a rate of unpardonable rant.[51]

According to Wilks, divine influence was evident in the French Revolution, because in returning the French clergy to their original simplicity the revolutionists purged Christianity of its unnatural hierarchy and superstitious popery. Also, in replacing the contrived complexity of the three estates with a simple, popularly elected single-chambered state, the French placed their government on a permanently natural basis, and brought their nation swiftly from medieval darkness to modern enlightenment.

After stating that his rebuttal of Burke was based largely upon Locke's *Essay on Civil Government*, Priestley's *Principles of Government*, and Paine's *Rights of Man*, the anonymous author of *The Political Crisis* (1791) set forth his idea of how man's "rights" in a state of nature became corrupted as civil society developed:

> I believe few will deny . . . that there was a time *prior* to any social compact in society. What, then, existed in that time? If man

existed, as I think is clear, had he not the power of willing and of acting as were most conducive to his happiness? . . . In a natural state, men had no established maxims or rules to guide them; but they were actuated by a law antecedent and paramount to all human institutions, Reason, which taught them to pursue their own happiness, without encroaching on the happiness of others. If one man made an unjust war upon another, he violated the law of Nature, for no one was so depraved as not to distinguish between right and wrong. . . . Man was not so much the enemy of man in the beginning, as he was afterwards; no one having a sufficiency to tempt the violence of his neighbor. Civil society was only made to remedy the inconveniences from a state of nature. These inconveniences were few in the infancy of the world, but they evidently increased in proportion as mankind increased.[52]

Since man's pride and depravity resulted from the increase in wealth and complexity of civil society, it was against the law of nature, the writer continued, for any man to store up goods while others lived in want. To fulfill all of man's economic needs, men had but to live in civil society without governments, as they had lived in a simple state of nature: "I see no reason why a large number of men may not live together, and carry on commerce with foreign nations, and yet be in a state of nature, because they act by no other law than the law of nature." In extending this point, the author of *The Political Crisis* interspersed his argument with several ideas borrowed almost verbatim from Paine:

The beasts of the field, and the fowls of the air, were made for the service of man, and man has a natural right to take them. . . . By nature, light is free; it is the gift of God; it descends spontaneously to everyone; but Government has cut off the design of Providence, by forcing its subjects to pay for it, in proportion as they receive it. . . . Government is itself simple, and does not require the aid of the learned sciences to explain it. . . . There is no inexplicable mystery in the Rights of Man, nor in the usurpations of men; though the usurpers may wish the world to believe there is an inexplicable mystery in both.[53]

The writer noted that "High Church Divines ridicule these natural rights, as being wholly hypothetical." Men like Burke, who would usurp nature by supporting artificially established churches which violate men's private conscience, rest their arguments on "the dusty Greek of Aristotle" rather than on the spontaneous impulses of the heart. What is worse, "they call in question the opinions of the greatest sages of modern times; those of Locke, Rousseau, the Utopia of Sir Thomas Moore, and the perfect Commonwealth of Hume, and bestow upon them the character of *visionary projectors.*" Such statements leave no doubt that the chief arguments against Burke's *Reflections* in *The Political Crisis* rested upon the assumption of a historical state of nature and an antithesis between natural and civil society.

Under the pretext of instructing the son of George III, David Williams wrote *Lessons to a Young Prince by an Old Statesman* (1791). This book was one of the most severe attacks on Burke. Williams, a deist, argued that the clear and simple God of nature had been artificially perplexed, and Christianity corrupted and made mysterious, by the "ambitious," "selfish," and "useless" Roman clergy. The Reformation and the invention of printing, by "diffusing knowledge into classes destined to be ignorant," had rid Christianity of some of its mystical absurdities, but except among the Quakers many great reforms were needed before Christianity could recapture its original rational simplicity. In political theory Williams claimed Locke, Hume, Rousseau, Sydney, and Harrington as his masters. Locke had made many fine observations in favor of civil liberty, Williams admitted, but his principles needed to be made more positive and greatly extended. Rousseau, through his principle of utility and his adaptation of "the periodical councils of Geneva" as the basis of a constitution centered in the "general will," had come much closer to the cardinal ideal of simplicity in politics. But the touchstone of all political constitutions was to be found in the simple, single-chambered, annually elected *mycel-gemot* of King Alfred. Williams condemned all constitutions with divided powers as mystical absurdities. The chief motif in Williams' strong criticism of Burke, in religion and politics, was mysticism and complexity. He condemned "the elaborate, intricate, and mystic production of Mr. Edmund Burke," which displayed and defended "a luxuriant wilderness, where tyranny, privilege, superstition, and intolerance, display their magic rites." Williams strongly implied that Burke's praise of chivalry and respect for artificial rites and ceremonies in religion proved he was a conscienceless Catholic in disguise. Burke's religious hypocrisy was revealed, according to Williams, in his attack on the revolutionists for their seizure of Church property. Williams' main purpose was to expose Burke's supposed Catholicism, but he also took sharp issue with Burke's belief that "government is both the institution of God and the invention of man." The assumed antithesis of nature and art was particularly evident throughout Williams' criticism when he contrasted Burke with the Dissenters in religion and with the natural rights tradition in English political thought.

Sir Brooke Boothby's *A Letter to Edmund Burke* (1791) is based on a conscious antithesis between natural simplicity and artificial complexity: "I think truth and sincerity and honesty and benevolence sufficiently lovely in the simplicity of their nature without that prodigality of ornament and decoration which you [Burke] seem to consider as so essential to them." Boothby wondered how Burke could claim to love liberty, or be a true Protestant, and not be pleased that the chief sources of corruption and poverty in France, the splendid court and the superstitious monkish hierarchy, had been dealt so strong a blow. Private conscience in religion and natural rights in politics, Boothby argued, were wholly a matter of private reason, and no church or state should come between a man's conscience and God. Most of Boothby's criticism of Burke occurred indirectly, by way of an attack on Catholicism and an appeal for further reforms in the "tautologous pharisaical liturgy" of the Church of England. He advised "a shorter and more rational form of prayer, rid of the remains of popery." As opposed to the "obscure language" and "pious frauds" of Rome, Hobbes had shown through natural reason and natural science the virtue of sincerity and simplicity in religion. Boothby concluded that Burke's main object in the *Reflections* was to shroud religion in "truths too sacred to be discussed" and to propound "mysteries of government."

In Boothby's second attack on Burke, *Observations on the Appeal from the New to the Old Whigs* (1792), he continued his vindication of "primitive simplicity" and condemnation of complexity and mysticism, but added one vital passage that reveals the whole source from which he drew the revolutionary principles contained in the antithesis of nature and art:

The moral writings of Rousseau seem to rest upon a principle which he is perhaps the first who has developed to any extent, and is I think founded upon truth and nature. *A distinction between the natural passions of man and those factious passions which are the produce of society*—the former all relate simply to our well being and preservation; are all in themselves good, and only become wrong by excess; and this *love of ourselves* (amour de soi) when confined to the desire of well-being which seems inseparable from conscious existence, is not only innocent in itself, but is the source of all the natural affections. Those passions on the other hand that *raise from comparing ourselves with others in order to obtain some preference or distinction,* such as ambition, avarice, envy, jealousy, and in general all the *hating* passions with all their infinite combinations, do not belong to the original nature of man, but are wholly generated by the artificial and complicated relations of society, which we ourselves create by our institutions and laws and opinions; and these factitious passions this writer seems to consider as the sources of all the vices and moral miseries of mankind. The writings of Mandeville, La Rochfoucault, Swift, Helvetius, etc. encourage the vices by representing them as inherent in human nature. Rousseau would lead us back to virtue and happiness as to our native rights and possessions. . . . His system of education goes upon the same . . . principles—to impress truth and right by the operation of inflexible necessity, moral and physical, rather than by the feeble and imperfect power of human institutions.[54]

In Boothby's interpretation and summary of Rousseau's "moral writings," the ingredients so common to revolutionary thought —sensibility, a monistic explanation of evil, a deterministic psychology, unbounded faith in human nature, and an implicit belief in progress and perfectibility—are clearly derived from an antithesis between the natural and artificial passions, in which man is conceived as being good by nature, and corrupted in his social passions by his artificial institutions and laws.

One of the most representative replies to Burke was Francis Stone's *An Examination of Burke's Reflections* (1792), in which Burke was answered point for point with positive alternative arguments centered in the antithesis of nature and art. After noting that Burke's thought was filled with "the various shuffling manoeuvres which characterize the designedly complex," and which prevented him from "discerning or relishing the beauty and excellence of a simple government," Stone asked: "Is not this . . . perfectly agreeable to your political principles that . . . the science and practice of government should be industriously involved in a mist of artificial confusion, in an affected obscurity, in a convenient labyrinth of mystery?" Like Granville Sharp, Major Cartwright, David Williams, and others, Stone found his touchstone of political simplicity in the Saxon institutions of King Alfred's time. It is noteworthy, among the confusions concerning "nature" held by Burke's opponents, that Stone identified his political ideal of simplicity with the law of nature:

When I speak of the Constitution, greatly as I admire it in its primordial Saxon purity, let me not be understood that it claims my respect in . . . its present abused and corrupt state, wherein . . . it has departed from its original beautiful simplicity, and has superceded those rights which the God of nature has given to mankind, and by which, as by an unerring standard, every political constitution should be at first formed, and if found defective reformed. . . . Our wise and good Saxon ancestors paid an especial regard to the law of nature in all their mild political institutions. The strictest attention to the equal rights of men is visible in the whole frame of their free government, a government as friendly to those rights, as the harsh, aristocratic, feudal system of the Normans is hostile. . . . By the law of our nature, adhered to in our free Saxon constitution of government, every man, arrived at least at the year of maturity, can claim a right to a voice in the choice of legislators. . . . Our Saxon patriot-king Alfred, enacted in conformity to the law of nature, [that] parliaments were to be annually elected, and oftener, if need be. . . . The Saxon form of government, in its native purity and simplicity is . . . congenial with the natural rights of men.[55]

To establish Britain's government on Stone's conception of the natural rights of men, he makes clear what must be done: "An absolute necessity exists for reforming our government according to its first, pure, unadulterated principle of nature, and of our Saxon constitution." Unfortunately, wrote Stone, "by a

weak and wicked policy the lower classes are kept in ignorance
of these rights; but their ignorance may be removed by the
distribution of short political catechisms among them." Stone's
use of the term "law of nature" as identical with Saxon simplicity in politics has nothing in common with classical or
Scholastic Natural Law, and his antithesis of the simple and
natural against the complex and artificial is clearly revolutionary.

As a Dissenter and minister, Stone assumed in religious
affairs that the primitive simplicity and popular sovereignty of
the early Church contained the only norm for Christianity:
"The whole tenor of the history of the first ages of the Church
is in point to prove, that such popular elections were peaceably
conducted, and the present elective practice of the dissenters
from the establishment corroborates the fact." Since establishments are "a manifest invasion of God's prerogative" which
"interfere" with private conscience, the French National Assembly, by abolishing the established religion and making
everyone free to choose for himself, moved toward the true
religious ideal. But it did not go far enough. Stone stated that
the French "should have ventured to proceed to a total annihila-
tion of their civil establishment in religion, and to put spiritual
concerns on the same footing they are among the Dissenters
in England. Thus their plan respecting church-matters, and
their triumph over church power and craft, would have been
complete." [56] Stone applied the same revolutionary argument
to the established Church of England. In the "enlightened
eighteenth century" the Church of England should not be "tied
down tight . . . by our less informed forefathers of the sixteenth." To Burke's question, "Is episcopacy to be abolished?"
Stone answered: "If the people at large, or their governors,
judge the abolition of episcopacy to be conducive to public
utility, they will of course abolish it." In anticipation that his
Saxon ideal in government would be established, Stone even
suggested a plan for disposing of the property of the Church
of England. Stone's desire to return to a simple or "natural"
form of worship made his view of religion and the Church
as revolutionary as his political theories.

In order to return to a simple Saxon government and a "primitive" Christianity, in which all men would have equal rights by having an equal share of power, Stone maintained that the unnatural distinctions created by existing artificial institutions, and therefore the institutions themselves, would have to be leveled:

You [Burke] assert, 'he feels no ennobling principle who wishes to level all artificial institutions.' I, on the contrary, maintain that he is destitute of this principle, who would wish to debase a man into a baby, tricked out with stars and ribbons, rather than elevate him into his rank as a man. He is truly noble, who approves of abolishing all external, fanciful distinctions, as serving no other end than to fill one set of men with pride, insolence, and a contempt of their fellow-men. . . . I am an advocate for an indiscriminate elevation of all men in the establishment of their natural equalization as men.[57]

In reply to Burke's statement, "Those who attempt to level, never equalize," Stone clarified how he would "elevate all men" to their natural equality:

To level and to equalize are synonymous. . . . I cannot discern the necessity that any one description of citizens should be uppermost. If by any means they attain any other distinction or superiority than what arises from a pre-eminence in integrity, they are filled with arrogance, insolence, and a contempt of their supposed inferiors, and ought to be instantly humbled, and reduced to their proper level.[58]

As an egalitarian, Stone's theory of simplicity or primitivism in politics and religion ignored all human differences which had resulted from historical continuity; he omitted all the civil institutions that come between man and a state of nature, and appealed directly to God:

We do not found our claim to liberty, and to the enjoyment of our property, and of every personal right, on any positive constitution of government, ancient or modern, but we fix it on that solid undestructible basis the rock of nature. . . . We derive all we possess in our political constitution not 'as an inheritance from our forefathers,' but as our birthright by nature, as an inheritance from God.[59]

Stone's idea that each man derives his civil rights directly from God or "nature," rather than indirectly through civil society, is clearly revolutionary. He conceived each man to be an abstract, self-contained being, independent of history, unaltered by time, place, or the influence of corporate institutions. In Stone's antithesis of the natural and artificial, the state of nature is the norm for man, and life in civil society is just and free in proportion to its approximation of the state of nature.

Locke's revolutionary "natural rights," based on the state of nature and an antithesis between nature and art, was one of the grand themes of the pamphleteers who replied to Burke's *Reflections*. An analysis of the numerous remaining "replies" would merely reveal a greater range of expressions and examples of the same theme. John Thelwall's *The Rights of Nature Against the Usurpations of Establishments* (1796) suggests even in its title the antithesis of nature and artificial institutions. These "natural rights" appear again in the later attacks by William Miles, Thomas Street, Gilbert Wakefield, and others on Burke's *Letter to a Noble Lord* (London, 1796). It is noteworthy, however, that Burke's more moderate critics, such as George Rous, William Belsham, and Sir James Mackintosh, scoffed at the whole idea of a state of nature and of any antithesis between nature and artificial society. They rested their criticism upon utilitarian principles and the general desire for political reforms. Yet they too were carried away by the universal passion for simplicity in religion and politics. Many of Burke's critics were not revolutionists but liberal Whigs; several experienced a considerable change in their political convictions, particularly concerning the state of nature. In his first reply to Burke, *Thoughts on Government; Occasioned by Mr. Burke's Reflections* (1791), George Rous invoked Locke's conception of equality and sovereignty: "The truth seems to be what Mr. Locke has taught. All men are by nature equal.—No authority can be exercised over them unless to exact that justice which independent communities yet in a state of nature may require from each other." [60] Rous concluded that if Burke did not accept the Lockian natural rights doctrines, as Charles Fox and his followers did, he had no right to consider himself a Whig. However, in his second reply, *A Letter to Burke in Reply to His Appeal from the New to the Old Whigs* (1791), Rous noted that "Mr. Burke does not deny the existence of natural rights . . . but these, according to Mr. Burke's system, refer wholly to a period antecedent to all civil government." [61] Rous did not distinguish between Burke's natural rights based on the classical and Scholastic Natural Law, and Locke's "natural rights" in a state of nature, but he condemned the latter in terms reminiscent of Burke himself:

> For since these rights cannot possibly exist but in the *absence of civil society,* and man in that condition (if, indeed, such a condition as the *total absence of civil society* ever did exist) must have been a rude unlettered animal . . . it seems to follow, that these speculations can have no other tendency but to *mislead man from his social duty.*[62]

This was precisely Burke's objection to the whole "natural rights" tradition in English political thought, from Locke to Dr. Price, Paine, Priestley, and the great majority of those who condemned his *Reflections.*

An excellent summary of Burke's essential objections to "natural rights" is contained in an anonymous pamphlet, *Six Essays on: Natural Rights, Liberty and Slavery, Consent of the People, Equality, Religious Establishments, the French Revolution* (1792). The first of these essays, "Natural Rights," expresses perfectly the position Burke held throughout his life toward the false "natural rights" of Locke and his disciples:

> It is the fashion with all modern philosophers, to lay down, as the basis of their systems, *Rights* which they assert to have existed in a state of nature, before any societies were formed amongst mankind, and for the maintenance of which they pretend men entered into society; they tell us that such *rights* are inseparable from our nature, and can never be superseded by any institutions of the Legislature. Upon these natural rights they build their pretentions to annul the most revered establishments of past times, and to overthrow, at pleasure, governments that have been the work of ages, whenever the people can be brought to think fit to exert the authority that is inherent in them. Surely it behoves us to examine carefully whether such rights did ever exist *in a state of nature,* before we allow the validity of them to invade every right which we claim

in a state of society, and upon which depends every blessing we derive from the protection of law and government. . . . In a state of perfect nature there can exist no right of any kind whatsoever. . . . The truest definition of a state of nature, is *a state previous to the institution of rights.* . . . But, in fact, no such state has ever yet existed; it is a mere creature of the imagination.[63]

Like Burke, the author of this pamphlet distinguished between true and false natural rights, and maintained that man's true natural rights must be fulfilled within the conventions of civil society, and are forever subject to the modifications of particular governments, of historical changes and the infinite variety of circumstances.

Burke's numerous later critics derived their faith in simple, direct, abstract, and original "rights" of nature, and in private sovereignty, from the nonutilitarian principles in the thought of Locke and Rousseau, and especially from their inherited religious nonconformity. The development of natural science also contributed much toward making simplicity the norm in social thought. Among Burke's opponents the love of simplicity in religion and "common sense" in morality was the positive side of their intense suspicion of anything mystical, "artificial," or aesthetic, of all that gave elegance to speech, refinement to dress and manners, or complexity to laws, government, and religion. The militant spirit of the seventeenth-century Dissenters permeated almost every criticism of Burke's *Reflections* on these vital points.[64]

The welter of confusions concerning "nature" among Burke's critics found a common denominator in their basic antithesis of nature and art, an antithesis which infused the whole revolutionary movement and became embodied in much of the revolutionary literature of romanticism.[65] Halévy has shown that among both utilitarian and natural rights English defenders of the French Revolution the great ruling passion was for simplicity in all things.[66] The intense desire for a Rousseauist simplicity sometimes passed over into primitivism. Man's religious ideal became deism or pantheism, the Dissenters' principle of private or popular sovereignty, or the primitive Christianity of the first three centuries. Man's ideal political constitution was thought to exist in simple forms of government, such as King Alfred's, or in the individual "natural rights" of a state of nature.

The desire to establish these simple and abstract norms in religion and politics caused many of Burke's opponents to skip over historical continuity, social prescription, and legal precedents, and to appeal directly to God or "nature." The result of the principle of simplicity and of the antithesis of nature and art was a revolutionary theory of society, and a conception of "natural rights" absolutely different from the traditional natural rights of Aristotle, Cicero, and Burke, derived from the Natural Law. The full measure of this difference will become abundantly clear in the next chapter, in which I shall examine the conception of human nature assumed by Burke in his acceptance of the classical and Scholastic Natural Law.

SIX

Human Nature

I. Man's Corporate Nature:
Burke's Rejection of Lockian Reason

One of the most ambiguous and challenging statements ever written about Burke is the following by Charles E. Vaughan:

> To say that reason finds expression in the whole of man's nature, instead of in the merely conscious and argumentative fragment of it which alone had been recognized by the general tendencies of eighteenth-century thought, implies a radical change, a change amounting to nothing less than a revolution, in the whole conception of man, and even of the world around him. To Burke, reason is no longer the purely passive and analytic faculty of Locke and his disciples; it is a creative faculty, which draws upon the darker and more mysterious, no less than upon the more definite and conscious, elements of man's experience.[1]

There are several points to be noted here. First, Vaughan's statement indicates that by 1789 Hobbes's a priori method of mathematical reasoning, together with Locke's empiricism, had been transmuted from a revolutionary conception of knowledge and human reason to the established and accepted norm. It is clear, also, that Burke had an altogether different conception of man's reason, and therefore it was his that appeared to be revolutionary. According to Vaughan, Burke's awareness of the mind as a creative faculty made him a precursor of Kant and the coming romanticism.[2] However, Burke's conception of man's reason and nature was distinct from both Kant's idealism and the mechanistic theory of Hobbes and Locke. Burke did not merely anticipate romanticism. He understood and rejected the Lockian theory, based upon empiricism and abstract reason, and by virtue of his conception of man as a corporate being, his view of history, and his adherence to Natural Law and Christianity, he became a counterrevolutionist on traditional grounds. Burke revolted against both the rationalist spirit and the "sensibility" of his era, because his conception of man as a rational and emotional being was richer and more unified by far than that of his Lockian and Rousseauist contemporaries. Burke's view of man had deep roots in history and was firmly imbedded in the ancient traditions of Natural Law and in the inbred piety of orthodox Christianity. In the age of the Encyclopedists and Jacobins, who were aware of history only as a negative force and who wished to amend human nature by emancipating it from history, Burke was unique in looking primarily to historical experience for his philosophy of man and civil society.

Vaughan is correct, however, that "to Burke reason is no longer the purely passive and analytical faculty of Locke and his disciples." Because of his understanding of the power of history in shaping human nature, Burke rejected "natural rights" and the whole theory of man proposed by Locke's rationalism. On this vital point Willey is far more sound than Vaughan:

According to the Jacobin philosophy, which derives from Locke, man brings nothing into the world with him except a sensitive percipience on which any sort of impressions may be inscribed. Heredity, history, physical environment, count for nothing. . . . If history has been for a long time inscribing erroneous impressions on the blank sheet of the mind, let us 'abolish' history—as d'Alembert suggested. Let us only begin to write reason and justice where history has written prejudice, slavery, and superstition, and we shall change human nature in one generation. To all this Burke replies by an appeal to psychological fact, and to history itself. Man is not a blank sheet at birth; he is born with a mass of predispositions inherited from an incalculable past, and these vary according to place and time.[3] *One writer likened B. to Darwin's concept of evolution. But above statement would link him to Lamarckian.*

In place of Locke's empirical-rational conception of man, so aptly summarized by William Godwin as "man Equal, unclassed, tribeless and nationless," Burke conceived man as the inheritor of an enormously complex historical tradition. As man was by nature a political animal, Locke's purely abstract or physiological conception of man contradicted his particular social nature as formed by the past. Reforms in civil society, Burke believed, should never be based upon Locke's *tabula rasa:* "I cannot conceive how any man can have brought himself to that pitch of presumption, to consider his country as nothing but *carte blanche,* upon which he may scribble whatever he pleases." [4] To Burke social knowledge was true and useful to the extent that it expressed the accumulated experience and wisdom of many generations. The revelations of history, which were for Burke "the known march of the ordinary providence of God," took complete precedence over social knowledge acquired through immediate sense perceptions and private reason. To Burke historical continuity was a human form of divine revelation. Through political, legal, and literary documents and social monuments, through the accumulated knowledge of the practical arts and sciences, and through moral philosophy, Christian Scripture, Church doctrines and traditions, history revealed the will of God in man's temporal affairs. Burke's profound veneration of antiquity, his awareness of the slow organic growth of institutions and nations and of man's restrictions under moral and civil laws, and, above all, his sense of the intricacy and ultimate mystery at the core of human nature flowed from his faith in a revelation beyond Lockian reason.

By "reason" Burke did not mean the immediate logical deductions of individuals, but the complex, historical, corporate revelations of the whole human race, as embodied in historical continuity and prescriptive artificial institutions. Burke distrusted intensely the tradition of individual logical reason. His reaction as a boy to the freshman text in logic at Trinity College, Dublin, which was Burgersdicius' *Institutionum libri duo* (Leyden, 1626), is a case in point. This famous compendium, based upon refutations of Aristotle's *Organon* by the followers of Peter Ramus, a Calvinist Dutch philosopher, provoked Burke's instinctive horror against "metaphysicians" and "refining speculatists":

Never look Burgy in the face! . . . The blackguard stuff, the hoard of exploded nonsense, the scum of pedantry and the refuse of the Boghouse school of Philosophy. . . . I assure you I stink of that crabbed stuff as any vile fresh. in the Univ. and I believe it will ruin me in my next Examination.[5]

Like Swift and Dryden before him, Burke always believed that the passion for private logical speculation, which set aside the experience of the whole human race, was the source of much evil in civil society. His intense dislike of abstract logic was the negative side of his veneration of historical continuity, prescription, and organically developed civil society. This antithesis between individual logic and corporate reason is a fundamental aspect of Burke's conception of human nature as the product of history.

Burke believed that social institutions such as the family, Church, and State, such things as race and nationality, even such broad concepts as "the Commonwealth of Europe," in their historical development, made Locke's isolated "natural" man a purely hypothetical being. Even such institutions as chartered cities and colonies, economic corporations, and political parties, which held their private sovereignty in fiat from the state, fulfilled the reasonable purposes of their individual members through corporate action. In 1771, when Burke's conduct in American affairs was imputed to purely personal motives, he replied in his capacity as a Rockingham Whig: "My principles, indeed the principles of common sense, lead me to act in *corps.*" He never thought of himself or conceived of "the people" in the abstract, apart from man's corporate character. He always thought ill of petitions to the government based solely upon numbers, because "such petitioners can only petition as so many individuals, and can have no corporate capacity or delegation whatsoever." [6] To Burke the individual isolated reason of man was an inadequate guide; in practical affairs "the general communion of mankind" or "the collected reason and representative majesty of mankind" was as the voice of God.

Burke's distinction between individual man and corporate man was first revealed when he was eighteen. The "Minute Book and Notes" for The Club, Burke's undergraduate society at Trinity College, contains the following entry for Tuesday, April 27, 1747: "Mr. Burke . . . says that there is a wide difference betwixt communities and private men, and that the interest of our country is the best motif for alliance." [7] This early awareness of man's corporate nature never left Burke. It was the foundation of all his attacks on the nominalism in any political theory of "natural rights" based on the state of nature. It was the basis of his constant opposition, during the 1780's and until his death in 1797, of every attempt to reform the representation of parliament on a "natural right" principle which ignored man's corporate nature:

> They who plead an absolute right cannot be satisfied with anything short of personal representation, because all *natural* rights must be the rights of individuals; as by *nature* there is no such thing as politic or corporate personality; all these ideas are mere fictions of law, they are creatures of voluntary institution; men as men are individuals, and nothing else.[8]

When Burke attacked Dr. Price in 1777 (and again in the *Reflections*) for having "split and atomized the doctrine of free government, as if it were an abstract question concerning metaphysical liberty. . . . ," he in effect rejected the whole Lockian theory of individual "natural" freedom. Man was free not by the standard of a state of nature, but by his willing adherence to the just rules and restrictions of his particular civil society. Like representation in parliament, civil liberty was not a subject for perpetual abstract speculation. Its practical fulfillment was a matter of moral prudence and veneration for civil society as a historical inheritance. Since man was by nature a corporate being, and civil society was the result of organic development over a long period of time, in discarding the state of nature Burke also rejected the conception of human nature taught by Locke and his disciples.

With admirable impartiality Burke applied to himself his principle that the authority of man's corporate nature and historical inheritance transcended his private reason. He therefore resisted every temptation to offer counterspeculations to other men's private theories. Thus, in 1775 he refused to engage the ministers of George III in a metaphysical debate over the "right" of parliament to tax the colonies:

> I set out with a perfect distrust of my own abilities; a total renunciation of every speculation of my own . . . I was resolved not to be guilty of tampering: the odious vice of restless and unstable minds. I put my foot in the tracks of our forefathers, where I can neither wander nor stumble.[9]

Because he had "well learned the important lesson of self-distrust," Burke placed his faith in Britain's corporate experience and wisdom, and cautioned: "Let us not be among the first who renounce the maxims of our forefathers." As I noted in Chapter Four, Burke refused in 1790 the request of his friend Dupont to submit a new constitution for France: "Never shall you find me aggravating, by the infusion of any speculation of mine, the evils which have arisen from the speculations of others." Moral prudence and historical continuity, rather than the raw, untried, arbitrary, and isolated speculations of any man's private reason, should determine the extent and manner of social reform.

Burke's writings abound with aphorisms on the vast superiority, within civil society, of "the collected wisdom of mankind" as against "the unsteady and precarious contributions of individuals." A few examples will indicate the sweet reasonableness and sociable temperament which Burke brought to his conception of man as a corporate being: "I prefer the collected wisdom of ages to the abilities of any two men living." "A conscientious person would rather doubt his own judgment, than condemn his species." "Personal self-sufficiency and arrogance are the certain attendants upon all those who have never experienced a wisdom greater than their own." "He is an ill-furnished undertaker who has no machinery but his own hands to work with." "We are afraid to put men to live and trade each on his own private stock of reason; because we suspect that this stock in each man is small, and that individuals would do better to avail themselves of the general bank and capital of nations and of ages." "I remember an old scholastic aphorism which says, 'that the man who lives wholly detached

from others must be either an angel or a devil.' " [10] In exalting
the wisdom of man's corporate nature Burke was not ignoring
the achievements in art and science of individual genius; the
wisdom of corporate man was centered not in art and science,
which required special individual talents, but in government
and the regulation of society:

> It is in direct opposition to all our theories and knowledge of
> human nature, to expect from one more than from many; or that
> the opinion of an individual, in all cases respecting the government
> and regulation of society, should be more solid than those which
> result from the joint experience and wisdom of multitudes com-
> bined and matured for that purpose.[11]

In political and civil matters, as Burke said in parliament,
"The mere *ignis fatuus* of private judgment" should not
"supersede the wisdom of Ages." Wholly apart from considerations of transmitted moral wisdom, man's corporate nature
afforded the only immediate practical means of sound political
action:

> Where men are not acquainted with each other's principles, nor
> experienced in each other's talents, nor at all practiced in their
> mutual habitudes and dispositions by joint efforts in business; no
> personal confidence, no friendship, no common interest, subsisting
> among them; it is evidently impossible that they can act a public
> part with uniformity, perseverance, or efficacy. In a connection, the
> most inconsiderable man, by adding to the weight of the whole, has
> his value, and his use; out of it, the greatest talents are wholly un-
> serviceable to the public. No man, who is not inflamed by vain-glory
> into enthusiasm, can flatter himself that his single, unsupported,
> desultory, unsystematic endeavours, are of power to defeat the subtle
> designs and united cabals of ambitious citizens. When bad men com-
> bine, the good must associate; else they will fall, one by one, an un-
> pitied sacrifice in a contemptible struggle.[12]

This passage, which explains why Burke attached such importance to political parties, reveals the broad grounds for his
glowing faith in the unfolding wisdom, maturing strength,
and predominant goodness of mankind as a corporate species.

Burke's faith in the wisdom and habits of man as a species was
connected with his principles of moral prudence and legal

prescription. His description of the corporate free will and reason of the British people in the "choice" of their constitution illustrates this relationship:

This is a choice not of one day, or one set of people, not a tumultary and giddy choice; it is a deliberate election of ages and of generations; it is a constitution made by what is ten thousand times better than choice, it is made by the peculiar circumstances, occasions, tempers, dispositions, and moral, civil, and social habitudes of the people, which disclose themselves only in a long space of time. It is a vestment which accommodates itself to the body. Nor is prescription of government formed upon blind, unmeaning prejudices —for man is a most unwise and a most wise being. The individual is foolish; the multitude, for the moment, is foolish, when they act without deliberation; but the species is wise, and when time is given to it, as a species it always acts right.[13]

When time is given to man, that is, through adherence to prescription and historical continuity, that known march of God's ordinary providence, which in essence is moral prudence, embodies God's divine purposes in man's civil institutions.

As the constitution is the foundation of civil liberty in Britain, prudence and prescription make civil liberty a "natural" part of each citizen's corporate nature, a valuable inheritance to be preserved, extended, and transmitted to posterity. Burke's appeal to prescription, far from making his political philosophy too rigidly conservative, as his liberal critics have commonly charged, is an essential element in the liberal side of his thought. It is the doctrinaire rationalist such as Dr. Price, or Paine, or Godwin who insists upon conformity to the logical conclusions of his private speculative system. As a true conservative, basing his principles upon moral prudence, prescription, and man's corporate nature, Burke made a generous allowance in his political philosophy for nonlogical elements in human nature and the processes of life. This is what made Burke's conservativism more truly liberal than anything in the political theories of his rationalist contemporaries.

His conception of man as a rational corporate being transcended by far the narrow emphasis upon direct sensory observation and logic which underlay the philosophy of Hobbes and

Locke, and was so common in the political speculations of the
Encyclopedists and Jacobins. Man was not to be explained
merely by his sense impressions being systematically organized
through mathematical science. Burke understood the more
mysterious elements in human nature, with its rich fusion of
the senses, reason, and faith, of prejudices, passions, and in-
tuitions, all enriched by fancy, imagination, and social habits.[14]
That is why he warned that "politics ought to be adjusted not
to human reasonings, but to human nature, of which the
reason is but a part, and by no means the greatest part." Burke
so emphasized that life does not proceed according to mathematical logic that he has been interpreted as an emotionalist.
According to John Lester, Burke set down as his first principle
that man is primarily a creature of emotions.[15] In a concordance
of Burke's writings, Wilson M. Hudson has shown that Burke's
discussions of man's nature contain many more references to
emotion than to reason: "The words relating to human nature
are chiefly of the kind that today we should call psychological.
There are hundreds of occurrences of *mind, passions, affections,
feelings, opinions, idea, temper, fear, admiration, ambition,*
and so on." [16] Both Lester and Hudson, however, make a needless separation between reason and emotion in Burke's thought.
Emotion, too, was but a part of human nature, and quite as
capable of error and evil as logical reason: "Leave a man to
his passions," Burke once wrote, "and you leave a wild beast
to a savage and capricious nature." [17] Burke's strong reaction
against the "sensibility" and emotion in Rousseau's theory of
man proves his deep distrust of a purely personal and intuitive
explanation of human nature. When reason and emotion were
integrated in man, they formed a safe guide in principles and
conduct. "Under the direction of reason," wrote Burke, "instinct is always in the right." [18] In discussing man, Burke's
writings are filled with such phrases as "the heart owns and the
understanding ratifies," and "it is felt in the heart; it is recognized by reason." His frequent appeals to "the common feelings
of nature," "natural sentiment," and "natural affections," are
invariably reinforced by supplications to man's right reason.
Both emotion and reason were conceived by Burke not as

private but as *corporate* guides to a true understanding of human nature. In this fusion of corporate emotion and reason Burke abandoned totally the conception of reason held by Locke and his "natural rights" followers.

In his conception of man's psychological and moral nature Burke also rejected the pleasure-pain calculus at the heart of the utilitarian strain in Locke's philosophy. The key to this aspect of Burke's complex theory of man is found in his moral dualism, which is most clearly revealed in his aesthetic theory. A firsthand knowledge of his *On the Sublime and Beautiful* is therefore prerequisite to an understanding of Burke's moral philosophy. Two critics of Burke's aesthetic theory, John Lester and Wilson Clough, indicate in their enormously oversimplified contradictions the general failure to understand this vital aspect of Burke's conception of man:

> The persistence of this idea of the external source of emotions, as well as other clearly Lockian ideas, in Burke's highly emotional aesthetic analysis, is again characteristic of Burke's respect for the authority of the tradition of Locke's psychology.[19]

> Burke's well-known conservatism in a later period, his horror at unreason, make it unlikely that he would have favored the full atomistic swing to subjectivity. Considering his youth . . . his essay was well-nigh a brilliant excursion into psychological esthetics. . . . For the 1750's he was a champion of Taste as a *subjective* imperative, freed from a static, methodized Nature by the indisputable facts of individual sensory equipment and their power to determine that pleasurable response which is the final arbiter of the claims of art.[20]

Burke's supposed respect for Locke's psychology led Lester to "the *external* source of emotions" in his aesthetics, whereas to Clough "the indisputable facts of individual sensory equipment" made Burke "a champion of Taste as a *subjective* imperative." This ambiguity or contradiction in the original active source of man's knowledge and responses, between man's mind and senses and the object of the senses when man thinks, has always plagued English empirical philosophy. In his theory of man's knowledge and in his conception of aesthetic and ethical reality, Burke certainly had a place for the individual senses and reason, but to him the mind of man was not a passive sensorium for collecting sense images, as Hobbes and Locke believed, nor was it, as Berkeley believed, the sole active principle in determining the reality of ideas.

From his undergraduate days Burke was familiar with Locke's works,[21] and in *On the Sublime and Beautiful* he utilized Locke's *Essay Concerning Human Understanding* for examples of the initial part played by the senses in experiencing aesthetic pleasure. But Burke was too Christian to make individual empiricism, logical reason, or pleasure the criterion for good taste and value judgments in aesthetics any more than in ethics. In both fields men were certainly entitled to their harmless private fancies, their preferences of schools and sects, but there was a broad area of social agreement on essentials in both beauty and goodness, or there could be no such thing as bad taste or evil behavior. Burke avoided this nihilism by always distinguishing between "descriptive" and "normative" nature; he never confused the impressions of his senses with the necessary principles of right reason. Nor did he assume the infallibility of his private ego in equating pleasure with good taste in art and desire with good action in ethics. In *On the Sublime and Beautiful* Burke examined at length and rejected the utilitarian ethics of Locke's pleasure-pain calculus, with its implicit monism:

Mr. Locke [*Essay Concerning Human Understanding,* I, ii, c. 20, sect. 16] thinks that the removal or lessening of a pain is considered and operates as a pleasure, and the loss or diminishing of pleasure as a pain. . . . Many are of opinion, that pain arises necessarily from the removal of some pleasure; as they think pleasure does from the ceasing or diminution of some pain. For my part . . . pain and pleasure, in their most simple and natural manner of affecting, are each of a positive nature, and by no means necessarily dependent on each other for their existence. . . . I can never persuade myself that pleasure and pain are mere relations, which can only exist as they are contrasted. Nothing is more certain to my own feelings than this.[22]

This is the key passage to Burke's aesthetic and ethical dualism. His conviction that pleasure and pain are each intrinsically real, that neither is merely the absence of the other, applies as well to the whole realm of ethics, and separates him completely from the common eighteenth-century utilitarian theory of ethics which derives from Hobbes and Locke.

Although neither Hobbes nor Locke had drawn the moral consequences of the pleasure-pain calculus, Burke saw implications in the theory which would have horrified Locke had he had the wit to perceive them. If pleasure was the absence of pain (and good the absence of evil), what would be a man's natural feeling and ethical response when witnessing the pain of others? The grounds of Burke's objections to Locke's ethical psychology become clear in his analysis of the normal moral feeling which follows witnessing an escape from some grave danger:

A man [who has] just escaped an imminent danger, the sort of mixed passion of terror and surprise, with which he affects the spectators, paints very strongly the manner in which we find ourselves affected upon occasions any way similar. . . . Pleasure has never its origin from the removal of pain or danger. . . . We have on such occasions found, if I am not much mistaken, the temper of our minds in a tenor very remote from that which attends the presence of positive pleasure; we have found them in a state of much sobriety, impressed with a sense of awe, in a sort of tranquillity shadowed with horror.[23]

Upon witnessing another's danger or suffering, a truly moral man experiences not pleasure in the knowledge that he is safe and free from pain, but pity and awe in the deepened awareness of the common frailty and tragic fate possible to all mankind. This sense of pity and awe, which was for Burke a source of the sublime, is natural to all uncorrupted men. It causes men to "enter into the concerns of others . . . we are moved as they are moved, and are never suffered to be indifferent spectators of almost anything which men can do or suffer." To feel indifference or pleasure rather than pity and awe toward another man's suffering, even when the other was an enemy, was for Burke the sign of a corrupted nature. Although Locke's conception of man was far more optimistic than the cynical and Epicurean philosophy of Hobbes, both assumed an egocentric pleasure-pain calculus which from Burke's point of view corrupted man's moral sensibility and principles.

It is worth while to note briefly how Burke's moral dualism

was connected in practice with his emotional responses to an actual historical event. His objections to Locke's pleasure-pain calculus in 1756 reappeared in another form in 1790, in his famous attack on Dr. Price's exultation over the "leading in triumph" of the fallen Louis XVI by the Paris populace:

Why do I feel so differently from the Reverend Dr. Price, and those of his lay flock who will choose to adopt the sentiments of his discourse?—For this plain reason—because it is *natural* I should; because we are so made, as to be affected at such spectacles with melancholy sentiments upon the unstable condition of mortal prosperity, and the tremendous uncertainty of human greatness; because in those natural feelings we learn great lessons; because in events like these our passions instruct our reason; because when kings are hurled from their thrones by the Supreme Director of this great drama, and become the objects of insult to the base, and of pity to the good, we behold such disasters in the moral, as we should behold a miracle in the physical order of things. We are alarmed into reflection; our minds (as it has long since been observed) are purified by terror and pity; our weak, unthinking pride is humbled under the dispensations of a mysterious wisdom. Some tears might be drawn from me, if such a spectacle were exhibited on the stage. I should be truly ashamed of finding in myself that superficial, theatric sense of painted distress, whilst I could exult over it in real life. With such a perverted mind, I could never venture to show my face at a tragedy. . . . Indeed the theatre is a better school of moral sentiments than churches, where the feelings of humanity are thus outraged. Poets who have to deal with an audience not yet graduated in the school of the rights of man, and who must apply themselves to the moral constitution of the heart, would not dare to produce such a triumph as a matter of exultation. There where men follow their natural impulses, they would not bear the odious maxims of a Machiavelian policy, whether applied to the attainment of monarchical or democratic tyranny.[24]

Being morally involved in mankind does not imply partisanship in what we pity. Morley's claim that Burke's moral sensibility was "only alive to the consecrated force of historic associations" is superficial nonsense, and misses the whole point in Burke's moral theory. (Burke had also written: "The poorest being that crawls on earth, contending to save itself from injustice and oppression, is an object respectable in the eyes of God and man." [25]) The point in Burke's criticism of Dr. Price is not that Burke favored Louis XVI or monarchy, which he did not, nor that Dr. Price had an ingrained prejudice against all kings, but that the suffering of *any* man, and perhaps especially one who symbolized his nation's greatness, should call forth not pleasure, nor a barbarous exultation over a fallen foe, but a generous pity and profound awe. Indeed, these are the only "natural" emotions. "It is *natural* to be so affected," Burke wrote, "because all other feelings are false and spurious, and tend to corrupt our minds, to vitiate our primary morals, to render us unfit for rational liberty." [26] Burke's attack on Dr. Price's "political computation" and application of the moral calculus, his "weighing, as it were in scales hung in a shop of horrors,—so much actual crime against so much contingent advantage," [27] is the measure of his hatred of the pleasure-pain calculus in utilitarian ethics. Burke's moral principles were founded in his Christian dualism, in which pleasure and pain, good and evil, mind and matter, wealth and poverty, peace and war, and all such opposites, were treated as intrinsic and not necessarily related realities.

In economic theory also Burke's moral dualism stands in the sharpest contrast with the implicit monism in the prevailing pleasure-pain calculus. Adam Smith, himself no revolutionist, expounded the radical thesis that wealth and poverty are proportionately related, an idea which implies that the wealth of the rich is a cause of the poverty of the poor: "Wherever there is great property there is great inequality. For one very rich man there must be at least five hundred poor, and the affluence of the few supposes the indigence of the many." [28] In answering Burke's *Reflections* Boothby agreed with Paine and invoked Rousseau on this point: "Rousseau has very truly observed, that to enrich one man many must be impoverished." [29] Halévy has shown that this implicitly monistic belief was common in eighteenth-century economic thought, particularly in Bentham, and that Godwin made it the basis of his leveling principle in attacking private-property rights.[30] Although Burke certainly disliked "the zealots of the sect of regulation" and believed that in economics "the great use of government is as a restraint," Halévy's conclusion that Burke adhered to Smith's theory of laissez faire errs by omitting the nonutilitarian moral basis of Burke's economics, which like all his thought was dualistic and religious. Burke applied to economics his dictum that "it is a poor exaltation which consists only in the depression of other men." [31] On this principle he opposed both the wealthy East India Company's exclusive monopoly on trade and radical egalitarian theorists on property, such as Godwin. In his conflict with his Bristol constituents over Irish trade Burke clearly rejected the utilitarian pleasure-pain calculus in economics, which was founded on avarice, in favor of a Christian conception of man and the universe:

I know that it is but too natural for us to see our own *certain* ruin in the *possible* prosperity of other people. It is hard to persuade us, that everything which is got by another is not *taken* from ourselves. But it is fit that we should get the better of these suggestions, which come from what is not the best and soundest part of our natures, and that we should form to ourselves a way of thinking, more rational, more just, and more religious. Trade is not a limited thing; as if the objects of mutual demand and consumption could not stretch beyond the bounds of our jealousies. God has given the earth to the children of men, and he has undoubtedly, in giving it to them, given them what is abundantly sufficient for all their exigencies; not a scanty, but a most liberal, provision for them all.[32]

Since wealth is not merely the absence of poverty, nor the necessary cause of someone else's misery, the security of Bristol's wealth through trade did not require the restriction and impoverishment of Ireland. Burke believed wealth was intrinsic and could be expanded socially without danger to anyone. This impartial liberality in Burke's economic theory is derived from his Christian dualism.

Burke took severe issue with the revolutionary theory that since pleasure is the absence of pain, and good the absence of evil, to increase the happiness and good of the greatest number men had but to eliminate the established evil impediments to social progress. Burke felt that those who on principle attributed all social evils to administrators, established institutions, and forms of government were at once dangerously naïve and petulantly cynical. Their oversimplified explanation of the causes of evil conditions in civil society, and consequently their facile interpretation of history, failed to take into account the natural limitations in all social contrivances and political systems, and ignored the illusions, passions, and vices common to all men:

> History consists, for the greater part, of the miseries brought upon the world by pride, ambition, avarice, revenge, lust, sedition, hypocrisy, ungoverned zeal, and all the train of disorderly appetites, which shake the public. . . . These vices are the *causes* of those storms. Religion, morals, laws, prerogatives, privileges, liberties, rights of men, are the *pretexts*. . . . As these are the pretexts, so the ordinary actors and instruments in great public evils are kings, priests, magistrates, senates, parliaments . . . judges. You would not cure the evil by resolving that there should be no more monarchs, nor ministers of state, nor of the gospel; no interpreters of law; no general officers; no public councils. You might change the names. The things in some shape must remain.[33]

To comprehend social evils fully, such as international wars, it was necessary to consult the internal nature of man and not merely the external arrangements of civil and religious institutions and administrators. Burke attacked the French revolutionists who naïvely supposed the violent destruction of evil kings and priests would result in universal peace:

> The French Propagandists, in attributing (as they constantly do) all wars, and all the consequences of wars, to the pride of those orders [Church and State] and to their contempt of the weak and indigent part of society . . . insist that even the wars which they carry on . . . are made to prevent the poor from any longer being the instruments and victims of kings, nobles, and the aristocracy of burgers and rich men. They pretend that the destruction of kings and nobles . . . is the only means of establishing an universal and perpetual peace. This is the great drift of all their writings from 1789 to the publication of the last Morning Chronicle.[34]

The hope of establishing universal peace by *any* means was for Burke an abstract speculation, contrary to the concrete facts of history, but seeking peace through the violent elimination of established corporate institutions was certain to bring on universal war. Forms of government (by whatever name they were called) might indeed be altered, but the passions and vices common to all men remained. For Burke's solution to the knotty problem of social evil one must turn to the Natural Law and Christianity as the basis of his conception of human nature.

II. Natural Law and Christian Revelation: Burke's Conception of Man's Moral and Spiritual Nature

Burke's hearty acceptance of the classical Natural Law implied among many other things that man's moral nature was created and fixed by God. Even legislators had no right to make a law prejudicial to the whole community, because, said Burke, "it would be against the principle of a superior law, which it is not in the power of any community, or of the whole race of man, to alter. I mean the will of Him who gave us our nature, and in giving impressed an invariable law upon it." [35] There was a direct correlation between the fixed moral principles of the Natural Law and man's moral nature. Through "right reason" and free will, even without the special grace of divine revelation, every man was capable of obeying the imperative ethical norms of the Natural Law. In 1771 Burke set down in unmistakable language his most fundamental criterion for judging all human behavior—the moral standard of the Natural Law:

My opinion of the truth or falsehood of facts related in history, is formed on the common rules of criticism; my opinion of characters, on those rules and the common principles of morality. I have no side in these matters. . . . My principles enable me to form my judgment upon men and actions in history, just as they do in common life, and are not formed out of events and characters, either present or past. History is a preceptor of prudence, not of principles. The principles of true politics are those of morality enlarged; and I neither now do, nor ever will, admit of any other.[36]

This is a key passage to an understanding of Burke's conception of man's moral nature. The Natural Law as an ethical norm, and not history as a descriptive science, supplied the criterion for moral judgments of man's behavior. History established a body of verifiable facts and dealt with empirical truth or falsehood; at best it was a preceptor of prudence and revealed

God's "divine tactic" to man. But neither historical events nor empirical data could be the basis of any moral judgment of human behavior. In *On the Sublime and Beautiful* Burke had written: "That chain of Causes, which links one to another, even to the throne of God Himself, can never be unravelled by any industry of ours. When we go but one step beyond the immediate sensible quality of things, we go out of our depth." In this statement Burke did not mean that everything beyond sensory perception is untrustworthy, but that the senses themselves are severely limited and tell us nothing about man's moral constitution, or the mystery at the core of life. Burke believed that the moral principles that guide men in public and private are not of our devising, but are molded into the nature and essence of the universe by God. Ultimately, the acceptance of Natural Law and belief in man's capability to fulfill its ethical norms is an act of religious faith.

He never fixed his attention so firmly upon the ethical norms of the Natural Law that he forgot the inherent fallibility of human nature. He always left room for "the ordinary frailties of human nature," and contended: "He knows little of mankind, and feels less for them, who . . . will not make a liberal allowance for our common and inevitable infirmity." [37] Although Burke held legislators most strictly accountable to God for abuses of power, even their occasional common weaknesses were exceptions implied and allowed for in the understood covenant by which power was delegated by fallible men to other men who were not infallible. Any failure to take into account the weaknesses natural to man was, in a real sense, impious: "He censures God, who quarrels with the imperfections of man." [38] Time and experience of the world taught Burke early in life to moderate his expectations of human ability, and this lesson underlay his many attacks upon political theorists who aim at perfection in human affairs: "That man thinks much too highly, and therefore he thinks weakly and delusively, of any contrivance of human wisdom, who believes that it can make any sort of approach to perfection." [39] A profound recognition of man's necessary imperfections,

Burke believed, was itself a corrective of the evils of theoretic perfection, and helped make possible the achievement of man's highest practical, but always imperfect, good:

There is, by the essential fundamental constitution of things, a radical infirmity in all human contrivance; and the weakness is often so attached to the very perfection of our political mechanism, that some defect in it,—something that stops short of its principle,— something that controls, that mitigates, that moderates it,—becomes a necessary corrective to the evils that the theoretic perfection would produce.[40]

Burke combined an infinite charity toward man as a finite and fallible creature and a strict acceptance of the imperative character of the Natural Law. In Burke's conception of human nature there was no contradiction or antithesis between personal charity, "the highest of the virtues," and the claims of social justice under the Natural Law.

Burke's willingness to bear with infirmities until they festered into crimes stands in the sharpest contrast to the dark and austere moral temperament of Robespierre and the moralists who organized and ran the Reign of Terror. Burke noted that such moralists, "by hating vices too much . . . come to love men too little." It is therefore no paradox that, like Othello, they sacrificed their victims for moral reasons, out of a muddy understanding and a surfeited and corrupted sense of human benevolence. Unlike Priestley and many other defenders of the French Revolution, who sanctioned the Reign of Terror as an inevitable evil accompanying the grand liberation of man, Burke never extended charity to include crimes against the Natural Law. Moral prudence was the regulator between the just claims of charity and justice, and Burke achieved an integrated conception of man's moral nature which included both. On the side of justice the first in rank of crimes against nature was homicide: "The act of homicide is *prima facie* criminal." [41] Violations against natural and civil rights to property and liberty also made their claims for redress.

In judging transgressions against the moral law Burke made a strict distinction between the intentions and consequences of men's actions. Where evil acts were sporadic and unsystematic he allowed room for the claims of pure intentions. This rule of charity did not apply to such a man as Warren Hastings, whose actions gave evidence of willful, premeditated and repeated violations of the Natural Law: "A *general evil intention,* manifested through a long series and a great variety of acts, ought to have much greater weight with a public political tribunal, than such detached and unrelated offences into which common human infirmity has often betrayed the most splendid characters in history." [42] Burke objected strongly that the House of Lords, in judging his argument for impeaching Hastings, made private intentions rather than social consequences and self-evident moral laws the basis for judgment:

> We are before a tribunal which, having conceived a favourable opinion of Hastings . . . will not judge of his intentions by the acts, but . . . will qualify his acts by the presumed intentions. It is on this preposterous mode of judging that he has built all the apologies for his conduct.[43]

To judge men by their presumed good intentions was to base the universal Natural Law upon an unverifiable subjective condition. Since Burke believed in man's right reason and free will, he held that the actions of men were the best criterion for moral judgment. He once said in parliament: "It was very natural to censure men from the event of their actions, for by what other criterion could you judge them?" In another speech he extended this statement: "He could not decide upon men's intentions; he could only speak of the outward and visible signs, and by these guess at the inward spirit." [44] For the same reason that Burke would not judge Hastings by his professed good intentions, he refused to judge George III's ministers by their patriotism, the persecutors of the Irish by their zeal for true religion, and the Jacobins by their logic, natural feelings, or social theories. After a due regard for man's ordinary weaknesses, in all moral judgments Burke estimated men simply by their actions, by their conformity to or divergence from the eternal moral Natural Law, and by nothing else.

However much Burke believed in the power of man's unaided right reason to perceive the moral law, compared with the "great illumination blaze and effulgence of light so gloriously demonstrated by the gospel," the glimmerings of natural reason were faint indeed. In Christianity grace supplemented reason and raised the whole level of man's nature, and of his understanding of the moral law and ability to abide by it, from a mundane to a supernatural level. Religion transcended morality not by violating natural reason, but by including it in supernatural revelation and grace. By adding to the natural powers of man the divine dispensations of God's grace, Christianity presented a far more intense, concrete, personal, and complete revelation of the moral law, and the practical means of its fulfillment. When the Natural Law was perceived only by individual reason, unaided by corporate religion, there was danger that men would construct a false antithesis between reason and faith, between works and contemplation and man and God; in short, there was danger that men would live under the shadow rather than under the body of the moral law. In time of crisis natural reason without supernatural faith often proved inadequate and untrustworthy, because human nature was subject to terrible illusions, weaknesses, and moral depravity. It is not surprising that some of Burke's most caustic criticism was directed against such English deists as Bolingbroke and Paine, who depended almost exclusively on the light of natural reason and had no corporate allegiance in religion. Deism was to Burke not the common denominator of man's revealed religions, but the halfway house to a rationalistic atheism. Burke's conception of man's rational and spiritual nature was centered in his Christianity, which at once paralleled and transcended the Natural Law.

Perhaps the most remarkable fact in Burke's Christianity was his early and consistent adherence to the *via media* of the High Church Anglican tradition. As Samuels has pointed out, even as an undergraduate Burke revealed the moderation characteristic of Anglicanism which later marked his political temper: "That preference of the *via media*, of the practically possible rather than the theoretically perfect, which characterized Burke's political philosophy, appears in the pages of the Proceedings of the Club." [45] Burke possessed a vast historical knowledge of the outstanding Anglican theologians, particularly the seven-teenth-century divines. He admired Hooker above all others, but he also enjoyed greatly the work of Donne, Stillingfleet, Hickes, Ussher, Jeremy Taylor, Isaac Barrow, Robert South, and Gilbert Burnet, while Browne's *Christian Morals* was a favorite book of his youth. When he visited France in 1773 he was agreeably surprised at the widespread knowledge of English divines he found among the French clergy. Swift's religious and political tracts were known to him, and Woehl has shown his acquaintance with many eighteenth-century Anglicans: "The churchmen of this period with whose works Burke was familiar included Joseph Butler, James Hervey, William Warburton, and the poet Edward Young. Burke presented Barry, the young painter whom he befriended, with a copy of Butler's *Analogy of Religion,* thus fixing Barry's belief in revealed religion." [46] Shortly before his death Burke said to his friend Mrs. Crewe, "Butler's *Analogy* is greatly in my estimation," [47] and his conception of man's intellectual and moral nature clearly reveals a profound indebtedness to But-ler.[48] Indeed, the influence of Hooker, Butler, and the whole Anglican tradition in Burke's thought is so profound that it deserves a separate study; we must be content here with a sum-mary of the cardinal principles in Burke's Christianity which shaped his moral temperament and determined his conception of man.

Following the complex *via media* of the seventeenth- and eighteenth-century Anglican writers on the Natural Law and Christianity, and particularly Butler's *Sermons* (1726) and *Analogy* (1736), Burke derived a dualistic theory of man which harmonized the claims of natural reason and divine revelation. Burke rejected both the cynical Hobbist theory that man, as a creature ruled by evil passions, is motivated solely by self-interest, and the sentimental theory of man's natural benev-olence put forth by the third Earl of Shaftesbury. If man were a creature of passions, whether evil or good, there would be no room for right reason in determining his moral behavior, and Natural Law would be a meaningless philosophy. Where Hobbes and Shaftesbury made a false antithesis concerning the nature of man's dominant passions, Calvinism and deism committed the same errors regarding grace and reason in the realm of religion. The Calvinist dogma of the elect made man's salvation depend entirely upon God's grace, and in effect denied that man's right reason and will had any part in his moral redemption. The deists exalted the natural reason of man and denied the need of any sanctifying grace. But the "reason" of the deists was not the Ciceronian "right reason" of the classical Natural Law, but merely the mathematical logic of natural science applied to moral problems. Olive Griffith has shown in *Religion and Learning* that between 1660 and 1800 Calvinism became thoroughly impregnated with the rationalistic spirit of natural science, and developed that love of simplicity which Hobbes and the deists venerated. Thus, not one of these philosophies was capable of harmonizing the classical Natural Law and Christianity. As a High Church Anglican Burke believed neither in the Hobbist and Calvinist theory of universal innate depravity, nor in the sentimental or rational natural benevolence of Shaftesbury, Rousseau, and the deists. Burke's Anglicanism prevented him from assuming any single, simple mainspring of human conduct, and enabled him to accept a philosophy of human nature in which the claims of passion, reason, and faith were synthesized.

Burke always strongly condemned any assertion which even suggested the Calvinist dogma of the "elect" and the "depraved," with its implied political corollary that some men are born to rule and others only to serve. To his son he wrote in 1792: "A religion that has for one of its dogmas the servitude of all mankind that do not belong to it, is a vile heresy." [49] In his *Letter to the Sheriffs of Bristol* Burke wrote: "He that accuses all mankind of corruption, ought to remember that he is sure to convict only one." Burke emphatically denied the repeated assertions of George III's ministers that the domestic and colonial disturbances of the 1760's and 1770's resulted "from the natural depravity of the people." "The ministers," he charged, "are the grand criminals," whose tyranny provoked rebellion. Burke always assumed the same ground against those who argued that an iron hand was necessary to constrain the turbulent natures of the Irish: "Those miserable performances which go about under the names of Histories of Ireland . . . would persuade us, contrary to the known order of nature, that indulgence and moderation in governors is the natural incitement in subjects to rebel." [50] Governors were themselves the truest sample of the nation: "If they are universally depraved, the commonwealth itself is not sound." Burke was aware of the corruptions in the House of Commons under George III, yet he defended it against the label of depravity: "An opinion of the indiscriminate corruption of the House of Commons, will, at length, induce a disgust of parliaments. They are the corrupters themselves, who circulate this general charge of corruption. . . . There are many amongst us who are free from all sorts of corruption, and of a most excellent spirit." [51] From whatever source and against whatever corporate group the cry of universal depravity was raised, Burke was certain to be found among the opposition.

Burke's early faith in man's "predominant proportion of active virtue and wisdom" was modified by his mature experience of the world: "Almost every body," he said late in life, "in the sanguine season of youth, looks in the world for more perfection than he is likely to find." Yet his early conviction was largely substantiated in his public life: "Never expecting to find perfection in men," he wrote in 1777, "and not looking for Divine attributes in created beings, in my commerce with my contemporaries, I have found much human virtue." [52] Two years later he wrote: "I am satisfied that there is so much good in mankind at large, that one of the main causes of the mutual hatred in parties, is our mutual ignorance of each other." And after more than a quarter century in parliament Burke wrote of his colleagues: "They are endowed with as many and as great virtues as the nature of man is capable of producing, joined to great clearness of intellect, to a just judgment, to a wonderful temper, and to true wisdom." [53] Nor did Burke restrict his praise to men like Rockingham, Portland, Savile, the Cavendishes, Windham, and Eliot: he praised also the virtues of Lord Chatham, Charles Townshend, Lord North, Erskine, Dundas, and the younger Pitt, men with whom he often strongly disagreed. Even more than his public statements, Burke's private letters are filled with glowing tributes to the moral and intellectual integrity and the liberal and humanized company of his peers.[54]

Yet Burke's admiration of his colleagues and general faith in the predominant goodness of man was totally distinct from the current belief in man's natural benevolence and sensibility. Compared with the theories of man's rational perfectibility put forth by Priestley and Godwin, or the intuitive moral sensibility preached by Rousseau, Burke's conception of man appears almost Augustinian. There are, however, only two statements in Burke's writings which suggest the severe doctrines of the Bishop of Hippo. The first was written to his friend Shackleton in 1744, during a period of mental depression: "Without the superior grace of God, I . . . find it very difficult to be commonly virtuous." The other probably was written during his middle years: "I have brought my mind to so exclusive a veneration for the Divine perfections, that I have no admiration left for those of men."

Although he was perfectly aware from both reading and observation of man's deeply sinful nature, Burke almost never exalted the glory of God at the expense of the real but limited dignity of man. His explanation of the problem of evil set him wholly apart from his rationalist and sentimentalist contemporaries. The rationalists, following their Lockian *tabula rasa,* assumed that personal and social evils originated and were maintained by a poor arrangement of the objects of man's perceptions and of the machinery of artificial institutions and government. The sentimentalists rejected Locke's *tabula rasa* in favor of man's innate or intuitive "moral sense," but they too explained evil as originating in external social conditions which impeded the free expression of man's natural goodness. Where the empiricists and rationalists saw only error in the computations of moral arithmetic, Burke saw original sin. Where the sentimentalists saw only the frustration of man's moral sincerity and good intentions, Burke saw original sin.

From early childhood, as an Anglican Christian Burke was

ever conscious of his non-Calvinist creed of original sin.[55] As Ross Hoffman has said, "The most important questions about the human race Burke answered from the Church of England's catechism." [56] Burke was too good an Anglican and too well acquainted with the history of human depravity to attribute personal corruption and social evils to any general cause other than man's inherent moral weaknesses. His study of history and his long and intimate political experience with the domestic corruptions of George III's reign, and of the affairs of Ireland, America, and India, supplied him with endless examples of man's sinful nature, of his willful and conscious inhumanity to man.[57] When English sentimentalists expressed shock at the social evils uncovered by the French Revolution, Burke wrote: "It is no soothing news to my ears, that great bodies of men are incurably corrupt." [58] Indeed, in Burke's conception of man's inherent moral nature, evil was only slightly subordinated to good.

Against the doctrine of original sin Burke placed his Christian faith in the redemptive capability of man as a being created in the spiritual image of God. Natural man, though in a fallen state, was capable through God's grace and his own right reason and free will of glorious worldly achievements and an even more glorious supernatural destiny. Burke eulogized the spiritual and civil achievements of man redeemed from sin: "That wonderful structure, Man—whose prerogative it is to be in a great degree a creature of his own making, and who, when made as he ought to be made, is destined to hold no trivial place in the creation." [59] The true Anglican *via media* for Burke was not a matter of religious sovereignty, which combined the historical continuity and traditions of Catholicism with the individualism of Calvinism; Burke's *via media* was centered in his conception of man's moral and spiritual nature, and combined the claims of reason and faith between the extremes of Pelagianism and Augustinianism:

We must soften into a credulity below the milkiness of infancy, to think all men virtuous. We must be tainted with a malignity truly diabolical, to believe all the world to be equally wicked and

corrupt. Men are in public life as in private, some good, some evil.
The elevation of the one, and the depression of the other, are the
first objects of all true policy.[60]

Clearly, Burke believed in man's inherent capacity for both
good and evil. But the natural inclination toward evil, or
original sin, was not total in some men (the depraved) and
totally lacking in others (the elect), but was mixed and partial
in all men. Consequently, through free will and right reason
all men were capable of adding sanctity to divine grace and of
achieving personal salvation. Those only were lost who willed
their own perdition. In short, Burke conceived of man as a
complex organic compound of many biological, psychological,
and spiritual elements, a dualism of flesh and spirit, a being so
complex and variable that it was almost impossible to generalize
about his nature. A passage written in 1764 summarizes Burke's
awareness of the complexity of human nature:

> This makes human nature so various and multiform in the indi-
> viduals that partake of it, that, in point of morals and intellectual
> endowments, it fills up all that gap which we conceive to be between
> brutes and devils below, and the celestial orders above; and such
> a prodigious diversity of minds must make it extremely difficult to
> discover the common principles of the species. . . . The savage
> hath within him the seeds of the logician, the man of taste and breed-
> ing, the orator, the statesman, the man of virtue, and the saint,
> which seeds, though planted in his mind by nature, yet, through
> want of culture and exercise, must lie for ever buried, and be hardly
> perceivable by himself or others.[61]

With the aids to natural grace supplied by family, Church,
State, and other artificial institutions, even the raw savage, in
a primitive state of nature, was capable of civil and religious
salvation. Without corporate institutions of dignity and authority to cover the defects of his naked and shivering nature, man
was little better than a wild beast.[62] Multitudes acting outside
of any corporate character are irrational and ruthless monsters.
Man's corporate institutions establish and sustain those laudable
restraints which make man happy in spite of his own nature.
It followed, therefore, as Burke wrote in a letter to his friend
Elliot, that "as the wisdom of men makes such institutions, the

folly of men destroys them." Burke's conception of man as a political animal, in constant need of artificial institutions, implied his total rejection of all primitivist theories of man's natural goodness, his belief in original sin, and his faith in the redemptive power of man.

The dark side of Burke's Christianity owes far more to the pagan Roman Stoics—to the spirit of Cicero and Epictetus— than to St. Paul or St. Augustine. Burke quoted Cicero more frequently than any other ancient author; as an undergraduate he had read and admired Epictetus, and had mentioned with approval Pascal's dictum that hard work is the best cure for personal sorrow and affliction.[63] The latter idea, which implies the stoical temperament, Burke repeated at various intervals throughout his life.[64] Like his friend Dr. Johnson, Burke poured out enormous energy and received great joy in his daily tasks. Nevertheless, he too believed that life contains little to be enjoyed and much to be endured. Kings and laws can cause or cure only a few of the evils which man, by the natural constitution of things, must suffer. Burke's Stoicism is evident in the high seriousness with which he approached life, and especially in his religious piety. He was ever conscious of all the mysterious powers by which external circumstances limit, condition, and weigh upon the hopes and plans of men.[65] He was convinced that God, "the benign and wise Disposer of all things," has established in man and the world "the nature of things with which we shall in vain contend." A few sentences taken at random will illustrate the spirit of Stoicism in Burke's thought: "The condition of our nature binds us to a strict law and very narrow limits." "The Author of our nature has written it strongly in that nature . . . that man shall eat his bread by his labour." "It is the common doom of man that he must eat his bread by the sweat of his brow." "But in all these things, we must acknowledge and revere, in silence, a superior hand." "We must take what God gives . . . submission is my duty and my policy." [66] In both personal and social affairs Burke's writings were permeated with Stoicism, and he found sense in life, and in the complex evolving forces of nature and society, by reverently accepting the basic order of the world and co-operating with unperceived powers and laws which transcended man's more than rational nature.[67]

Burke's acceptance of the unalterable constitution of things was by no means pessimistic or fatalistic, but rather implied faith in the salutary terms of man's existence on earth. "Providence," he wrote to Franklin in 1781, "has not done its work by halves," and he was convinced that nature was perfectly capable of fulfilling all of man's physical and moral needs: "There is nothing that God has judged good for us, that He has not given us the means to accomplish, both in the natural and the moral world." Burke learned early in the House of Commons that the real problem was how to make men perceive their glorious place in the natural order, and to make themselves worthy of it: "We ought to elevate our minds to the greatness of that trust to which the order of Providence has called us." [68] Through his strong belief in free will, Burke always held man morally responsible for his own destiny: "Let those rail at free will," he wrote, "who have sinned in consequence of it." Without free will man could not have any responsible control over his behavior; if necessity governed man, there could be no such things as liberty and morality: "It is better to cherish virtue and humanity, by leaving much to free will, even with some loss to the object, than to attempt to make men mere machines and instruments of a political benevolence. The world on the whole will gain by a liberty, without which virtue cannot exist." [69] In an early letter to Shackleton Burke objected vigorously to the Cartesian theory that nonhuman animal life is totally mechanistic, and also rejected any belief that man's actions are predetermined. Burke applied his anti-mechanistic conception of man in the *Reflections*, throughout much of his criticism of the revolutionary social theory. Although he believed man was strictly bound by the physical and moral order of the universe, in his individual and corporate capacity man was free to shape his destiny to the full measure of his nature.

He was aware that in practice it was often difficult to determine precisely how, within the "divine tactic," which had disposed and marshalled man within the sovereign nature of things, men could exercise their reason and free will to improve themselves and society without violating the Natural Law. On the one hand was the power and law claimed by physical and moral nature. Burke's constant thesis was that man must submit to that which is "laid deep in the natural constitution of things," to "that power [which] steps in . . . limits the arrogance of raging passions and furious elements, and says, 'So far shalt thou go, and no farther.' Who are you, that you should fret and rage, and bite the chains of nature?" On the other hand was Burke's belief that God has given man natural reason and free will to mold his destiny with his own hands, that "after this allowance to Nature, something is always left in our own power." How was the line between the claims of man and nature to be drawn? In 1777 Burke felt that the British public, in its attitude toward the American rebellion, attributed to nature evils which lay within the power of man to correct: "I find that, generally speaking, they bear their calamities as they bear the seasons; not as arising from the faults of those who rule them, but as dispositions of Providence, at which they ought not to repine, and are not able to oppose." [70] Burke knew that America had rebelled not against nature, but against British misrule.

John Morley felt that in 1789 Burke should have applied the same principle and reasoning to the misrule of the old régime in France, where the people had rebelled against an unnatural tyranny of long standing.[71] Burke was convinced, however, that the primary cause of the French Revolution was not economic hardship and political misrule, but a new and revolutionary theory of man and society. The French Revolution resulted from the dogma that all men were and should be by nature intellectually and morally equal, that individual differences and all existing social evils and imperfections were caused and maintained by man's inherited institutions, by priests and kings, and that the established order in Church and State had to be destroyed in order to found a new and perfect social order on a rational basis. Burke's basic criticism of the French revolutionists was that in attempting to establish a perfect society according to their abstract reason, they refused to subordinate their will and logic to the Natural Law.

In practical politics the conflict between nature and man was to Burke more apparent than real. This conflict was the result of a false humility or excessive pride, and appeared because men could not achieve in practice the abstract perfection of their social and political theories. To the extent that men were made through their institutions morally in tune with their highest instincts and reason, they were in perfect harmony with the Natural Law. When conflicting claims between nature and man's will arose, the problem could not be settled on any abstract principle. Moral prudence, together with man's corporate experience through history, supplied the best guide in determining whether social evils should be endured as natural and necessary, or resisted as the artificial product of tyrants.

The complete antithesis of Burke's Stoical Christian conception of human nature is found in Epicurean-atheism, in which pleasure and private will usurped the place of moral duty and right reason. It is in Stoicism that the spirit of Burke's Christianity meets with the classical Natural Law, in opposing Epicurean-atheism. As early as 1773 Burke had actually identified Epicureanism with atheism.[72] Two years later he wrote: "I think . . . general affection to religion . . . will make a common cause against Epicurism, and everything that corrupts the mind and renders it unworthy of its family." [73] In essence Epicureanism exalted the private ego and will of men at the expense of their corporate reason and in defiance of prudence and the ethical norms of the Natural Law. Burke was keenly aware that without civil institutions it was "a difficult thing to the corrupt, grasping, and ambitious part of human nature . . . to put bounds" on its power and submit to "the rules and principles of law." [74] It was the chief function of man's just institutions, produced by the legislative wisdom of ages, to check and control these selfish appetites and depraved passions of man in his fallen state, to convert his latent energy into constructive action in harmony with Natural Law. To Burke nothing was stronger proof of individual depravity than an unwillingness or inability to live under the moral law as that law was variously embodied in man's inherited institutions. There was something satanic in such men as Paine, Priestley, Price, and the leaders of the French Revolution, who sought to rid society of its economic and social evils by destroying the solid work of generations, and who frequently objected to all civil and religious authority on principle. Burke perceived that the fusion of two anti-Stoical and anti-Christian strains of thought gave tremendous power and social prestige to eighteenth-century Epicureanism— the revolutionary dogma of man's intellectual equality, and Rousseauist sensibility.

The Natural Law and Christianity supplied Burke with his conception of the moral equality of man under divine law— the equal value of each man's soul to God. It was a conception of equality centered in equity,[75] in what men had in common as men, as members of the same species, and also in an equal regard for their individual differences, as members of a particular race, religion, nationality, or other corporate group in civil society. To Burke individual and corporate differences among men were natural, salutary, and necessary, and made possible that "natural aristocracy" of talents and virtues in every free, well-ordered and just society. Clearly, Burke's Christian conception of equality, with its hierarchy of values and classes, was totally at variance with the doctrinaire egalitarianism of eighteenth-century revolutionary thought. Paine and other levelers, who wished to destroy as "unnatural" all inherited or acquired social distinctions, filled Burke with a profound fear for civil society. The radicals assumed that utility and the rights of man in a state of nature were the soundest norms for establishing equality in civil society. Burke rejected the utilitarian pleasure-pain calculus as an inherently false and rationalistic method; utilitarianism was indistinguishable from the ancient Epicurean principle that pleasure and enlightened self-interest were man's highest good. Man was fitted by his divine nature for a higher destiny than anything imagined in such a calculating philosophy.

The radicals' attempt to establish in civil society the "rights of man" in a state of nature would violate true moral equality.

Individual differences and legitimate distinctions would be leveled, and men would be reduced to a mere equality of condition. The whole basis of the radical conception of equality was the assumption, derived from empirical philosophy, that men were literally equal in intellectual capability. As Thomas Cooper put it in his *A Reply to Mr. Burke's Invective Against Mr. Cooper and Mr. Watt in the House of Commons* (1792), all men have "equal rights and capacities for improvement." [76] Paine also believed that "men are all of *one degree,* and consequently all men are born equal, and with equal natural right." [77] Burke was castigated by William Belsham for rejecting the theory that men were literally equal: " 'Men, with them,' says Mr. Burke, i.e., with the National Assembly of France, 'are strictly equal, and entitled to equal rights.' This, we have long been taught by Mr. Locke, and others in this country, to consider as a simple, just, and noble principle, lying at the very foundation of all just reasonings on the subject of Government." [78] Another opponent of Burke, Benjamin Bousfield, stated well the revolutionary implications of belief in man's literal equality: "The principle of primaeval equality is a sacred principle, which neither injustice nor ambition can erase; which exists in every breast, and to exert itself requires only to be awakened among the numerous and oppressed classes of mankind." [79] The hypothetical equal "rights of man" in a state of nature could not be established except by leveling out all the natural and inherited distinctions found in civil society.

Nothing so violated Burke's faith in the corporate nature of man, in the classical Natural Law and in moral prudence and temperance, as the sensibility of Rousseau. The theory that morality was based upon private intuitive feeling also contradicted Stoicism and Christianity. It implied belief in the inherent goodness of natural man. To Burke, who believed that nine out of ten of the moral virtues taught men the need of restraint upon their passions, sensibility was but another form of Epicurean self-indulgence. In his extensive attack on Rousseau in *A Letter to a Member of the National Assembly,* Burke recognized that Rousseau's type of sensibility had infused a sentimental idealism into the private sensations, pleasures, fancies, and rational calculations of revolutionary thought. The blaze and whirlwind of Rousseau's emotion supercharged eighteenth-century radical theory with a militant religious fervor. It enabled modern Epicureanism to disguise itself as a pseudo-religion, and to make claims as a full-fledged moral philosophy. It taught a personal religion of social salvation through works alone. It was no longer necessary to reflect and act according to the dictates of right reason and the revelations of Christianity; it was enough to be touched vitally by a delicate distress. To Burke sensibility permeated a vile philosophy of pleasure, power, and will with moral feeling; it corrupted men by teaching them to justify evil means in practice for noble ends in theory, to act without restraint or a conscious reference to any legal precedents or moral code. Against sensibility and salvation through feeling alone, Burke took his stand on traditional Christian grounds.

It should now be evident that Burke's Stoical and Christian conception of man was the foundation of his whole social and political philosophy. His conviction that man had free will and was capable of right reason enabled him to maintain a close connection between morality and politics. For Burke there was no Machiavellian separation between sound political principles and practice. Since God had "willed the state" and man was by nature a political animal, Burke regarded legislators as God's instruments, acting in trust, responsible for their conduct to the great Master, Author, and Founder of society, and fulfilling in the temporal world the divine purposes of the Creator. Burke's statements that civil society was of divine origin and that commonwealths were not physical but moral essences, were also the logical consequence of his Christian conception of man. By a "divine tactic" man had been formed that at his best he might rule himself rationally and morally. Burke had a mystical conception of society, not because he was a mystic or irrationalist, but because he saw the reality in society of spiritual powers which transcended the merely rational understanding of man, and even the complex processes of history itself. When reason and history had revealed all that man was capable of knowing about government and the art of politics, there still remained for Burke the power and wisdom of God, whose spirit touched the innermost springs of human nature.

SEVEN

Church and State

I. The Historical Function of the Church: Civil Manners

The essential distinction between natural and civil society, which Burke made in all his attacks on the revolutionary "rights of man," also permeates all of his discussions of the origins, functions, historical development, and structural relationships of the two chief artificial institutions of civil society —Church and State. To appreciate the rich significance of this distinction in Burke's political philosophy, it is necessary first to consider separately how Church and State developed historically, and their respective functions under the law of nations. It will then be clear how, together, they fulfilled Burke's grand principle of moral prudence under the Natural Law, and established the civil justice and liberty which made possible the delicately balanced and magnificent order of European civilization.

Burke always believed that from history "much political wisdom may be learnt . . . as habit, not as precept . . . as an exercise to strengthen the mind, not as a repertory of precedents for a lawyer." [1] But he was far too wise, both as a historian and as a political philosopher, to philosophize about theories of history. He always suspected theorists and refining speculators whose fondness for simple categories, analogies, and logical systems caused them to ignore established facts and the changing historical circumstances of mankind. History did indeed reveal "the known march of the ordinary providence of God." But in its origins, means, and ends history was shrouded in mystery, and Burke was too self-skeptical to assume that he was one of God's elect, chosen for special insights into its ultimate meaning. In limiting himself within history, Burke was always starkly practical in his conception of Church, State, and other civil institutions. The religious mysticism which infuses his political philosophy was embodied within the known events of European history.

Apart from the purely personal function of religion, to expand man's charity and to give men hope through their love of God, Burke conceived an exalted historical and social function for religion. It was "the chain that connects the ages of a nation." It was the force which made men conscious of "the great mysterious incorporation of the human race." By definition, "religion [was] one of the great bonds of human society; and its object the supreme good, the ultimate end and object of man himself." [2] Religion enabled man to judge passing temporal events against the background of eternal moral laws. As the basic religion of Europe, Christianity was to Burke not only "the foundation of our common hope," but also "the foundation upon which all our laws and institutions stand as upon their base." [3] Christianity was the spiritual equivalent of Burke's conception of a worldly "Commonwealth of Europe." In the eighteen centuries of its existence, through historical continuity and legal prescription, it had added immeasurably to the richness and stability of European civilization.

In his view of the grand sweep of European history, from the gradual fall of the Roman Empire to the French Revolution, Burke was acutely conscious of the enormous social task the Church had assumed and carried successfully for almost eighteen hundred years. Burke noted in his historical survey, *An Abridgment of English History* (1757), that "the barbarians, after destroying the Empire, at length submitted their necks to the gospel." In the struggle to subdue the barbarians, the Church had preserved, transcribed, and spread the learning, literature, science, laws, and manners of the ancient world. Throughout Europe she had spread a system of Christian charity, patronized the arts, and founded the great cathedral schools and universities. Burke's *An Abridgment of English History*, which extends from the invasions of Caesar to the Magna Carta, leaves no doubt that he revered the great social achievements of the Church in the Middle Ages. Under the

Romans, whom Burke considered the "conquerors, civilizers and legislators of mankind," the ancient Britons had been best subdued not by force of arms, but "by reconciling them to Roman manners." [4] After Rome recalled her legions, Burke noted, the Britons "fell into a disregard of religion and into loose, disorderly manners." With the fall of the Roman Empire sound civil manners were replaced by the crude tribal customs of the ancient Celts.

During the critical period after Rome withdrew from Britain, the greatest social function of the Church, infusing the arts and civil manners through the spiritual nature of man, first revealed itself: "Light scarcely begins to dawn until the introduction of Christianity; which [brought] with it the use of letters and the arts of civil life." [5] Burke constantly iterated that the essential struggle between the Church and the Germanic and Celtic barbarians was over civil manners: "The chief difficulties which Christianity had to encounter . . . [were] the gross and licentious manners of a barbarous people." But, he noted, "Christianity soon made a sensible change in these rude and fierce manners," and "by degrees the sanctions of religion began to preponderate." [6] Even by the eighth century the relation of Church to State, of civil manners to political laws, was clearly evident: "The manners of the Saxons underwent a notable alteration by this change in their religion; their ferocity was much abated; they became more mild and sociable; and their laws began to partake of the softness of their manners." [7] Burke retained this view of the relation of Church and State, of civil manners and laws, in his interpretation of the French Revolution.

Since the barbarian invasions had not destroyed all of civilization, the Church was never wholly alone in her great task of social reconstruction. Ancient Rome was still so revered that for centuries men refused to admit she had fallen. She was still "the asylum of what learning had escaped the general destruction . . . even in her ruins she preserved something of the majesty of her ancient greatness." Burke noted that throughout Europe, in the midst of barbarous chaos, "there were principles at work which reduced things to a certain form, and gradually unfolded a system, in which the main springs were the papal and imperial powers." [8] The Church, together with the remnants of the Roman civil state, sought to Christianize and civilize the raw Germanic barbarians, to transform them through artificial manners and laws into tractable, cultured, civil-tempered European Christians. Only by submitting to the authority of Church and State, and assuming a just system of manners and laws, could the barbarians be brought to live in peace according to the spirit of Natural Law.

The Church transformed the uncouth manners of the Germanic barbarians directly through a simple, rational presentation of Christian morality in the Scriptures. But in the aesthetic appeal of ceremony, liturgy, and tradition, though fraught with dangers, the Church found a more indirect, and far more subtle, refined, and effective method of softening crude manners. Burke noted the appeal of the Church "in music, in decoration, in speech, in the dignity of persons, [in the] mild majesty and sober pomp . . . modest splendour and unassuming state," which made the Church "the public ornament, consolation and hope." [9] As art was inseparable from man's social nature, the art of the Church was for Burke one of the best means of raising man from a crude primitive society into a refined civil society. The use of liturgy was to Burke intrinsically sound as a Christian means of worship. The desirable social consequences of art in religion were not its justification, but merely the by-product of a sound Christianity. But as neither ethics nor aesthetics could guarantee that the barbarians would submit their necks to the gospel, the Church sought to break down the warlike natures of men close to a state of nature by turning barbaric power against itself. To fulfill this practical social end it instituted chivalry. No one who has read Burke's account of Britain in the Middle Ages can possibly be under the delusion, so common to his critics, that he regarded the dim past as an heroic age of high romance. Burke felt that chivalry, which transformed wild boors into gentle Christian knights on horseback who used their strength to protect rather than to pillage the weak, arose out of a grim moral necessity to combat, with truly great heroism, the "deplorable condition of those barbarous times." [10] Chivalry was adapted to the warlike customs of the Germanic barbarians; it was probably the most powerful practical weapon the Church wielded in infusing sweetness and light into the untransformed souls of men.

While Burke was yet in his twenties he wrote a sketch entitled "The Character of a Fine Gentleman," which expressed the beau ideal of his time and revealed the great importance he attached to the gentlemanly character.[11] The man of gentle manners was for Burke the foundation of that "true natural aristocracy" which, as he said in 1791, formed "an essential integrant part of any large body rightly constituted." The gentleman, blending the humanistic and social ideals of Aristotle's *Ethics,* the courtly traditions of chivalry, Castiglione, and Elyot, was in all ages the conserving force of civil society. In the France of 1789 the gentleman was the natural enemy of atheists and sans-culottes. Burke pointedly reminded his readers in the *Reflections* how much European civilization owed to the good manners inculcated by Christian chivalry:

It was this [chivalry] which, without confounding ranks, had produced a noble equality . . . which mitigated kings into companions, and raised private men to be fellows with kings. Without force or opposition, it subdued the fierceness of pride and power; it obliged sovereigns to submit to the soft collar of social esteem, compelled stern authority to submit to elegance, and gave a dominating vanquisher of laws to be subdued by manners. . . . Nothing is more certain, than that our manners, our civilization, and all the good things which are connected with manners and with civilization, have, in this European world of ours, depended for ages upon two principles; and were indeed the result of both combined; I mean the spirit of a gentleman, and the spirit of religion.[12]

For ages in the strongly localized autonomies of medieval life chivalric manners had worked wonders in transforming tyrants into gentlemen who submitted their arbitrary wills to Christian morals, manners, and laws. It is unnecessary here to trace the progress of religion and chivalry upon the social life of Europe. There is no doubt, however, that Burke conceived the social function of the Church—the refinement of civil manners—as the same in all ages. In all of his defenses of the Church against

French Jacobins and English Nonconformists, nothing is so evident as Burke's conviction that religion and "the ancient chivalry" had established "a system of manners . . . which softened, blended and harmonized" the whole character of modern Europe.[13]

The great importance of the social function of Christianity in Burke's political philosophy cannot truly be understood apart from his belief in the classical Natural Law, and the historical development of Christian churches. The Natural Law taught Burke to stress what men have in common before giving his characteristically generous regard for their national, sectarian, or individual differences. This principle, together with his belief that "veneration of antiquity is congenial to the human mind," [14] caused Burke to emphasize "the similitude throughout Europe of religion, laws and manners. At bottom these are all the same." [15] Since "all the principal religions of Europe stand upon one bottom," [16] Burke found reasonable worship in them all. Every important branch of Christianity was consonant with the Natural Law. But so far as religion was considered solely as a vehicle for civilizing man, Burke had far less regard for the various Calvinist sects than for Roman Catholicism or Anglicanism. In his *Speech on Conciliation with the Colonies* he noted that "the dissenting interests have sprung up in direct opposition to all the ordinary powers of the world, and could justify that opposition only on a strong claim to natural liberty." The claim to private natural liberty in religion contradicted Burke's conception of man as a corporate being. Noncorporate abstract liberty tended to reduce man to a state of nature within civil society. By regarding civil institutions as impediments to the abstract claims of private conscience, the Dissenters weakened or destroyed the historical continuity and prescriptive sense which united the generations of man. Their conception of man's relation to society was voluntaristic. Finally, their whole view of man's moral nature, centered in the Old Testament, was far more Augustinian than that of Burke. Despite these fundamental differences, Burke recognized the positive contributions of the Dissenters to the national life of Britain and always championed their civil rights against those who would impose disabilities upon them.

Burke always retained a high reverence for the common unity of Catholic Christendom throughout history. It was from this common base that all the national and individual branches of Protestantism had originated. I have already remarked upon Burke's deep appreciation of the achievements of the medieval Church in civilizing the Germanic barbarians through morals, arts, and manners. But as the source of the common religion of Europe, Catholicism was also the great unbroken chain of historical and cultural continuity, and was the closest in spirit to that "wisdom of our ancestors" which connected men and nations with the classical Natural Law. No theology was more in harmony with the ancient traditions of Natural Law than that of Roman Catholicism. Throughout its history the conservative spirit of Catholicism had retained an unbroken spiritual and cultural continuity among its adherents. Burke defended the Catholics of Ireland for resisting persecution because, among other reasons, they acted "upon a principle which of all others is perhaps the most necessary for preserving society, an implicit admiration and adherence to the establishments of their forefathers." [17] Burke appreciated much in Catholicism that was opposed to a simple primitive society, much that fostered the social virtues which made possible the slow, natural growth of a sound civil society.

Burke's own religious convictions might well be described as Catholicism qualified by British nationalism. He was educated, as he once remarked in the House of Commons, "as a Protestant of the Church of England, by a dissenter," and he remained loyal to the religion of his birth throughout his life. Since his mother, sister, and wife were Catholics, there were personal as well as theological and political reasons why Burke was strongly attracted to the Catholic elements in the Anglican Church.[18] A constant yet semi-detached adhesiveness marked Burke's connection to the Anglican Church. In his theological convictions he was essentially Catholic; in his loyalty to the sovereign authority of his church he was a true Protestant.

Froude's observation of Burke's position in religion is probably correct: "Burke was not himself a Catholic, but as little was he a Protestant. His sympathies were with the old faith. His most intimate friends were Catholics to the end, and at the end even more than at the beginning." [19] Certainly Burke's interpretation of the Natural Law was identical with the Catholic principle, taught by all the Scholastic philosophers, that sovereignty lies in God's reason and justice, rather than, as the Calvinists held, in His private will and power. On this essential point Burke was in the main stream of the High Church Anglican tradition of Hooker, Laud, Lancelot Andrewes, Bramhall, Jeremy Taylor, and many other seventeenth-century Anglican divines. It was a position Burke shared with his friend Dr. Johnson.

As a High Church Anglican Burke believed that at the Reformation the Church of England did not merely protest against the doctrines and authority of Rome, but remained, as before, a Church *"positive in its doctrine and its discipline."* [20] To Burke the Church of England was Protestant in her national sovereignty, but essentially Catholic in her inherited doctrines and forms of worship. Burke accepted the High Church theory that doctrinally Anglicanism differed from Roman Catholicism in degree rather than in kind: "The Catholics of Ireland . . . have the whole of our *positive* religion; our difference is only a negation of certain tenets of theirs. If we strip ourselves of that part of Catholicism, we abjure Christianity." [21] Like Hooker and other High Church Anglicans, Burke consciously made or tacitly assumed the distinction between Catholicity and apostolicity, between things "necessary" and things "recommended" for salvation. With Burke this Anglican principle never became the grounds for latitudinarian indifference to religious dogmas; rather, it fulfilled the same function in Burke's religious beliefs that moral prudence served in his political philosophy.

In modes of worship, as well as in doctrines, Burke was essentially Catholic. He described the Roman Catholic Mass as "a church-service in the Latin tongue, not exactly the same as our liturgy, but very near it." [22] Indeed, Burke's veneration of antiquity, his spirit of moderation and belief in historical continuity, prompted him to minimize the importance of the changes which had taken place in the Church of England:

So tenacious are we of the old ecclesiastical modes and fashions of institution, that very little alteration has been made in them since the fourteenth or fifteenth century: adhering in this particular, as in all things else, to our old settled maxim, never entirely nor at once to depart from antiquity.[23]

The doctrinal and historical position of the Anglican Church in Burke's conception of civil society cannot be appreciated unless it is remembered that to him it was the institution which united England with her spiritual past, to the lost but enduring Latin civilization which had endowed Britain with her religion, art, manners, laws, and government.

Burke believed that at the Protestant Reformation the changes made in the Church of England were consistent and parallel, on a national scale, with changes in the political order of the commonwealth of Europe. These changes in religion were like the modifications of Natural Law by the political law of nations. They were like the alterations of the abstract Roman law, that "living voice of reason," by the distinctions of race and national custom, into English common law: "A Church, in any legal sense, is only a certain system of religious doctrines and practices, fixed and ascertained by some law; by the difference of which laws, different churches (as different commonwealths) are made in various parts of the world." [24] The historical phases through which the Church of England had passed had kept alive the essential ancient doctrines and forms of worship of the common Catholic religion of Europe, but had meliorated and adapted them to the political sovereignty of England:

There never has been a religion of the state, (the few years of the parliament only excepted) but that of *the episcopal Church of England* . . . before the Reformation, connected with the see of Rome, since then, disconnected and protesting against some of her doctrines, and against the whole of her authority, as binding in our national Church.[25]

Although Burke's loyalty to the Church of England claimed his primary and sovereign allegiance, he never lost sight of the greater common cause of Christianity and religion: "The cause of the Church of England is included in that of religion, not that of religion in the Church of England." [26] But there was nothing in the sovereignty or doctrines of the English national Church contrary to Christianity or the universal Natural Law: "A religious establishment in this state is not contrary to the law of God, or disagreeable to the law of nature, or to the true principles of the Christian religion." [27]

In the principles and history of Anglicanism, no less than in Catholicism, Burke found much that opposed theories of primitive or "natural" society, much that nourished a system of civil manners which made possible the peaceful development of a free and just society. Before examining how Burke's conception of the Church is related to the state and the community, it is necessary to investigate the nature and function of the state in Burke's political philosophy.

II. The Nature and Function of the State: Civil Laws

To discuss Burke's conception of the state with intelligence, it is essential to understand precisely what he meant by such terms as "natural," "artificial," and "divine." The failure to understand Burke's use of these terms invalidates the following critical summary by Robert M. Hutchins:

> The violently emotional character of Burke's expressions on this subject [the French Revolution] makes it difficult to take his theoretical arguments seriously. Either they are contradictory or they are hypothetical: if the state is natural, nature decrees that it shall not be altered; if it is artificial, change is a breach of contract; if its origin is divine, God wills that it shall always remain the same. When he is talking about France, it is impossible to discover whether Burke had a theory of the state and, if so, what it was.[28]

Burke's emotional reaction to the French Revolution was totally extraneous to his conception of the state, and his arguments were neither contradictory nor hypothetical. Since the French Revolution forced him to shift from practical party politics to political philosophy, his conception of the state is clearest in his discussions of French affairs. The errors in Hutchins' criticism flow from a complete failure to understand the importance of Burke's vital distinction between natural and civil (or artificial) society, and from a refusal to take Burke at his word when he said that "God willed the state." Finally, it is nonsense to assert that because the state is natural, artificial, or divine it is therefore unalterable. Although Hutchins touched upon every important facet of Burke's view of the state except its development through history, in the complex relationships between God, man, and nature he failed to distinguish between direct and indirect origins, between necessary means and ends, and Burke's formulation of the state eluded him.

To Burke the state was divine, artificial, and natural. Without contradiction it was all three at once, being a kind of mystical trinity of three substances in one nature. Burke believed that all power to govern was from God, and that to be just, power had to be exercised in conformity to the Natural Law. It was imperative, therefore, that all men, and particularly rulers, should "acknowledge the existence of God as a moral governor of the world" [29] and that "all persons possessing any portion of power ought to be strongly and awfully impressed with an idea that they act in trust, and that they are to account for their conduct in that trust to the one great Master, Author, and Founder of society." [30] To Burke the state was the gift of God to man; it was one of the greatest and most necessary tools by which man was to be brought to perfection. Nothing could be more explicit and clear than Burke's insistence upon the divine origin of the state:

He who gave our nature to be perfected by our virtue willed also the necessary means of its perfection. He willed therefore the state. —He willed its connection with the source and original archetype of all perfection.[31]

The state was divine, therefore, in its ultimate indirect origin from God. But the state was also "artificial" and "natural." Unlike his Lockian contemporaries, who in various degrees made an antithesis between their hypothetical "state of nature" and civil society, Burke used the words "artificial" and "natural" as synonymous or complementary terms. The state was "artificial" in the sense that it was not an organic natural growth, like an unattended seed springing to maturity, but the product of man's conscious reason and will. Burke admitted that the origins of government were veiled in mystery, and that a particular civil society often might originate through a voluntary contract. But the continuance of any society was not a matter of private reason and choice. By a "wise and salutary neglect" the social covenant blandly assimilated men to their civil duties, so that man was *by nature* a political animal. Because civil society was "natural" to man, and man was by his nature a rational animal, everything which was the sound product of human reason, that is, "artificial," was also "natural." Burke even described civil society as "a state of nature—and much more truly so than a savage and incoherent mode of life." It was natural, therefore, for men to develop the arts and sciences, including the art of governing through the state, to the highest degree: "Never, no, never did nature say one thing and wisdom say another. . . . Nature is never more truly herself than in her grandest forms." [32] The wild paradoxes of primitivists who made an antithesis between "nature" and civil society were answered, once and for all, by Burke's aphorism: "Art is man's nature." The state, as Burke conceived it, was *divine* in its ultimate indirect origin from God, *artificial* in its penultimate direct origin and use as a product of man's reason and will, and *natural* because it was a necessary institution for man in his normal state. In Burke's political philosophy God was like a silent, supreme, invisible dramatist; man was like the director and cast, and civil society was the "natural" stage on which the human drama unfolded itself through time and history. [33]

The true significance of Burke's conception of the state as at once divine, natural, and artificial cannot be understood apart from his principle of the social contract. Precisely what did Burke mean when he said the state is connected with the source and original archetype of all perfection? A complete answer to this vital question would supply the key to Burke's whole conception of the state and civil society. The essential answer is contained in Burke's famous and much misunderstood passage on the social contract:

> Society is indeed a contract. Subordinate contracts for objects of mere occasional interest may be dissolved at pleasure—but the state ought not to be considered as nothing better than a partnership agreement in a trade of pepper and coffee, calico or tobacco, or some other such low concern, to be taken up for a little temporary interest, and to be dissolved by the fancy of the parties. It is to be looked on with other reverence; because it is not a partnership in things subservient only to the gross animal existence of a temporary and perishable nature. It is a partnership in all science; a partnership in all art; a partnership in every virtue, and in all perfection. As the ends of such a partnership cannot be obtained in many generations, it becomes a partnership not only between those who are living, but between those who are living, those who are dead, and those who are to be born. Each contract of each particular state is but a clause in the great primaeval contract of eternal society, linking the lower with the higher natures, connecting the visible and invisible world, according to a fixed compact sanctioned by the inviolable oath which holds all physical and all moral natures, each in their appointed place.[34]

The conception of the social contract expressed in this passage is a world apart from that of Hobbes, Locke, Hume, and Rousseau, and the revolutionary "rights of man" theorists, who for all their differences[35] accepted the pre-civil "state of nature" and conceived of the social contract either as irrevocable or as revocable at the pleasure or arbitrary will of the monarch or the people at large. Historically, Burke's social contract is a brilliant eighteenth-century expression of the traditional conservative Christian view of society and the state. Its antecedents are to be found in St. Thomas Aquinas and Suarez and in Hooker, Bramhall, and other seventeenth-century Anglicans. Burke's social contract depended upon belief in the ultimate sovereignty of the classical and Scholastic Natural Law.

The whole school of positivist scholars either ignored Burke's statement on the social contract, or dismissed it as "a mere metaphor," "unintelligible," and "resounding nonsense." [36] Since Burke's conception of society and the state was posited on a firm belief in God, from the point of view of atheism, agnosticism, or rationalist secularism, his conception of the state must have appeared unintelligible or hypothetical. His passage on the social contract has not even been understood as a metaphorical statement of his conviction that society and the state were at once divine, natural, and artificial. To Burke, God was no "mere metaphor," but the ultimate reality of all existence. His interpretation of the social contract was therefore based upon his Christian view of God, man, and the universe. God, the original archetype of all perfection, had established "a fixed compact" with Himself and with man, sanctioned by an "inviolable oath," that the physical and moral universe He had created would not be changed by His or anyone's arbitrary will, but that all things would hold in their appointed place. This did not mean that the state, as one element in the moral universe of man, was unalterable, but that all changes in the organic and temporal nature of the state were to be made in conformity with the Natural Law. Within the infinitely fixed moral norms of the Natural Law, changes in the state were not only possible, but necessary and good. Man could no more remain in an "original" static civil state than in any hypothetical natural or primitive state. As a rational creature possessing free will, man certainly had the power, but he had not the right, to transgress the moral imperatives of the Natural Law. These imperatives were equally binding upon all men at all times. Without adherence to the Natural Law, the state ceased to fulfill its divine purpose of bringing man to social salvation. Since the temporal state was a divine instrument, a necessary aid to grace, Burke could not regard it merely as a business partnership in a commercial enterprise. To clarify how each state was for Burke a clause in the total spiritual partnership between man and God, I shall explore briefly Burke's conception of the historical development, structure, and general function of the British state.

As a Christian Burke was deeply skeptical of all naturalistic attempts to define the precise origins of government from a state of nature, or even from primitive historical conditions. To Burke "a sacred veil" was "drawn over the beginnings of all governments." He noted with approval that Montesquieu, in praising the British constitutional state, never indulged in a speculation concerning its ultimate origins, but simply called it "a fine system . . . invented in the woods." [37] Burke believed that many of the best principles of justice, liberty, and good order contained in the British constitution developed gradually, without conscious human contrivance or systematic design, from the dramatic tensions of English history.

The basic structure of the British constitutional state, centered in divided and balanced powers, was the product of history rather than of human will or reason. In his *An Abridgment of English History* Burke pointed out that beginning with William the Conqueror it became the custom of English kings who had doubtful or disputed claims to the crown to placate and win support from the landed gentry and London merchants by granting, confirming, and extending charters which guaranteed them political rights and civil liberties.[38] These medieval charters culminated in the Magna Carta, which according to Burke "disarmed the Crown of its unlimited prerogatives, and laid the foundation of English liberty." [39] Thus Burke's basic principle that "states . . . will best exist with a partition of civil powers" [40] was established early in Britain. The ancient system of the Germanic barbarians, based upon a simple, single-chambered government centered in absolute monarchical and popular will, with all its usual attendant dangers of fanaticism and dogmatism, yielded gradually to the principle of divided civil powers, with its attendant prudence and spirit of conciliation. Through the natural course of history the British constitutional state became divided into king, Lords, and Commons. This basic division and balance of power always remained the keystone of Burke's conception of the civil state. Through the principle of divided power the state best fulfilled its general function—the guarantee of civil order, distributive and commutative justice, and liberty under constitutional law.

Throughout its development the British state absorbed many admirable characteristics which expressed the temperament of the British people. Therefore, the state was not to be regarded by the private citizen with suspicion, or with a cold objective eye, or as the object of perpetual speculation concerning its possible improvement. To Burke the relationship most proper for a citizen and his state was analogous to that of a son toward his father; the state was the social father of each citizen. This kinship was particularly evident when Burke considered the weaknesses of the state. He believed that citizens "should approach to the faults of the state as to the wounds of a father, with pious awe and trembling solicitude." [41] Burke's feeling of "filial reverence" toward the state was no mere ornamental figure of speech. It was the natural consequence of his conception of the state as a divine instrument given to man for his social salvation. Therefore, if the state were sick, Burke would in Pope's words "nurse its venerable age, and with lenient arts extend a parent's breath." [42] He would never seek quick cures for social ills in the quack remedies of private metaphysical speculation or revolutionary innovation. He would consult the nature of the state and fit his prescription for improvement to all that has contributed to its organic growth.

The close kinship between citizen and state in Burke's political philosophy helps to explain his deep veneration for antiquity and tradition, his great caution in social reforms,[43] and his insistence that the state was a complex living organism which waxes to maturity through centuries, rather than an inanimate mechanism that can be altered at any time, according to every theorist's hope of a contingent improvement. His repeated insistence that men were born into civil society without their own consent, and that all their civil liberties and obligations were derived to them as an inheritance from their forefathers, was closely connected with the patristic element in his view of the state.

In Burke's conception of the British constitutional state, the principle of divided and balanced powers may best be understood by examining separately his view of the structure and function of its constituent parts—Crown, Lords, and Commons. The British constitution exemplified "the method of nature in the conduct of the state" quite as much in its structure as in its historical development. Burke reprobated no form of government on abstract principles. The historical circumstances of a

corporate people, their character and habits, determined
whether some form of monarchy, oligarchy, or democracy was
best suited to them. The history of England and the character
of Englishmen led Burke to prefer "a monarchy directed by
laws, controlled and balanced by the great hereditary wealth
and hereditary dignity of a nation; and both again controlled by
a judicious check from the reason and feeling of the people at
large, acting by a suitable and permanent organ." [44] Burke's
warm acceptance of Britain's constitutional monarchy was the
unpardonable sin in the minds of English and French Jacobin
democrats, particularly after 1789, and has been the source of
much misunderstanding of his conception of the state. Unlike
absolute monarchists and democratic absolutists, Burke had no
vulgar admiration or vulgar antipathy toward kings. He once
remarked that "kings are naturally lovers of low company," [45]
and he was aware (more profoundly than any nonconstitutional-
minded democrat) that too often they had abused their trust and
misused their power.[46] Because of man's fallen and fallible nature, Burke believed that "there are, and must be, abuses in all
governments." [47] But abuses of power were not evidence against
the form of any government, nor against any part of a constitutional state. Would any zealous democrat admit that the House
of Commons should be abolished whenever it abused its constitutional powers? True reformation, Burke maintained, was
the opposite of revolution and aimed at conserving the forms,
offices, and true functions of institutions by ridding them of
abuses. "A monarchy," Burke wrote, "is . . . perfectly susceptible of reform; perfectly susceptible of a balance of power;
monarchy is not only reconcilable to liberty, but . . . it may
be rendered a great and stable security to its perpetual enjoyment." [48] Despite all its faults and past abuses, the Crown
was the chief glory and ornament, "the keystone" of the
British constitutional state, and Burke defended its legal powers
and essential functions. In addition to the king's negative on
legislation, and his right to dissolve parliament, he had "dis-
cretionary powers . . . for the execution of the laws, for the
nomination to magistracy and office, for conducting the affairs of peace and war, [and] for ordering the revenue." [49]

These powers were exercised under the limits of constitutional and Natural law. In addition, since the Protestant Reformation formally united the English Church and State, the Crown was the link between Britain's mixed ecclesiastical and political constitution. Under the union of Britain the Crown united the four nations which comprised the United Kingdom, and through parliament it was the sole political connection with the overseas empire. In national civil affairs it was a necessary stabilizing bulwark against the dangers of aristocratic or democratic absolutism. Burke favored a "properly regulated" monarchy as essential to "a limited and balanced government." [50]

Burke also always respected the inherited political position and function of the House of Lords. Egalitarian democrats who despised social distinctions based on class, and held "artificial" prerogatives in contempt, generally assumed that Burke identified "the spirit of a gentleman" with the nobility. Nothing could be further from the truth. To Burke gentlemanliness was not a class prerogative, but a matter of personal character and temperament. He once observed: "Kings may make a nobleman, but they cannot make a gentleman." [51] Burke made his general attitude toward the nobility very clear: "I am accused of being a man of aristocratic principles. If by aristocracy they mean the peers, I have no vulgar admiration, nor any vulgar antipathy, towards them." [52] On occasions he expressed himself more strongly: "I am no friend to aristocracy, in the sense at least in which that word is usually understood." [53] Nobility as the basis for government met with some of Burke's most severe criticism: "The worst imaginable government [is] a feudal aristocracy." [54] Yet his criticism of the aristocracy was not an abstract distrust, and his defense of its role in the state was not less generous than his defense of a qualified Crown: "I hold them [the Peers] to be of absolute necessity in the constitution, but I think they are only good when kept within their proper bounds." [55] The aristocracy was to Burke the least important element in the formal structure of the state.[56] Although their general lack of spirit prevented the nobility from usurping arbitrary power, men like the Duke of Bedford were too often the willing lackeys of monarchical or aristocratic intrigue and popular fanaticism. However, at their best, throughout the county seats and country parishes of Britain, the nobility frequently displayed "that unbought grace of life," a tradition of selfless personal honor in the performance of their civil duties. Apart from their role in the state and the community, and despite all their faults or virtues as individuals or a class, the nobility served to remind men that a just society was essentially hierarchical, not egalitarian, that liberty was safest when connected with property, that good order was best preserved through legal prescription and the preservation of artificial manners.

Burke considered the popular or republican element in the British constitutional state of paramount importance. The House of Commons most nearly reflected the corporate character and temperament of the people, and furnished the practical means of fulfilling political prudence. It brought the government and the people into close harmony with each other and with constitutional and Natural law. The House of Commons was to Burke "the representatives of the people" and the "natural guardians of the constitution" and of "the purity of parliament . . . conveying the collective sense of the people to the throne." [57] So far as the constitutional voice of the people could be considered the voice of God, the House of Commons was not the sole exclusive representative of the people, because in a mixed form of government the corporate sense of the people was expressed through every branch of the state:

The king is the representative of the people; so are the lords; so are the judges. They all are trustees for the people, as well as the Commons; because no power is given for the sole sake of the holder; and although government certainly is an institution of Divine authority, yet its forms, and the persons who administer it, all originate from the people.[58]

Two things are to be noted in this passage. First, since Burke believed a nation is not a local and individual momentary aggregation, but includes the moral, civil, and social habits of a people through many ages and generations, the true voice of God is not to be found in any particular act of government, or

even in the general policy of an administration, but is "formed
upon the known march of the ordinary providence of God."
Thus, to say that God willed the state is but another way of
saying that God's will is revealed in history. Second, as Ernest
Barker noted, Burke's belief that government is of divine authority and that the forms and offices of the state originate from
the people is a perfect expression of St. Thomas Aquinas' political philosophy.[59] However, Barker failed to perceive that
Burke's principles of political sovereignty and prudence derive
respectively from these two cardinal principles. Political sovereignty based on Natural Law and Burke's reverence for the
corporate character of the people are the two supreme principles
of his political philosophy.

The House of Commons was for Burke the ideal practical
vehicle by which the state fulfilled the sovereignty of the Natural Law in the spirit of prudence: "The desires of the people,
when they do not militate with the stable and eternal rules of
justice and reason (rules which are above us and above them)
ought to be as a law to the House of Commons." [60] But like
monarchical and aristocratic will, popular republican will had
to operate within the moral limits of the Natural Law: "No man
carries further than I do the policy of making government pleasing to the people. But the widest range of this politic complaisance is confined within the limits of justice." [61] So long as the
moral imperatives and spirit of the Natural Law were obeyed,
so long as constitutional limits were observed, Burke venerated
the will of the people above all else. He had none of Carlyle's
animus against the common people. He once said: "I reverentially look up to the opinion of the people, and with an awe
that is almost superstitious." [62] On the floor of the House of
Commons Burke generally followed the advice he gave to Fox:
"Lay your foundations deep in public opinion." [63] A true representative of the corporate sense of the people was obliged to
judge the immediate desires of his constituents against the general will of the total nation and the Natural Law to see that
they conformed. A self-elected aristocracy of wealth or talent,
ruling through the decrees of delegates, had no place in the
House of Commons. As the chief link between the government

and the people, and aware of its highest civil and divine duties, the House of Commons served an exalted function in Burke's conception of the British constitutional state.[64]

In addition to connecting British civil society through the constitution with the sovereignty of the Natural Law, the House of Commons helped to maintain the balance of the state. If the Crown was a safeguard against popular excesses, the House of Commons on its part often helped to preserve the liberty of the Crown and the nobility:

> By the true republican spirit, paradoxical as it may appear, monarchies alone can be rescued from the imbecility of courts and the madness of the crowd. This republican spirit would not suffer men in high place to bring ruin on their country and themselves. It would reform, not by destroying, but by saving, the great, the rich, and the powerful . . . [it] would not suffer monarchs, or senates, or popular assemblies, under pretences of dignity, or authority, or freedom, to shake off those moral riders which reason has appointed to govern every sort of rude power.[65]

The true republican spirit of the House of Commons moderated the other parts of the state, and compelled them to submit their wills to constitutional law. Thus, the House of Commons helped to maintain the political means by which the people at large lived according to the spirit of the Natural Law.

In its history, structure, and functions the British state revealed a natural complexity proper to the achievement of the great ends of civil society—good order, liberty, and justice. In rebuttal to those who favored one-chambered government, Burke wrote of himself: "He always thought any of the simple, unbalanced governments bad: simple monarchy, simple aristocracy, simple democracy; he held them all imperfect or vicious: all were bad by themselves; the composition alone was good." [66] The continued existence of civil liberty made necessary a complex constitution: "We are members for a *free* country; and surely we all know, that the machine of a free constitution is no simple thing; but as intricate and as delicate as it is valuable. . . . A constitution made up of balanced powers must ever be a critical thing." [67]

Burke believed that a well-balanced state should contain a

rich diversity of contending corporate interests, both in the structure of the state and the community. Opposing interests invigorated and tempered the diverse virtues of human nature, and drew out the complex harmony of every just society. This, in essence, was his answer to those French revolutionists who attacked the principle of checks and balances in the British constitution, and who proposed to establish a one-chambered government which would express the general will of the majority:

> These opposed and conflicting interests, which you considered as so great a blemish in your old and in our present constitution, interpose a salutary check to all precipitate resolutions. They render deliberation a matter not of choice, but of neccessity; they make all change a subject of compromise, which naturally begets moderation; they produce temperaments preventing the sore evil of harsh, crude, unqualified reformations; and rendering all the headlong exertions of arbitrary power, in the few or in the many, for ever impracticable.[68]

To describe the delicate and intricate spirit of the British state, which, Burke said, "without question pursues the greatest variety of ends," [69] he frequently used an image in which the idea of balance is heavily stressed:

> Our constitution stands on a nice equipoise, with steep precipices and deep waters upon all sides of it. In removing it from a dangerous leaning towards one side, there may be a risk of oversetting it on the other. Every project of a material change in a government so complicated as ours . . . is a matter full of difficulties; in which a considerate man will not be too ready to decide; a prudent man too ready to undertake; or an honest man too ready to promise.[70]

In its slow growth the divided and balanced British state exemplified for Burke the ideal structure by which the sovereignty of Natural Law and the spirit of prudence might best be fulfilled in civil society.

Since Burke believed that "natural moderation . . . is the best corrective of power," [71] any absolute concentration of all political power into the hands of one person, or one group of persons, whether the holders of such power were hereditary, usurped, or elected, was to him tyranny. To prevent tyranny from any quarter Burke always sought to preserve the balance of power in the state, and his impartiality in adhering to this principle has been the cause of much misunderstanding among partisan-minded royalists and Jacobin democrats. When the balance of constitutional power in the state and corporate community is destroyed, the result is despotism: "It is the nature of despotism to abhor power held by any means but its own momentary pleasure; and to annihilate all intermediate situations between boundless strength on its own part, and total debility on the part of the people." [72]

Historically, the source of danger to the British constitution had largely shifted from monarchical to popular despotism: "The distempers of monarchy were the great subjects of apprehension and redress in the last century; in this, the distempers of parliament." [73] After the triumph of parliament over Charles I, and particularly after 1688, the direct executive powers of the Crown had been greatly reduced. Since 1714 most of the executive power was exercised by the prime minister. However, according to Burke, beginning about 1765 the indirect power of the Crown had "grown up anew, with much more strength, and far less odium, under the name of influence," through "a cabal of the closet and back stairs." [74] George III, who thought himself the essence of Bolingbroke's "patriot king," threatened to destroy the traditional balance of power by establishing personal rule. Burke sympathized with the American colonists on constitutional grounds. He opposed George III because he wished to defeat the king's absolutist ambitions and to restore the balance of power in the state. Because Burke persistently opposed the extension of unconstitutional powers to the king, nonconstitutional-minded royalists and democrats condemned or praised him as a hater of kings.

The intense reaction of the British public against the failure of the king's colonial policy shifted the source of danger from monarchical to popular arbitrary will. Burke sensed this danger from the moment it appeared, around 1780, in the form of popular demands for reform in the representation of parliament.[75] Nine years before the French Revolution Burke warned against government by popular factions: "Such a constitution of freedom, if such can be, is in effect no more than another name for the tyranny of the strongest faction; and factions in republics have been, and are, full as capable as monarchs, of the most cruel oppression and injustice." [76] The French Revolution greatly intensified the danger to the balanced British state from popular will. Burke maintained his constitutional ground, but changed his front to repel the new source of attack. In his conception of a balanced state, the monarchical, aristocratic, and republican elements represented "three very different natures," united as one. Like the three main branches of British Christianity, they were independent yet joined; they were "the triple cord which no man can break." Each could be vindicated only "on the several principles peculiarly belonging to them." Because all three "are brought into one harmonious body," it was often necessary to oppose that part of the state which sought to usurp the functions of the others. Burke made no apology for "defending such various, and, at first view, discordant parts of a mixed constitution," because "as any one of the members . . . happens to be endangered, he that is a friend of all of them chooses and presses the topics necessary for the support of the part attacked. . . . He is not to embarrass his hearers by bringing into view at once all that may be said in favour of the other members." [77] This was Burke's reply to those Englishmen who charged him with political inconsistency because they never understood his conception of the constitution and were themselves involved in the heresy of Jacobin democracy. Against absolutism in any form and from any source, Burke advocated adherence to the principle of divided power centered in a balanced constitutional state.

If the social function of the Church was to promote civil manners, the State, through its power to pass statutes, assumed all other strictly public functions. Burke summarized the outstanding public concerns of the state:

The state ought to confine itself to what regards the state, namely, the exterior establishment of its religion; its magistracy; its revenue; its military force by sea and land; the corporations that owe their existence to its fiat; in a word, to everything that is *truly and properly public.* . . .[78]

In maintaining social order and civil liberty, and in administering justice, the state had no right to touch purely private domestic interests. But as government was "a contrivance of wisdom to provide for human wants," the state could not abjure its rightful responsibility in essential public concerns. Burke therefore distrusted not only "the zealots of the sect of regulation," who would replace constitutional liberty with regulating restraints, but also theorists of laissez faire who denied that the state was morally responsible for establishing limits to abstract liberty. He knew that self-interest alone was not a safe or sufficient guiding principle in economic affairs. The case of the East India Company attested that laissez faire on the part of government led to economic despotism under the monopolistic charters and unrestricted usurped powers of the company. Burke's fear of an arbitrary leviathan state applied as well to any powerful corporate group which owed its existence to the fiat of the state, and whose plenitude of power could intimidate or defy the state. Such corporations were quite as subject to the moral imperatives of the Natural Law and the legal prescriptions of the constitution as the state itself.

To prevent abuses of liberty in a free society, Burke believed that government should be active and strong in protecting the largest public welfare. The great function of the state in maintaining the maximum of individual and corporate civil liberty under the constitution was fulfilled not by any abstract rule, but by a public and enlarged prudence in applying the Natural Law to the diverse circumstances of men.

III. Burke's Idea of Church and State: A Balanced Civilization

Since Church and State were to Burke the chief institutions of society by which man fulfilled "the ends for which society was formed . . . temporal prosperity and eternal happiness," [79] both were absolutely essential for the perfection of man's civil and divine nature. That was what Burke meant when he said that every sort of moral, civil, and politic institution, aiding the rational and natural ties that connect the human understanding and affections to the divine, were necessary to build up that wonderful structure, man. In this profound sense of the total nature of man, spiritual as well as social and biological, Burke believed that "in a Christian commonwealth the church and state are one and the same thing, being different integral parts of the same whole." [80] In their marriage Church and State maintained "an indissoluble union" so "inseparable" that "scarcely is the one ever mentioned without mentioning the other." [81] Burke conceived Church and State as closely knit national corporate social bodies, possessing a totally distinct yet closely parallel sovereignty and function, striving together by different means to realize the highest divine and civil potential of man. In their union the mysticism and practicality which infuses every part of Burke's political philosophy are perfectly united; religion sanctifies government and animates its forms with the spirit of the Natural Law, and government protects religious liberty and enables men to fulfill their purely civil needs on earth in an orderly and just society.[82]

It is remarkable that no scholar has ever discussed Burke's strong emphasis upon the inner spirit, rather than the outer forms of national constitutions and the Church and State relationship. This omission in Morley, Stephen, Vaughan, and other positivist scholars helps to explain their general neglect of the importance of manners and their more serious failure to perceive the Natural Law in Burke's thought. Because the Natural Law connected man in civil society to God, who was "the source and original archetype of all perfection" and "the one great Master, Author, and Founder of society," Church and State were not to be regarded merely as formal arrangements of physical power, alterable at man's will, but rather as moral essences whose inner spirit was determined by the eternal and unalterable Natural Law. Church and State were the instruments through which men, under a great variety of constitutional arrangements, fulfilled the Natural Law. Burke's criticism of the paper constitutions of the Abbé Sieyès,[83] his frequent admonitions of the political projects of French Jacobins and English radical reformers, reveal how vital to his political philosophy was the distinction between the inner spirit and the outer forms of government. This distinction was at the core of his insistence that politics was a practical, not a theoretical science, and it underscored all of his attacks on metaphysical speculation, proportionate arithmetic, and political geometry. In the *Reflections* Burke noted that in the constitution of the French revolutionists "not one reference whatsoever is to be found to anything moral." [84] The same charge appeared throughout Burke's criticism of "the strong Jacobin faction" in Britain for their proposed innovations in the constitution:

They are always considering the formal distributions of power in a constitution: the moral basis they consider as nothing. Very different is my opinion: I consider the moral basis as everything; the formal arrangements, further than as they promote the moral principles of government . . . to be of little importance.[85]

The moral basis of every constitution supplied the inner spirit of all its parts. Thus, Burke was concerned not with the House of Commons' *"legal form* and power, but . . . its spirit" [86] in fulfilling its part in the state. The essential spirit supplied by the Natural Law was that of moral prudence, that spirit of equity and temperance, of conciliation, forbearance, and sweet reasonableness, so characteristic of the unwritten, invisible parts of the British constitution. Yet in all his criticism of revolutionary and doctrinaire theory, Burke never once recommended the form of the British constitution; always he held up as a model its spirit of equity in law and moral prudence. Burke knew that Church and State could maintain social order and civil liberty and administer impartial justice under a variety of constitutional forms, centered in monarchy, oligarchy, or democracy, and that the substance of good government under any form consisted in its adherence to the spirit and principles of the Natural Law.

Burke's complete absorption in practical political affairs, together with his Christian humility and moral prudence, resulted in a thoughtful skepticism toward human reason and prevented him from ever attempting to define the relationship between the outer forms and the inner spirit of Church and State. Burke never cast his cardinal political principles into any logical or ordered system. The "wise and salutary neglect" for which he praised the American colonies as "a vast, disconnected, infinitely diversified empire" aptly describes this element in the complex genius of his own political philosophy. Yet the essential relationship between the forms and spirit of Church and State is perfectly clear in Burke's political thought: Church and State are related in their purely social function as manners are to laws. Burke believed that all churches and states have their own particular forms, laws, and spirit, but that in general the State maintains the national laws and formal structure of society, whereas the Church, like the family, fosters its local manners and inner spirit.

In the division of powers and functions between and within Church and State, nowhere does Burke suggest precisely where the sovereignty of manners leaves off and that of laws begins. Each institution is supreme in its own sphere; the Church in things spiritual and in social manners, the State in things temporal and in civil laws. Moral prudence, whose rules are fixed not by any a priori law or reason, but by a passion for moderation and a strict moral and intellectual regard for particular circumstances, determines where and how far the rights and powers of Church and State should be exercised. In Europe the sovereignty of local parish manners was so strong, and so intimately connected with the dominant temperament of the people, that every statesman should refrain prudently from trespassing within the jurisdiction of manners:

Statesmen who know themselves will, with the dignity that belongs to wisdom, proceed only in this the superior orb and first mover of their duty. . . . But as they descend from the state to a province, from a province to a parish, and from a parish to a private home, they go on accelerated in their fall. They cannot do the lower duty; and, in proportion as they try it, they will certainly fail in the higher. They ought to know the different department of things; what belongs to laws, and what manners alone can regulate.[87]

In descending from the province to the smaller division of society, the local parish, Burke shifted significantly from a political to a religious term. This was consistent with his conception of the general sovereignty and particular functions, nationally and locally, between state laws and church manners. In this complex relationship both Church and State were subject to the constitution, which in turn rested upon the Natural Law.

Since the soft spirit of moral prudence transcended in importance the forms of sovereign power in civil institutions, it was natural, according to Burke, that the social manners inculcated by the Church should take precedence and give the spirit to the laws of the State:

Manners are of more importance than laws. Upon them, in a great measure, the laws depend. The law touches us but here and there, and now and then. Manners are what vex or soothe, corrupt or purify, exalt or debase, barbarize or refine us, by a constant, steady, uniform, insensible operation, like that of the air we breathe in. They give their whole form and colour to our lives. According to their quality, they aid morals, they supply them, or they totally destroy them.[88]

Burke felt that the moral basis of laws was manners; customs supply social force and justness to the law: "Whilst manners remain entire, they will correct the vices of law, and soften it at length to their own temper." [89] Conversely, "When manners [are] corrupted the laws are relaxed, as the latter always follow the former." [90] Burke believed that in general "manners are required sometimes as supplements, sometimes as correctives, always as aids to law." [91] Manners and customs achieved locally through natural, imperceptible means the same or better civil order that statutory laws achieved nationally through conscious effort. Manners included the collected wisdom of many generations, and were the habit of mind and temper of a whole people, whereas statutes were at best the right reason of the present moment. Manners were primary, therefore, because they established those "local partialities from which nations derive the first principles of their stability." By forming the temperament and character of the people, manners made legal sovereignty follow prudence; through the Church, social diversity was maintained within a spiritual unity. Through manners the Church fostered and maintained the division of power which prevented a ruthless uniformity and tyranny in the State.

Thus, Burke believed that "the observance of conventions is of infinitely more consequence than the making of them." [92] Manners were to Burke essential in mitigating raw political power; prudence was the first of political virtues because it assimilated manners with morals and afforded the practical means of living under the spirit of the constitution and the Natural Law.

In view of the enormous practical political importance Burke attached to social manners, he was not indulging in sentimental rhetoric or a nostalgic love of a hypothetical romantic past when he lamented that "the age of chivalry is gone." That large body of critics, from Philip Francis and Tom Paine to the twentieth-century critics, which has attacked Burke as the defender of "pure foppery," has missed the point totally in Burke's defense of Marie Antoinette.[93] It is nonsense to regard Burke's picture of 10,000 swords leaping from their scabbards to avenge any threat or insult to the French queen as a defense of Marie Antoinette's personal character. Should a physician who saves the life of an alleged adulteress be charged with favoring adultery? In politics, no less than in medicine, it is necessary to rise beyond personality to principle. By raising good manners to the level of principle, chivalry taught men to defend weakness in every station of life, without inquiry as to moral status or regard to personal merit. As an institution chivalry illustrated perfectly Burke's conception of how religion and manners, apart from laws, sustain civilized social order. The whole history of the social function of the Church, as it related to manners, was contained in the conversion of the Germanic warrior and Roman soldier into the Christian knight, and finally into the gentleman.

Burke was aware that good manners might be assumed as a *substitute* for ethical principles, as was often true of Charles II.[94] But when in the *Reflections* he wrote that through the code of honor in chivalry men possessed that "unbought grace of life" which "inspired courage whilst it mitigated ferocity, which ennobled whatever it touched, and under which vice itself lost half its evil, by losing all its grossness," Burke clearly made manners and morals *auxiliary* to each other. By contrast

with the honor and manners of chivalry, the proudly rational
"Enlightenment" of his era appeared to Burke an age of
"sophisters, economists and calculators," without much "generous loyalty to rank and sex" or respect for the traditional
values of Christianity. The destruction of this system of manners by the French Revolution, Burke believed, was an ir-
reparable loss to the political and social life of Europe. The
alternative, he feared, was a secularized leviathan state based
upon utilitarian economics and military power. In such a
state the most direct means to self-interest would predominate;
the simplest, strongest, most numerous, or most barbarous
power would establish an arbitrary and absolute rule without
reference to any constitutional safeguards, or to the Natural
Law. Burke warned: "Power of some kind or other will survive
the shock in which manners and opinions perish; and will find
other and worse means for its support." Under such crude
power, "laws are to be supported only by their own terrors, and
by the concern which each individual may find in them from
his own private speculations, or can spare to them from his
own private interests." [95] In view of the ruthless spirit of
Napoleon's power politics and of nineteenth-century economic
utilitarianism, Burke's fear that refined manners and respect
for the Natural Law were being weakened has been vindicated
by history.

Perhaps the most important single visible function of Church
and State, as Burke conceived them, was that throughout
Europe and between and within every Christian nation they
established and maintained, through common manners and
different laws, that division and balance of spiritual and secular
powers which made possible the greatest degree of liberty,
order, and justice in civil society. In ecclesiastical affairs the
balance of power was divided between the Papacy and the
Protestant churches. In political affairs, Burke felt that the
balance of power between nations had been for centuries centered in the Holy Roman Empire:

If Europe does not conceive the independence and the equilibrium of the empire to be in the very essence of the system of balanced power in Europe, and if the scheme of public law upon which

that independence and equilibrium are founded, be of no leading
consequence as they are preserved or destroyed, all the politics of
Europe . . . have been miserably erroneous.[96]

Burke held that the partition of Poland in 1773 was a gross
violation on the part of Prussia, Russia, and the Empire, of the
Natural Law as it applied to nations. This partition also violated the political balance of power which France, the natural
guardian of the independence and balance of Germany, might
have prevented.[97] Similarly, Burke argued that "it is always
the interest of Britain that the power of France should be kept
within the bonds of moderation." But, he added, "it is not her
interest that that power should be wholly annihilated in the
system of Europe," because through the balance of power the
common liberty of all nations could best be "secured against
the single or the combined ambition of any other power." [98]

Burke was impartial in his adherence and application of the
principle of balanced powers. He reminded his countrymen,
as Fénelon had reminded Louis XIV, that in her ambitions
Britain was also subject to the balance of power.[99] The object
of this principle was to establish throughout Europe that "political equilibrium" necessary for a balanced civilization, so that
"no power is able absolutely to predominate, or to prescribe
laws to others." [100] Burke's sense of history permeated all of
his arguments about the "balance of power throughout the
Christian world." [101] He considered it axiomatic that "the
balance of power had been ever assumed as the known common
law of Europe at all times, and by all powers." [102] The result
of this division of powers between churches and states was a
complex, various, yet harmonious spiritual and secular European civilization, a vast diversity within a flexible common
social unity, in which no single ecclesiastical or secular power
could achieve absolute control, and under which all the individual differences of men in race, customs, language, religion,
manners, and laws, could find their highest self-fulfillment in
harmony with the spirit of the Natural Law.

According to Burke's political conception of Church and
State, the same sensitive equipoise and spirit of prudence that
was achieved by the Papacy, the Protestant churches, and the

nations of Europe, was also maintained on a national level in Britain through her "mixed" ecclesiastical and secular constitution:

The whole scheme of our mixed constitution is to prevent any one of its principles from being carried as far, as, taken by itself, and theoretically, it would go. To avoid the perfection of extremes, all of its several parts are so constituted, as not alone to answer their own several ends, but also each to limit and control the others.[103]

All the Christian churches of Britain shared in the general civil function of religion, to make men aware that they lived in a society governed by the Natural Law. In this general sense all three great branches of British Christianity were part of the ecclesiastical half of the constitution:

All the three religions prevalent . . . in various parts of these islands, ought all, in subordination to the legal establishments, as they stand in the several countries, to be all countenanced, protected, and cherished.[104]

Burke's fundamental principles of sovereignty and prudence, and of the primary right of individual and corporate conscience operating within constitutional law, are evident in this passage. He placed the practical will and reason of individual sects under the law of "legal establishments," yet retained a positive place for their individual differences and social liberties. He achieved a diversity within a single national unity, because in religion, as in government, he was always interested not in the triumph of a faction or sect, not in simplicity and uniformity, but in a harmony and prudent balance of contending functions and interests, and in the fulfillment of the Natural Law.

Apart from its general social function, the prescriptive, established Church of England had for Burke a unique function. "There is nothing of more consequence in a state," Burke believed, "than the ecclesiastical establishment," because it was the "great link towards holding fast the connexion of religion with the state"; it "consecrated the state" by giving it stability, virtue, and historical continuity.[105] Through the king, who was "bound by law to be in communion with the Church of England," [106] the Establishment was the only branch of Christianity officially connected with the British state, commonwealth, and empire. It was the official and conscious means of spiritual unity holding together the essential civil corporations of Britain, and it had an intrinsic importance in religion which Burke highly revered:

> I wish it [the Established Church] well, because it is more closely combined than any other of the Church-systems with the *Crown,* which is the stay of the mixed constitution; because it is the sole connecting *political* principle between the constitutions of the two independent kingdoms. I have another, and infinitely a stronger, reason for wishing it well; it is that I consider it as one of the main pillars of the Christian religion itself. The body and substance of every religion I regard much more than any of the forms and dogmas of the particular sects. Its fall would leave a great void, which nothing else of which I can form any distinct idea might fill. I respect the Catholic hierarchy, and the Presbyterian republic. But I know that the hope or the fear of establishing either of them is, in these kingdoms, equally chimerical, even if I preferred one or the other to the Establishment, which certainly I do not.[107]

As part of the "legal establishment," the sovereignty of the Church of England in the mixed constitution, unlike that of Catholicism or Presbyterianism, was, like the Catholic Church in medieval times, parallel rather than subordinate to that of the political state.

In Burke's political philosophy Church and State together established in "the Commonwealth of Christian Europe," and in Britain, the civil order, justice, and liberty which he held to be the highest social end of man, and which was revealed in history. Through "the known march of the ordinary providence of God," Church and State had raised Europe from the dark ages of pagan barbarism to the magnificence of Western civilization. The French Revolution, Burke feared, would destroy the traditional conception and function of Church and State and would reverse the natural meliorative process of history. In his *Letter to a Noble Lord,* after reviewing the "whole revolutionary system" of the Jacobin "rights of man" theory, and the devastation which had occurred and would yet result from the attempt to establish that theory in practice, Burke summarized for the aristocratic English Jacobin, the Duke of Bedford, the traditional function of Church and State to the enduring civil order and liberty of Britain:

But as to *our* country and *our* race, as long as the well-compacted structure of our church and state, the sanctuary, the holy of holies of that ancient law, defended by reverence, defended by power, a fortress at once and a temple, shall stand inviolate on the brow of the British Sion—as long as the British monarchy, not more limited than fenced by the orders of the state, shall, like the proud Keep of Windsor, rising in the majesty of proportion, and girt with the double belt of its kindred and coeval towers, as long as this awful structure shall oversee and guard the subject land—so long the mounds and dykes of the low, fat, Bedford level will have nothing to fear from all the pickaxes of all the levellers of France. As long as our sovereign lord the king, and his faithful subjects, the lords and commons of this realm,—the triple cord which no man can break; the solemn, sworn constitutional frank-pledge of this nation; the firm guarantees of each others' being and each others' rights; the joint and several securities, each in its place and order, for every kind and every quality of property and of dignity:—as long as these endure, so long the Duke of Bedford is safe: and we are all safe together—the high from the blights of envy and the spoliations of rapacity; the low from the iron hand of oppression and insolent spurn of contempt.[108]

This significant passage summarizes in its implications almost all that Burke believed about Church and State in civil society. It reveals his mysticism and practicality, his veneration for antiquity and concern for the present moment. It discloses his sense of the power, the enduring glory, enormous complexity, and vast range in history, of the intimate yet separate relations and functions of Church and State. It indicates how the spirit of Britain's mixed and balanced constitution is infused through the whole harmonious civil life of Britain.

This passage may be used as a gauge of Burke's vigorous style and thought in political philosophy. It illustrates the inexhaustible wealth of ideas, the great poetic eloquence and even greater reflective wisdom, which characterizes his political reflections. Burke does not repeat a few meager, isolated facts or simple commonplace slogans until the reason, feeling, and truth in them is worn threadbare, or distorted by the attempt to make them fit into a universally logical system. He suits his style prudently to his subject and the temperament of his readers, and without trying to be logical or systematic, like the metaphysical poets and prose writers of the seventeenth century, he combines through intense and rapid sense impressions the most diverse ideas in the whole intellectual history and equipment of man, and shapes a new, illuminated, and unsystematic harmony. Can anything be more metaphysical, more intellectually ironical and dramatic, or startling in the novelty with which remote and apparently disparate ideas are yoked together, than a passage which begins with the highest mysticism, "the holy of holies" of God's divine and Natural Law, transcends human events and concerns, includes the vast sweep of British institutions and history, and finally comes to rest upon the concern of a brief moment, willfully anticlimactic, in the lowly character of the young, insipid, spiteful fifth Duke of Bedford? There is nothing more witty or dramatic in the styles of Hooker, Taylor, or Burton, or in the poetry of Donne, Herbert, or Crashaw. Even in the Duke of Bedford Burke could perceive how the Natural Law, embodied in the constitutional safeguards of Church and State, operated for all men. The common humanity of man applied even to this "poor rich man," who had so little of it himself. Even in trivial historical events Burke perceived the operation of the eternal past upon the temporal present. Church and State were the embodiment of the divine and Natural law working through history, the instruments of man's temporal and spiritual redemption.

EIGHT

Burke and the Sovereignty of Natural Law

I. The Consistency of Natural Law in Burke's Thought

Throughout this study of the classical and Scholastic Natural Law in Burke's political philosophy, as revealed in his reflections and actions in the practical affairs of Ireland, Colonial America, Britain, India, and revolutionary France, no attempt has been made to describe the "development" of the Natural Law in Burke's thought and statesmanship. What was most remarkable in Burke was the sustained consistency of the Natural Law in his thought and career. However much John Morley failed to perceive the Natural Law in Burke, his famous remark that Burke "changed his front but he never changed his ground" is literally true. Morley's insight was applied merely to Burke's fundamental political consistency between the American and French revolutions, and not to his early and habitual adherence to the primary principles of the Natural Law. Even as an undergraduate at Trinity College, Dublin, Burke indicated in his private correspondence his full acceptance of primary Natural Law principles. Undoubtedly, his inherited High Church Anglican religious principles and his early wide reading in the classics, particularly in Cicero, were instrumental in shaping the Natural Law as the foundation of his political philosophy.

The Natural Law is fundamental in Burke's conception of man and civil society. As principle or as the spirit of prudence, Natural Law permeates his view of Church and State and all international relations; it transcends all national, geographical, and historical considerations, all religious and political loyalties, all man-made legal systems and forms of government. It achieves this higher moral synthesis without in any way violating the right reason or true interests of man. But the Natural Law is also evidenced consistently in the negative side of Burke's thought; it supplied the moral and legal weapons for his attacks on various eighteenth-century radical theories and innovations, and on existing abuses in government. From his "Tract on the Popery Laws" (1761?) to the last of his *Letters on a Regicide Peace* (1797), Burke conceived of the Natural Law as an ethical norm by which to judge the social and political behavior of men. This study has made it abundantly clear that in every period of his political life, from before his entrance into parliament through the crisis of the French Revolution, he consistently appealed to the Natural Law for the standard of redress against tyranny, chaos, and injustice.

Burke's faith in the Natural Law secured him firmly to the most vital ethical and political traditions of Europe, so that he was able to ride out the storm of ideas that swept over Europe during the last half of the eighteenth century. The appeals of deism and pantheism in religion left him untouched. His faith that the basic principles of Natural Law were self-evident to right reason, and that man had inherent rights by virtue of his innate spiritual nature, made him skeptical of the whole tradition of Locke's empiricism and rationalism. To Burke the revolutionary conception of an idyllic "state of nature," whether historical or hypothetical, was a childish and dangerous illusion, and led directly to such theories as the revocable social contract.

Burke was always convinced that no civilization, however just, could long survive the application of the revolutionary abstract "rights of man" to civil society. He was equally untouched by Rousseauist and other eighteenth-century theories of "sensibility," simplicity, and primitivism. The moral calculus of Bentham and the utilitarians likewise was wholly rejected by Burke. In short, from the beginning to the end of his life he remained a Christian humanist, an Anglican who recognized that the particular revelations of Scripture were supplemented by Church tradition and by the historical continuity of man as a corporate rational being living under the general sovereignty of the Natural Law. Burke's theological consistency as a Christian paralleled his political consistency as a humanist adherent of the Natural Law. In his religion and politics, man as a corporate being was obliged to recognize and submit to the superiority of God's law, whether perceived as revelation or through right reason. The persistent antithesis to divine law and man's corporate reason was the arbitrary will or power of men.

II. The Natural Law and Political Sovereignty

Throughout European history those who have accepted the classical and Scholastic Natural Law have asserted a conception of religious and political sovereignty in which right reason supersedes any appeal to will or power. The chief question in every problem of sovereignty is—what makes an act or law just or unjust? In theological debates during the Middle Ages, the question of sovereignty depended ultimately upon the essential nature of God: is God primarily a Being of will and power, or of reason and law? The answer to this question determined whether God's power created or followed His reason, whether a law was just because God willed it, or whether God willed it because it was inherently just.

In choosing between these alternatives, as they apply to sovereignty in both God and man, theologians in the tradition of St. Augustine were generally voluntarists, and tended to minimize the Natural Law, whereas the rationalist tradition of St. Thomas Aquinas exalted the Natural Law. The distinctions in doctrine between St. Augustine and St. Thomas Aquinas were not differences of principle, but of emphasis. The crucial points involved how right reason and the higher will are related, and what part man can play in securing the divine grace necessary for salvation. The conflicting claims of reason and will were applied to man far more than to God, because since God was held to be a spirit infinitely perfect, there could not really be any separation of the divine mind and the divine will, because God's reason or justice is equal to His power. Therefore, whether a law is just because God has willed it, or whether He has willed it because it is just, is a problem which does not exist for God. But for man in his fallen state this problem is paramount; part of the imperfection of man, resulting from original sin, involves the natural insufficiency and tragic separation of his intellect and emotion. In his natural state, unaided by divine grace, man's moral reason is clouded, his higher will is weak, and the divided elements in his spiritual nature are in perpetual war with themselves and with the world.

In the struggle between reason and will as the basis of sovereignty, St. Thomas Aquinas granted a superiority to the intellect in both man and God. He held that a law is not bad because God forbids it, but that God forbids it because it is bad. The same applies to God's commands of good laws.[1] Hence there is a Natural Law, intrinsic and immutable, created by God and distinct from the order of revealed Scripture, though not contrary to it. In this theological argument St. Thomas laid the foundation of political sovereignty in the Natural Law and man's right reason.

After the Protestant Reformation, the struggle for religious and political sovereignty in Britain remained centered in the conflicting claims of men who exalted the arbitrary will of a sect or party above the right reason of revelation and the Natural Law. The philosophical and practical nature of this vital conflict, from the reign of Queen Elizabeth to the Petition of Right, has been well described by George L. Mosse in *The Struggle for Sovereignty in England*.[1a] During this crucial period the conception of sovereignty based on the Natural Law, which had been expounded by St. Thomas Aquinas and Bracton, found skillful advocates in Richard Hooker and Sir Edward Coke. As thinkers and as defenders of an inherited religious and constitutional liberty, both of these men were greatly admired by Burke. Hooker argued in his theological debates with the Calvinists that to say a thing was good because God willed it, without any moral reason, was to conceive of God as an arbitrary tyrant. He held that God necessarily chooses to follow His created Natural Law: "They err therefore who think of the will of God to do this or that, there is no reason besides His will."[2] To Hooker sovereignty implied a divine contract by which God, out of His perfect fusion of reason and will, fixed forever the original constitution of all physical and moral nature. Thus, the immutable and eternal Natural Law was to

Hooker "that order which God, before all ages, has set down with Himself to do all things by." The self-imposed limits established by "that law Eternal which God Himself hath made to Himself" [3] prevented God from acting by arbitrary will, and made His laws reasonable and just. Throughout *Of the Laws of Ecclesiastical Polity* Hooker formulated the Natural Law principles of sovereignty which Bishop Bramhall and other seventeenth-century High Church Anglicans utilized in their debates with Calvinists, who exalted the will of God, and with Hobbists who identified sovereignty with the absolute will of the monarch.[4]

The essential principle of political sovereignty under Natural Law was stated in the thirteenth century by Henry de Bracton: "The King himself ought not to be subject to any man, but he ought to be subject to God and the law, since law makes the King. Therefore let the King render to the law what the law has rendered to the King, *vis,* dominion and power, for there is no King where will rules and not the law." [5] This principle was illustrated dramatically early in the seventeenth century when Coke opposed the desire of James I to rule by his private arbitrary will.[6] In opposing the king Coke in no way wished to limit or destroy the legitimate prerogatives of the English monarchy, as did many Puritan parliamentarians. Like Burke, Coke conceived of English society as a *dominium politicum et regale,* a commonwealth evolving through historical continuity into a complex and harmonious whole, in which the king, Lords, and Commons exercised their respective functions in conformity with the sovereignty of the common law, Magna Carta, and all the customs and manners that formed the constitution of England. Throughout his *Institutes* and by his appeals to "fundamental law," "legal reason," and "equity," Coke sought to preserve the traditional harmony of balanced interests in England, by which civil liberty and justice were maintained. To Coke neither the king nor parliament was the sole foundation of political sovereignty, but both together were the necessary instruments through which the sovereignty of the constitution and the Natural Law were fulfilled. Because of the absolutist pretensions of James I, Coke's constitutional conception of sovereignty brought him into direct conflict with the king. As Mosse has shown, this circumstance rather than agreement on principles made him the ally of parliament:

> In Coke's lifetime the king rather than the Parliament seemed to advance a theory of sovereignty which presented the greater menace to the liberties of Englishmen. Indeed, it must have seemed, at the moment, that Parliament in fighting the king was standing on the traditional ground of the constitution rather than itself elaborating a rival concept of sovereignty. . . . It was no small wonder, then, that Coke in the end sided with Parliament while trying to preserve the traditional concept of the constitution.[7]

Coke's constant thesis that not even the king was superior to the common law applied equally to parliament. Coke did not live long enough to realize how much the pretensions of parliament were quite as arbitrary and absolutist as those of James I and the other Stuart kings.[8] But it was Coke's great achievement that in a reign which inaugurated an era of competing claims to absolute political sovereignty between both kings and parliaments, he defended the natural and civil rights of Englishmen by an appeal to constitutional law. No eighteenth-century Englishman venerated the memory of Coke, nor appreciated the courage and wisdom in his achievement, more than Edmund Burke.

The course of the various competing claims to absolute political sovereignty from the time of Hooker and Coke to Burke was devious. At different times Puritans, Anglicans, or Catholics, parliamentarians or royalists, Whigs or Tories advanced claims of a "right" to absolute political power. In Burke's conception of the structure, relationship, and social function of Church and State was his conviction that the English constitution always maintained a delicate balance of power between all corporate groups within civil society, so that none might triumph and all could enjoy their natural rights under the constitution. Burke's constitutional view of the structure and spirit of English society was also clearly apparent in his interpretation of the great events of 1688, 1775, and 1789. As a constitutional-minded statesman, Burke interpreted *every* attempt to assume absolute power, regardless of the source, as the assertion of arbitrary will, of political sovereignty in violation of the Natural Law. His interpretation of the Revolution of 1688, his defense of the American Revolution, and his attack upon the French Revolution—all are but various revelations of Burke's basic conviction that political sovereignty had to transcend all personal, sectarian, partisan, and popular expressions of will, and had always to be rooted in the constitution and the Natural Law.

To Burke, 1688 was "a revolution not made but prevented." The real rebel, from a constitutional viewpoint, was not the British nation but James II. Burke contended that James II was a bad king with a good title. Therefore, those Englishmen who opposed his reign not because he violated the constitution, but because they denied that a Catholic had any legal right to be king, were quite as arbitrary as James II himself. For Burke 1688 was the final defeat of a Stuart monarch's attempt to make royal absolutism supreme over the constitution. The defeat of James II resulted in a Protestant qualification for holding the Crown and a further restriction of the monarchy in the English constitution. The American Revolution was likewise a rebellion of subjects who wished to preserve their political and constitutional rights against the arbitrary and absolutist pretensions of a king. According to Burke, the real rebels during the decade before 1775 were not the colonies, but George III and his Tory ministers. The king was in rebellion against the political ascendency of the Whigs and the House of Commons and wished to reverse the republican emphasis which had been given to the British state by the Revolution of 1688, and the long rule of Sir Robert Walpole. The ambition of George III to achieve "personal" rule threatened to subvert the established balance of power in the constitution. The American Revolution, Burke contended, exactly paralleled the Revolution of 1688: "He [Burke] always firmly believed that they [the Americans] were purely on the defensive in that rebellion. He considered the Americans as standing at that time, and in that controversy, in the same relation to England, as England did to King James the Second, in 1688." [9] It took the French Revolution to reveal beyond any doubt that just as some Englishmen had opposed James II on religious rather than on constitutional grounds, some of Burke's radical contemporaries had opposed George III on the revolutionary ground that popular sovereignty was the *only* legitimate basis for government. To such doctrinaire theorists as Price, Priestley, and Paine, the abdication of James II signified that the English Crown was not held by hereditary right, but that George III, and indeed all executive heads of states, held their power at the discretion or arbitrary will of the populace. This radical conception of popular sovereignty received respectable support in Britain from such "new Whig" liberals as Chatham and Fox, who sometimes ignored parliamentary methods and constitutional restraints and appealed directly to the people at large. In the light of Burke's faith in the Natural Law and from the vantage point of his strict constitutional position toward the revolutions of 1688 and 1775, the full significance of his conflict with the French Jacobins over the question of popular sovereignty is revealed.

Throughout Burke's career there is ample evidence of his profound respect for the corporate will of the English people when it functioned within constitutional forms and according to the principles of the Natural Law. In his *Thoughts on the Cause of the Present Discontents* (1773), Burke had stated that the constitutional forms of government were themselves a product of the people's will: "Although government is an institution of Divine authority . . . its forms, and the persons who administer it, all originate from the people." In the same year he confessed: "I reverentially look up to the opinion of the people, and with an awe that is almost superstition." [10] In 1780 Burke expressed his complete faith in the positive will of the people as against any negative will that might circumscribe it: "It would be a dreadful thing if there were any power in this country of strength enough to oppose with effect the general wishes of the people." [11] In his *Speech on the Economical Reform* (1780), Burke defined the relationship between the general national will and the will of parliament, and of both to the Natural Law: "The desires of the people, when they do not militate with the stable and eternal rules of justice and reason (rules which are above us and above them) ought to be as a law to the House of Commons." Veneration for popular will was a deep and abiding conviction of practical policy with Burke, but it was not the final test of conscience for legislators, nor the ultimate moral basis of government:

When we know, that the opinions of even the greatest multitudes are the standard of rectitude, I shall think myself obliged to make those opinions the masters of my conscience. But if it may be doubted whether Omnipotence itself is competent to alter the essential constitution of right and wrong, sure I am that such *things*, as they and I, are possessed of no such power. No man carries further than I do the policy of making government pleasing to the people. But the widest range of this politic complaisance is confined within the limits of justice. I would not only consult the interest of the people, but I would cheerfully gratify their humours. We are all a sort of children that must be soothed and managed . . . I would bear, I would even myself play my part in any innocent buffooneries, to divert them. But I never will act the tyrant for their amusement. If they will mix malice in their sports, I shall never consent to throw them any living, sentient creature whatsoever, no, not so much as a kitling, to torment.[12]

There was certainly nothing in Burke's conception of political sovereignty under the Natural Law which in any way prevented the corporate will of the people from fulfilling the just ends of government.

After 1789 Burke's faith in the Natural Law and in constitutional political sovereignty came into direct conflict with a fundamental dogma of the French Revolution—that the general will of the people at large was the sole legitimate criterion for making changes in society and the only allowable basis for sovereignty in government. The anonymous author of *The Political Crisis* (London, 1791) summarized this cardinal principle in the revolutionists' creed: "The people have an undoubted right . . . to alter the government when they think fit, for any cause, or for no cause at all; if they will it, it is sufficient." [13] This "right" exists because "mankind are a law to themselves."

Burke's rejection of this theory of popular sovereignty forms a major theme in his attacks on the French Revolution. (For the essential passages on Burke's objections to the Jacobin theory of popular sovereignty, see Appendix II.) Since Natural Law contained the moral norms of every nation, and constitutional law established its legal and political norms, *every* form of sovereign power had to be exercised within these necessary limits. The great object of law was to make ruling authority morally responsible to the citizens at large, and ultimately to "the one great Master, Author, and Founder of society," God himself. Thus, by "subjecting . . . occasional will to permanent reason," good order, liberty and justice would prevail. Nothing was more dangerous, Burke contended, than to say that any power was above the law, or that power made rather than followed law. This cardinal principle applied to *every* form of government, to democracy quite as much as to monarchy. Actually, because responsibility was more dispersed under a democracy, and therefore harder to assess, Burke held that those who composed the collective sovereignty under a democracy should be particularly impressed with the principle that they act in trust to God and the people. Abuses of power exercised with the apparent consent of the people at large were particularly difficult to redress.[14] It is important to note that in appealing to the Natural Law, "that eternal, immutable law," against the claims of arbitrary will centered in popular sovereignty, Burke used the phrase "in which will and reason are the same." Like St. Thomas Aquinas and Hooker before him, Burke recognized that in the nature of God there was the perfect fusion of will and reason or power and law. While Burke subordinated man's will to the ethical norms of right reason, he also knew that man's corporate right reason was capable of conforming to the Natural Law. Under these conditions, Burke believed profoundly that the voice of the people was as the voice of God.

Implicit throughout Burke's strong objections to the revolutionary theory of popular sovereignty was his principle that the Natural Law supplied the moral basis of all political sovereignty, regardless of the *form* of government under which power was exercised. Since government was a trust for the entire nation, Burke denied that a present numerical majority had any absolute rights of sovereignty. The revolutionary theory that the majority will could reconstruct the whole social order according to each impulse of the heart's desire was completely contrary to Burke's faith in historical continuity, moral prudence, legal prescription, the restrictive safeguards of constitutional law, and above all the ethical norms of Natural Law and the moral inviolability of the divine contract.

In his *Thoughts on French Affairs* (December 1791), Burke resumed his earlier attack on the revolutionary theory of popular sovereignty. He noted that the Jacobins no longer restricted themselves to France, but applied their new "political dogma" to all the countries of Europe:

The political dogma which, upon the new French system, is to unite the factions of different nations, is this, 'That the majority, told by the head, of the taxable people in every country, is the perpetual, natural, unceasing, indefeasible sovereign; that this majority is perfectly master of the form, as well as the administration, of the state; and that the magistrates, under whatever names they are called, are only functionaries to obey the orders (general as laws, or particular as decrees) which that majority may make; that this is the only natural government; that all others are tyranny and usurpation.[15]

Burke's last three works on domestic affairs, *The Present State of Affairs* (1792), *The Conduct of the Minority* (1793), and *Letter to a Noble Lord* (1796), reveal that his greatest fear was that an English-French revolution might establish a government centered in absolute arbitrary popular will. To combat this possibility he defended the "sovereign reason" of the British constitution as a prescriptive instrument grounded upon the Natural Law.

Almost from the beginning of the French Revolution Burke had perceived that its fundamental principle of authority was based upon absolute popular sovereignty. Burke was certainly aware that during the last half of the eighteenth century, through the works of Rousseau and many other writers, including a vast number of journalists and pamphleteers, the theory of political sovereignty based upon *la volonté générale* had become a widespread and popular myth.[16] In August 1793, looking back upon all the events and declarations which had occurred since the first meeting of the Estates General on May 5, 1789, Burke quoted the revolutionary theory of sovereignty and even ventured a guess as to its origin:

'La souveraineté est *une, indivisible, inaliénable, et imprescriptible:*—Elle appartient à la nation: Aucune *section* du peuple, ni aucun *individu* ne peut s'en attribuer l'exercise.' This confounds, in a manner equally mischievous and stupid, the origin of a government from the people with its continuance in their hands. I believe that no such doctrine has ever been heard of in any public act of any government whatsoever, until it was adopted (I think from the writings of Rousseau) by the French assemblies, who have made it the basis of their constitution at home, and of the matter of their apostolate in every country.[17]

Although the theory of popular sovereignty and the phrase *la volonté générale* did not originate with Rousseau,[18] Burke was essentially right in surmising that by 1793 the spirit of Rousseau dominated the ideas of the Jansenist abbés, Sieyès and Grégoire, and of the Left Wing interpreters of the Declaration of the Rights of Man, such as Rabaut de St. Étienne and the "incorruptible" Robespierre.[19]

On June 27, 1789, after more than a month of grim maneuvering among the various orders and delegates of the Estates General, the king agreed to the union of the three orders into a unicameral National Assembly, with the vote *par tête* rather than *par ordre*. This triumph of the Third Estate in effect established the principle of popular absolute sovereignty and determined the whole course of the revolution. On June 17 the Abbé Sieyès, who had coined the phrase "National Assembly," also had defined its power: "The right of interpreting and determining the general will of the nation belongs to it and can belong to no other body. No veto, no power of negation can exist between the throne and the Assembly." [20] Thus, before the revolution was two months old, the possibility of establishing an effective check upon popular despotism through a division of power was destroyed by the triumph of the general will. As Burke remarked in the *Reflections*, the revolutionists forgot to establish a senate, and the rights of corporate minorities, in stitutions, and individuals were thereby left up to the arbitrary will of a prevailing majority.

When the National Assembly was moved from Versailles to Paris, more than three hundred of the more conservative deputies quit the government out of fear for their lives, and the prevailing "majority" came more and more to consist of the Paris political clubs and mobs.[21] By the middle of July 1789, the moderate deputies were too intimidated to oppose the radical revolutionists of the Hôtel de Ville and the Palais Royal. In August 1789 the National Assembly issued its famous Declaration of the Rights of Man, a system of abstract "rights" of universal validity, which supplied the theoretical justification of the revolution. Article Three of the Declaration of the Rights of Man stated, *Le principe de toute souveraineté réside essentiellement dans la Nation. Nul corps, nul individu ne peut exercer d'autorité qui n'en émane expressément.* However, Article Six declared that *La loi est l'expression de la volonté générale.* Since all "rights" were subject to the law, it was inevitable that the declared universal "rights" of man would depend in practice upon the general will of the National Assembly. Thompson has shown that by August 1789, "the growing tendency to insist upon the subordination of the natural rights of men to the authority of the 'general will' is reflected again and again in the speeches of deputies." [22] It was an easy transition from Sieyès' insistence that "all individual wills must be subordinated to the general will," [23] to the denial that any individual "rights" existed independent of the general will of the majority in the National Assembly. As Burke perceived in the *Reflections,* individuality was wholly left out of the revolutionary system, the state had become all in all, and the stage was set for the Reign of Terror and Napoleon.[24]

Burke's attack in 1790 on the Jacobin theory of popular sovereignty was construed by Fox and other "new Whigs" as a departure from his liberalism during the American Revolution, and an abstract contempt for all democratic forms of government. Much of Burke's *An Appeal from the New to the Old Whigs* is devoted to refuting both of these charges.[25] For a constitutional democracy such as the Americans had established, based upon the Natural Law, centered in the principle of divided power, established to maintain good order, to protect life, liberty, and property, and to administer justice, Burke had great respect. It was not democracy as a form of government but the Jacobin theory of the general will that Burke attacked in 1790. He had even attacked this revolutionary theory in 1780, during the American Revolution:

> Such a constitution of freedom [based upon popular sovereignty] if such can be, is in effect no more than another name for the tyranny of the strongest faction; and factions in republics have been, and are, full as capable as monarchs, of the most cruel oppression and injustice.[26]

When Burke said in 1790 that "the tyranny of a multitude is but a multiple tyranny," [27] he was not departing from any former belief. He had always maintained that regardless of the *forms* of government men who lived under the Natural Law never sophistically confounded the "rights" of the people with their "power": "They would not bear the odious maxims of a Machiavellian policy, whether applied to the attainment of monarchical or democratic tyranny." [28] Thus Burke rejected both Hobbes's monarchical absolutism and Rousseau's democratic absolutism, both of which had more in common with each other than either has with constitutional monarchy or constitutional democracy.[29] Burke attacked the Jacobin theory of the general will because it was subversive of all the great ends of civil society—good order, liberty, and justice under the Natural Law.

Burke's distinction between a true constitutional democracy and the popular despotism of Jacobin "democracy" has been summarized perfectly by Lord Acton:

> The true democratic principle, that none shall have power over the people, is taken to mean that none shall be able to restrain or to elude its power. The true democratic principle, that the people shall not be made to do what it does not like, is taken to mean that it shall never be required to tolerate what it does not like. The true democratic principle, that every man's free will shall be as unfettered as possible, is taken to mean that the free will of the collective people shall be fettered in nothing.[30]

Burke believed not in the Jacobin or Rousseauist heresy of *vox populi, vox Dei,* but in a civil order founded upon constitutional law and the Natural Law, in which majorities and minorities, corporate groups and individuals, rulers and ruled alike, all are *sub Deo et sub lege.* To Burke the will or power of the political sovereign, whether monarchical, oligarchical, or democratic, could never be the ultimate source of law, because law itself made the political sovereign. In human affairs the ultimate *political* law of any nation was its constitution, which proceeded from the will of many generations of men and institutions, as regulated by corporate right reason. But as government was an instrument given to man by God, all human affairs were also subject to God's reason and will, so that the ultimate *moral* basis of political sovereignty was the Natural Law.

Once it is clearly understood that Burke applied his belief in the Natural Law and his principle of political sovereignty with complete impartiality to every ruler and every form of government, the problem of his consistency, which has harassed all his interpreters since 1789, should perplex no one. Without once mentioning the Natural Law or political sovereignty, Woodrow Wilson sensed the true answer to Burke's consistency: "He was applying the same principles to the case of France and to the case of India that he had applied to the case of the colonies." [31] The key to Burke's consistent love of liberty and justice under a political sovereignty based on the Natural Law is contained in such statements as the following: "If I were to describe slavery, I would say with those who hate it, it is living under will, not under law." [32] This principle applied equally to the Americans and the Irish living under the monarchical arbitrary will of George III, to the people of India under Hastings' oligarchical arbitrary will, and to the French under the democratic "general will" of the National Assembly. Burke opposed Price, Priestley, Paine, and other English radical reformers, and the revolutionists in France, on exactly the same grounds on which he had opposed Hastings and George III.

As Burke's writings on French affairs reveal, the greatest failure of the revolutionists was their refusal to subordinate and circumscribe arbitrary popular will to the legal processes of constitutional law and the ethical norms of the Natural Law. Burke was convinced that the revolutionists, in fulfilling their theory of political sovereignty, would destroy all the religious, legal, and social traditions of France, all existing statutes and courts of law, the monarchy, nobility, and clergy, the system of chivalric manners, all habits of local loyalties, in short, everything in the ancient constitution of France that had stood between the people at large and unbounded power in the hands of one person or group. Burke's position toward the French Revolution was not a departure from his earlier convictions, but the culmination of a consistency in the primary principles of the Natural Law applied to political sovereignty.

III. The Contemporary Need of Burke's Political Philosophy

There is little doubt that Burke's intense moral integrity is the chief source of his greatness as a political thinker. Among a great variety of religious and political thinkers, from his own era to the present, Burke has enjoyed a supreme reputation for political knowledge and wisdom. On their tour of the Hebrides, Dr. Johnson once said to Boswell: "I do not grudge Burke being the first man in the House of Commons, for he is the first man everywhere." The "new Whig" Charles James Fox admitted that Burke had taught him more about politics than he had learned from all the books he had ever read and all that experience of the world had taught him. Burke's erstwhile opponent James Mackintosh said that "his works contain an ampler store of political and moral wisdom than can be found in any other writer whatever." After his disillusionment in the French Revolution, Wordsworth admitted that "Burke was . . . by far the greatest man of his age." William Hazlitt, whose faith in the French Revolution remained unshaken, even made it a test of the good sense of its proponents that they had to admit the greatness of Burke as a man and political thinker. Macaulay pronounced Burke "the greatest man since Milton."

Lord Acton's praise indicates the enormous prestige of

Burke's influence and reputation late in the nineteenth century: "Systems of scientific thought have been built up by famous scholars on fragments that fell from his table. Great literary fortunes have been made by men who traded on the hundredth part of him. Brougham and Lowe lived by the vitality of his ideas. Mackintosh and Macaulay are only Burke trimmed and stripped of all that touched the skies." As if to confirm Acton's words, Lord Brougham wrote: "No one can doubt that enlightened men in all ages will hang over the works of Burke." In the twentieth century Sir Frederick Pollock remarked that "Burke is full of ideas more instructive than other men's systems." These eulogies reveal the respect of men who recognized that in any sensible estimate Burke must be regarded as one of the greatest writers on man as a political animal. Many of these learned and critically minded men did not recognize the vital element of the Natural Law in Burke's political philosophy, but all of them sensed the validity and profundity of his answers to man's eternal problems concerning the uses of power, the rule of law, and the moral and prudent means of achieving good order, civil liberty, and social justice as the great temporal ends of man.

The whole of Burke's political career is profoundly instructive in the moral wisdom of Christian statesmanship. No one has defined the just relationship between mother country and colony better than Burke. No one has made a better case for individual and minority corporate rights under constitutional law. No English writer has so ably defended historical continuity and legal prescription as the wise and just method for social growth. In all these and many related matters Burke saturated politics with thought and provided the model for applying first principles to practical affairs. However, his reply to the totalitarian challenge of the French Revolution has a special significance to twentieth-century man. We too are confronted with Jacobin types of popular collectivism which would make society and the state everything and the individual nothing. We have witnessed the rise of impersonal leviathan states, claiming the sanction of the popular will, in which every local corporate interest and every personal human right is extinguished or exists solely at the discretion of a centralized sovereign power. This cosmic struggle between the might of the state and the natural rights of man as man is the central conflict to be resolved during the second half of the twentieth century. If the commonwealth of Christian Europe is to survive and form the ethical norms of civilization throughout the world, all men but particularly Americans will have to learn the great lessons in Burke's political philosophy.

To a very considerable degree contemporary man is the heir of the same elements in the "Enlightenment" which Burke opposed throughout his life. The eighteenth-century rationalists who constructed a priori social projects, based on infallible mathematics and moral computation, without reference to history or to human nature, find their familiar counterparts among the sophisters, economists, and calculators of our century. Burke's philosophy is the best cure for the complex satanic disease of the soul that deludes fallen man to the Faustian illusion of superman. Neither a cynic nor a despairing pessimist, Burke was fully aware of the sins and moral paradoxes which resulted from man's moral and intellectual pride. He spent his life opposing all theories which presupposed an idyllic primitive or simple state of nature, because such naïve optimism about the natural goodness of "natural" man was destructive of the ethical norms of civilization and the Natural Law. He perceived that the Encyclopedists and later the Jacobins, in their unbounded confidence in logical reason, science, and progress, pointed toward the Reign of Terror and political despotism. He knew there was no harder heart to be found anywhere than that of a refining metaphysician and logician. On grounds of morality, social utility, or abstract "truth," a convinced and zealous utopian, bent upon reshaping civilization on a scientific basis, could justify even mass murder. By degrees inhumane methods become the systematic and necessary means for superhuman ends. Political reforms that begin in abstract and unrestricted liberty end in absolute and unlimited despotism. A doctrine of popular sovereignty, interpreted by the majority counted by the head, will produce perfect anarchy until, interpreted by Napoleon, it will produce perfect tyranny.

A homogenized *vox populi,* in servitude to a bureaucratic elite disguised as *vox Dei* and fed with journalist slogans on liberty, equality, and fraternity, becomes sooner or later a cannibal state that eats its weaker young and makes war on its neighbors. All this Burke perceived in revolutionary France, and his analysis is profoundly instructive beyond the events which provoked him. In the later political writings of Burke, contemporary lovers of constitutional democracy will find effective armor and powerful weapons against every form of totalitarianism.

The powerful revival of interest in the Natural Law is strong evidence of the need for a greater knowledge of Burke, whose Natural Law principles vitalize the moral cohesion for Western civilization. If totalitarian theories of arbitrary power are to be checked, if government with the consent of free corporate groups is to replace government by the compulsion of party cliques, Burke is our master teacher. No one has proved better than Burke that statism, as cause and effect, is the attempt to make the state the sole source of human rights and to remake man and society without regard to the Natural Law. To restore faith in man as an end in himself, as a distinctly personal creature, contemporary man must learn Burke's great principle that the political sovereign is subject to the law, that God only is the ultimate sovereign. Informed Christians need not read Burke for any original revelations, but their faith may be restored and enriched by the powerful insights he continuously supplies in the practical application of Christian and Natural Law principles to political affairs. Acceptance of the Natural Law made Burke's moral imagination transcend sectarian differences. He is the perfect bridge between utilitarians or positivists and Christians, and between Catholics and Protestants. Essentially a Thomist in his political philosophy, he is the embodiment of all that is best in the Anglican tradition. For a vast number of people, therefore, Burke is a restorative of the Christian-humanist wisdom of Europe, based on the Natural Law.

Today the very existence of law and liberty, founded on a universal ethical norm, is questioned and denied, not only by tyrants whose actions prove their political philosophy is frankly centered in force, but also among many well-intentioned but confused people. To a world in which secular rulers make ultimate appeals to nationalism, race, class interest, social utility, descriptive science, popular will, and so on, in which subjects are told they must give up civil liberty to enjoy economic security, and in which the rights of private conscience are treated with contempt, Burke will always have much to say. The destiny of free men may depend largely upon their ability to understand and choose wisely between the philosophies of Caesar and Cicero, between "the fanatics of popular arbitrary power" and "a manly, moral regulated liberty" based upon constitutional law and Natural Law. Throughout Western history the Natural Law has played a vital role in the dramatic struggle to preserve and extend the traditions of civil and religious liberty, and men who wish to gain fresh insights into its applied principles will have their faith in liberty renewed by turning to the political writings of Edmund Burke.

APPENDIX I

These quotations should be read not merely as an illustration of the consistency and duration of Natural Law principles; they are vital to an understanding of Burke's political philosophy. I return frequently to the philosophical ideas expressed in these passages on the Natural Law:

ca. 340 B.C., Aristotle: Political justice is partly natural, partly legal. Natural justice is that which everywhere has the same force and does not exist by people's thinking this or that (*Ethics,* v, 7). Particular law is that which each community lays down and applies to its own members. . . . Universal law is the law of nature. For there really is, as everyone to some extent divines, a natural justice and injustice which binds all men (*Rhetoric,* i, 13).

ca. 54 B.C., Cicero: Right reason is indeed a true law which is in accordance with nature, applies to all men, and is unchangeable and eternal. By its commands this law summons men to the performance of their duties; by its prohibitions it restrains them from doing wrong. Its commands and prohibitions always influence good men, but are without effect upon the bad. To invalidate this law by human legislation is never morally right, nor is it permissible ever to restrict its operation, and to annul it wholly is impossible. Neither the senate nor the people can absolve us from our obligation to obey this law. . . . It will not lay down one rule at Rome and another at Athens, nor will it be one rule today and another tomorrow. But there will be one law, eternal and unchangeable, binding at all times upon all peoples; and there will be, as it were, one common master and ruler of men, namely God, who is the author of this law, its interpreter, and its sponsor. The man who will not obey it will abandon his better self, and, in denying the true nature of man, will thereby suffer the severest of penalties, though he has escaped all the other consequences which men call punishment (*De republica,* iii, 22).

533 A.D., Justinian: Natural laws which are observed among all nations are due to a divine providence. They remain in full force and are immutable (*Pandects,* I, 2).

ca. 1268, Henry de Bracton: The King himself ought not to be subject to any man, but he ought to be subject to God and the law, since law makes the King. Therefore, let the King render to the law what the law has rendered to the King, *vis,* dominion and power, for there is no King where will rules and not the law (*Tractatus de legibus,* f. 5b).

1275, St. Thomas Aquinas: Since all things subject to Divine providence are ruled and measured by the eternal law . . . it is evident that all things partake somewhat of the eternal law, in so far as . . . from its being imprinted on them, they derive their respective inclinations to their proper acts and ends. Now among all others, the rational creature is subject to Divine providence in the most excellent way, in so far as it partakes of a share of providence, by being provident both for itself and for others. . . . This participation of the eternal law in the rational creature is called the natural law. . . . Every human law has just so much of the nature of law as it is derived from the law of nature. But if at any point it deflects from the law of nature, it is no longer a law but a perversion of law (*Summa theologica,* I, 2, Q. xci, art. 2; Q. xcv, art. 5).

1593, Richard Hooker: This [natural] law we may name Eternal, being that order which God, before all ages, has set down with Himself to do all things by. . . . The [natural] laws . . . do bind men absolutely even as they are men, although they have never any settled fellowship, nor any solemn agreement among themselves what to do or not to do. . . . Human laws are measures in respect of men whose motions they must direct. . . . Such measures have also their higher rules to be measured by: which rules are two, the law of God and the Law of Nature. So that laws must be made according to the general law of nature (*Of the Laws of Ecclesiastical Polity,* I, ii, 6; I, x, 1; III, 9).

1608, Edward Coke: The Law of Nature was before any judicial or municipal law and is immutable. The Law of Nature is that which God at the time of the creation of the nature of man infused into his heart for his preservation and direction; and this is the Eternal Law, the Moral Law, called also the Law of Nature (*Calvin's Case,* note 7, Rep. 12a).

1612, Francis Suarez: The rational basis of the Law of Nations . . . consists in the fact that the human race, howsoever many the various peoples and kingdoms into which it may be divided, always preserves a certain unity, not only as a species, but also, as it were, a moral and political unity called for by the natural precept of mutual love and mercy, which applies to all. . . . For just as in one state or province law is introduced by custom, so in the human race as a whole, it was possible for laws to be introduced by the habitual conduct of nations, and all the more because the matters comprised within this latter system of law are few, and very closely related to the Natural Law, and most easily deduced therefrom in a manner so advantageous and so in harmony with nature itself, that while this derivation of the law of nations from Natural Law may not be self-evident, that is, not essentially and absolutely required for moral rectitude, it is nevertheless quite in accord with nature and universally acceptable for its own sake (*De legibus ac de Deo legislatore,* Vol. II, Chap. xix).

1625, Hugo Grotius: The Natural Law is the dictate of right reason which points out that a given act, because of its opposition to or conformity with man's rational nature, is either morally wrong or morally necessary, and accordingly forbidden or commanded by God, the Author of nature. . . . Many human laws may be established supplementing the Natural Law, but they cannot contradict it (*De jure belli et pacis,* I, i, 10).

1672, Samuel Pufendorf: We may call it [Natural Law] likewise the law Universal or Perpetual, the former, in regard that it binds the whole Body of the Human Race, the latter, because it is not subject to change (*Of the Law of Nature and Nations,* Oxford ed. [Oxford, 1703], p. 95).

1690, John Locke: Municipal laws are only so far right as they are founded on the law of Nature, by which they are to be regulated and interpreted (*Second Treatise on Civil Government,* chap. 2, sec. 12).

1758, Emmerich de Vattel: As men are subject to the laws of nature and as their union in civil society cannot exempt them from the obligation of observing those laws . . . the whole nation remains subject to the laws of nature and is bound to respect them in all its undertakings (*Le droit des gens,* Int. 5).

1765, William Blackstone: This law of nature, being coeval with mankind, and dictated by God himself, is of course superior in obligation to any other. It is binding over all the globe, in all countries, and at all times: no human laws are of any validity, if contrary to this; and such of them as are valid derive all their force, and all their authority, mediately or immediately, from this original (*Commentaries on the Laws of England,* Chitty ed. [New York, 1832], I, 27–28).

1776, Thomas Jefferson: When in the Course of human events, it becomes necessary for one people to dissolve the political bands, which have connected them with another, and to assume among the powers of the earth, the separate and equal station to which the Laws of Nature and of Nature's God entitle them, a decent respect to the opinions of mankind requires that they should declare the causes which impel them to the separation. We hold these truths to be self-evident, that all men are created equal, that they are endowed by their Creator with certain unalienable Rights, that among these are Life, Liberty and the pursuit of Happiness (The Declaration of Independence, p. 1).

APPENDIX II

The following passages from Burke's *Reflections* and *An Appeal from the New to the Old Whigs* reveal that his rejection of popular sovereignty is based upon his faith in the ultimate claims of the Natural Law:

It is indeed difficult, perhaps impossible, to give limits to the mere *abstract* competence of the supreme power . . . but the limits of a *moral* competence, subjecting . . . occasional will to permanent reason, and to the steady maxims of faith, justice, and fixed fundamental policy, are perfectly intelligible, and perfectly binding upon those who exercise any authority, under any name, or under any title, in the state. . . . Otherwise competence and power would soon be confounded, and no law be left but the will of a prevailing force. Law . . . emanating from the common agreement and original compact of the state . . . is equally binding on king and people too, as long as the terms are observed, and they continue the same body politic.

Reflections, pp. 294–295.

The old fanatics of single arbitrary power dogmatized as if hereditary royalty was the only lawful government in the world, just as our new fanatics of popular arbitrary power maintain that a popular election is the sole lawful source of authority.

Reflections, p. 300.

By these theorists the right of the people is almost always sophistically confounded with their power . . . but till power and right are the same, the whole body of them has no right inconsistent with virtue, and the first of all virtues, prudence.

Reflections, p. 335.

They always speak as if . . . there is a singular species of compact between them and their magistrates, which binds the magistrate, but which has nothing reciprocal in it, but that the majesty of the people has a right to dissolve it without any reason, but its will.

Reflections, p. 360.

All persons possessing any portion of power ought to be strongly and awfully impressed with an idea that they act in trust: and that they are to account for their conduct in that trust to the one great Master, Author, and Founder of society. This principle ought even to be more strongly impressed upon the minds of those who compose the collective sovereignty, than upon those of single princes.

. . . The share of infamy that is likely to fall to the lot of each individual in public acts is small indeed: the operation of opinion being in the inverse ratio to the number of those who abuse power. Their own approbation of their own acts has to them the appearance of a public judgment in their favor. A perfect democracy is therefore the most shameless thing in the world. As it is the most shameless, it is also the most fearless. No man apprehends in his person that he can be made subject to punishment. Certainly the people at large never ought: for as all punishments are for example towards the conservation of the people at large, the people at large can never become the subject of punishment by any human hand. It is therefore of infinite importance that they should not be suffered to imagine that their will, any more than that of kings, is the standard of right and wrong. They ought to be persuaded that they are full as little entitled . . . to use any arbitrary power whatsoever. When the people . . . are conscious that they exercise, and exercise perhaps in a higher link of the order of delegation, the power, which to be legitimate must be according to that eternal, immutable law, in which will and reason are the same, they will be more careful how they place power in base and incapable hands.

Reflections, pp. 365–366.

Have these gentlemen never heard, in the whole circle of the worlds of theory and practice, of anything between the despotism of the monarch and the despotism of the multitude? . . . Is it then a truth so universally acknowledged, that a pure democracy is the only tolerable form into which human society can be thrown, that a man is not permitted to hesitate about its merits, without the suspicion of being a friend to tyranny, that is, of being a foe to mankind? . . . I reprobate no form of government merely upon abstract principles. . . . An absolute democracy, no more than absolute monarchy, is to be reckoned among the legitimate forms of government. . . . If I recollect rightly, Aristotle observes that a democracy has many striking points of resemblance with a tyranny. Of this I am certain, that in a democracy, the majority of the citizens is capable of exercising the most cruel oppressions upon the minority, whenever strong divisions prevail . . . and that oppression of the minority will extend to far greater numbers, and will be carried on with much greater fury, than can almost ever be apprehended from the dominion of a single sceptre. In such a popular persecution, individual sufferers are in a much more deplorable condition than in any other. Under a cruel prince they have the balmy compassion of mankind to assuage the smart of their wounds . . . but those who are subjected to wrong under multitudes, are deprived of all external consolation. They seem deserted by mankind, overpowered by a conspiracy of their whole species.

Reflections, pp. 395–397.

In July 1791, when Burke published his *An Appeal from the New to the Old Whigs,* he expressed his deep concern that in Britain, quite as much as among the Jacobins in France, the theory of absolute popular sovereignty found many adherents among the radical reformers and liberal "new Whigs":

These new Whigs hold that the sovereignty, whether exercised by one or many, did not only originate *from* the people, (a position not denied nor worth denying or assenting to,) but that in the people the same sovereignty constantly and unalienably resides; that the people may lawfully depose kings, not only for misconduct, but without any misconduct at all; that they may set up any new fashion of government for themselves, or continue without any government at their pleasure; that the people are essentially their own rule, and their will the measure of their conduct. . . . These doctrines concerning the *people* (by which it is plain enough they mean their own faction) tend to the utter subversion, not only of all government, in all modes, and to all stable securities to rational freedom, but to all the rules and principles of morality itself.

An Appeal from the New to the Old Whigs, pp. 44–45.

The factions, now so busy amongst us . . . endeavour to propagate an opinion that the *people,* in forming their commonwealth, have by no means parted with their power over it. . . . Discuss any of their schemes—their answer is— It is the act of the *people,* and that is sufficient. Are we to deny to a *majority* the right of altering even the whole frame of their society, if such should be their pleasure? . . . The French Revolution, say they, was the act of the majority of the people; and if the majority of any other people, the people of England for instance, wish to make the same change, they have the same right. Just the same undoubtedly. That is, none at all. Neither the few nor the many have a right to act merely by their will, in any matter connected with duty, trust, engagement, or obligation. The constitution of a country being once settled upon some compact, tacit or expressed, there is no power existing of force to alter it, without the breach of the covenant, or the consent of all the parties. Such is the nature of a contract. And the votes of a majority of the people . . . cannot alter the moral any more than they can alter the physical essence of things. The people are not to be taught to think lightly of their engagements to their governors; else they teach governors to think lightly of their engagements towards them. . . . As no one of us men can dispense with public or private faith, or with any other ties of moral obligation, so neither can any number of us. The number engaged in crimes, instead of turning them into laudable acts, only augments the quantity and intensity of the guilt. . . . Men love to hear of their power, but have an extreme disrelish to be told of their duty. This is because every duty is a limitation of some power. Indeed, arbitrary power is so much to the depraved taste of the vulgar of every description, that almost all the dissentions which lacerate the commonwealth are not concerning the manner in which it is to be exercised, but concerning the hands in which it is to be placed. . . . Men [who] thirst after power . . . should be taught, and by their civil constitutions they should be compelled, to put many restrictions upon the immoderate exercise of it.

An Appeal from the New to the Old Whigs, pp. 76–77.

NOTES

Notes to Chapter One

1. H. G. Wells, *Mind at the End of Its Tether* (New York: Didier, 1946), pp. 1–4.

2. Alfred Cobban, "The Return of Natural Law," in his *The Crisis of Civilization* (London: J. Çape, 1941), p. 94.

3. A large number of works on Natural Law have appeared during the twentieth century. There is no comprehensive bibliography on the contemporary revival of Natural Law, but the following works should be consulted: James Bryce, "The Law of Nature," in his *Studies in History and Jurisprudence* (New York, 1901); Sir Frederick Pollock, *Essays in the Law* (London, 1922); Roscoe Pound, *Law and Morals* (Chapel Hill, N.C., 1924); Charles G. Haines, *The Revival of Natural Law Concepts* (Cambridge, Mass.: Harvard University Press, 1930); Ernest Barker, "Ernst Troeltsch on Natural Law and Humanity," in *Natural Law and the Theory of Society: 1500–1800*, ed. Otto Gierke (Cambridge, Eng.: At the University Press, 1934); John Walter Jones, "The Law of Nature," in his *Historical Introduction to the Theory of Law* (New York: Oxford University Press, 1940); Cobban, *The Crisis of Civilization;* Richard O'Sullivan, "Natural Law and Common Law," in the *Grotius Society Transactions for the Year 1945,* Vol. XXXI (London: Longmans, Green and Co. [1946]); Ernest Barker, "Natural Law and the American Revolution," in his *Traditions of Civility* (New York: The Macmillan Co., 1948); *University of Notre Dame Natural Law Institute Proceedings* (Notre Dame, Ind.: University of Notre Dame Press, 1949–1951); A. P. D'Entreves, *Natural Law* (London: Hutchinson's University Library, 1951); Louis I. Bredvold, "Jus naturale redivivum," in *The History of Ideas News Letter*, Vol. I, no. 1 (Dec., 1954). For the revival of Natural Law in France and Germany see the following: Joseph Charmont, *La renaissance du droit naturel* (Montpellier: Coulet et fils, 1910); François Geny, *Science et technique en droit privé positif* (Paris: L. Tenin, 1914–1924); Louis Le Fur, *La théorie du droit naturel depuis le XVII siècle et la doctrine moderne* (Paris, 1928); Jacques Maritain, *Les droits de l'homme et la loi naturelle* (New York: Éditions de la Maison française, Inc., 1942); Ernst Troeltsch, *The Social Teaching of the Christian Churches* (1912), tr. Olive Wyon (New York: The Macmillan Co., 1931); Ernst Troeltsch, *Naturrecht und Humanität in der Weltpolitik* (Berlin, 1923); Johannes Sauter, *Die philosophischen Grundlagen des Naturrechts* (Vienna: Springer, 1932); Heinrich Rommen, *The Natural Law*, tr. Thomas R. Hanley (St. Louis: B. Herder Book Co., 1947).

4. Roscoe Pound, "The Scope and Purpose of Sociological Jurisprudence," *Harvard Law Review*, XXV (Nov., 1911), 162. In 1945 Richard O'Sullivan also observed: "Even before the outbreak of the war of 1914–

1918 the minds of men . . . were seeking to restore jurisprudence to its proper state and its ancient dignity by a revival and a restatement of the principles of natural law" (*Grotius Society Transactions for the Year 1945,* p. 137).

5. Charles Haines has proved from a rich source of American court cases that *in practice* the Natural Law has always been applied: "In public law the use of natural law theories for various purposes has been continuous from Colonial times to the present day." Haines has demonstrated "the significance of natural law ideas in the interpretation of the state and federal constitutions in the United States, where natural law doctrines have been extensively applied" (*The Revival of Natural Law Concepts,* p. 220). According to Roscoe Pound, the same use of Natural Law ideas is to be found in practical legal decisions throughout Europe: "All nineteenth-century theories of judicial decision in one way or another grow out of the natural law thinking of the seventeenth and eighteenth centuries" ("The Theory of Judicial Decision," *Harvard Law Review,* XXXVI [May, 1923], 802).

6. For two excellent essays on the Natural Law as viewed by these writers, see Robert N. Wilkin, "Cicero and the Law of Nature," and Thomas E. Davitt, S.J., "St. Thomas Aquinas and the Natural Law," in *Origins of the Natural Law Tradition* (Dallas: Southern Methodist University Press, 1954). In Cicero's time three types of law were clearly distinguished: (1) *Jus civile* was a positive law applicable only to Roman citizens. (2) *Jus gentium* was generally contractual law, commercial in its content, and was a kind of common or international law which applied both to Roman citizens and foreigners. It possessed a "universal" element as distinct from the local or national peculiarities of *jus civile.* (3) *Jus naturale* was the Natural Law, the law imposed on all men by virtue of their common humanity. Its moral essence was contained in the Stoic principle of equality: *omnes homines natura aequales sunt.* In St. Thomas Aquinas there were four types of law: (1) *lex divina,* the law revealed to man by God in the Scriptures; (2) *lex humana,* man's positive laws which conformed to God; (3) *lex aeterna,* the law of all creation, revealing the will of God in natural phenomena and to all His creatures; and (4) *lex naturalis,* the Natural Law, by which man's right reason can comprehend the will and reason of God.

7. Compare these points for similarities and differences with Lois Whitney's account of the laws of nature in the eighteenth century, in *Primitivism and the Idea of Progress* (Baltimore: The Johns Hopkins Press, 1934), p. 10.

8. Cobban, *The Crisis of Civilization,* p. 86.

9. See Etienne Gilson, *Reason and Revelation in the Middle Ages* (New York: Charles Scribner's Sons, 1950).

10. See Troeltsch, *The Social Teaching of the Christian Churches.*

11. O'Sullivan, *Grotius Society Transactions for the Year 1945,* XXXI, 120. See also p. 122.

12. *Ibid.,* p. 123.

13. *Ibid.*, p. 135.

14. John S. Marshall, "Richard Hooker and the Origins of American Constitutionalism," in *Origins of the Natural Law Tradition*, p. 68.

15. "The American Revolution, as it ran its course from 1764 to 1776—from the first beginnings of resistance down to the Declaration of Independence and the creation of new colonial constitutions—was inspired by the doctrines of Natural Law" (Ernest Barker, in *Natural Law and the Theory of Society: 1500–1800*, ed. Otto Gierke [Cambridge, Eng.: At the University Press, 1934], I, xlvi). See also Randolph G. Adams, *Political Ideas of the American Revolution* (Durham, N.C., 1922); Ernest Barker, "Natural Law and the American Revolution," in *Traditions of Civility;* Carl Becker, *The Declaration of Independence* (New York: Alfred A. Knopf, 1942); Clarence Manion, "The Natural Law Philosophy of the Founding Fathers," *University of Notre Dame Natural Law Institute Proceedings* (Notre Dame, Indiana: University of Notre Dame Press, 1949), Vol. I; John C. H. Wu, "The Natural Law and Our Common Law," *Fordham Law Review*, XXIII (March, 1954), 13–48.

Notes to Chapter Two

1. John Quincy Adams, *An Answer to Paine's Rights of Man* (London, 1793), p. 17. This work has been attributed frequently to his father, John Adams.

2. Jacques Maritain, *The Rights of Man and Natural Law*, tr. Doris C. Anson (New York: Charles Scribner's Sons, 1943), p. 36.

3. Alfred Cobban, *The Crisis of Civilization* (London: J. Cape, 1941), p. 85.

4. The revolutionary implications of this point were drawn by Leo Strauss: "During the modern period natural law became much more of a revolutionary force than it had been in the past. This fact is a direct consequence of the fundamental change in the character of the natural law doctrine itself" (*Natural Right and History* [Chicago: University of Chicago Press, 1953], p. 183).

5. Leo Strauss, *The Political Philosophy of Hobbes* (Chicago: University of Chicago Press, 1952), p. xii.

6. See A. P. D'Entreves, *Natural Law* (London: Hutchinson's University Library, 1951), pp. 51–53 and 58–59. "The tendency to regard natural law in moral and legal science as analogous to axioms in geometry was well settled in seventeenth-century thought after Grotius" (George Sabine, *A History of Political Theory* [New York: Henry Holt, 1937], p. 530).

7. For an example of the common failure among scholars to cut through the eighteenth-century confusions regarding "nature," see Carl Becker, *The Heavenly City of the Eighteenth-Century Philosophers* (New Haven: Yale University Press, 1932), pp. 54–63.

8. See Strauss, *The Political Philosophy of Hobbes*, p. 104.

9. Strauss, *Natural Right and History*, p. 184. See also p. 185.

10. Sabine, *A History of Political Theory*, p. 456. Hobbes's absolute sovereignty would sanction a popular or democratic despotism quite as much as a monarchical or oligarchical despotism. See Strauss, *Natural Right and History*, pp. 192–193.

11. Thomas Hobbes, *Leviathan*, ch. 15.

12. See William Hazlitt, *The Complete Works of William Hazlitt*, ed. P. P. Howe (London, 1930), II, 123–191; XVI, 123; and XX, 69–83.

13. Hobbes, *Leviathan*, ch. 2.

14. For Hobbes's secular "natural rights" in his social thought see Strauss, *Natural Right and History*, pp. 120–164. Strauss is not sufficiently aware that Hobbes's theory of human nature is paramount in his "natural rights" philosophy.

15. For example, Ernest Barker asserts that Locke is "the exponent of the sovereignty of Natural Law." Yet the ambiguities in Locke's political philosophy compel Barker to admit that "Locke has no clear view of the nature or residence of sovereignty" (*Essays on Government* [London: Oxford University Press, 1951], pp. 94 and 102–103).

16. Strauss, *Natural Right and History*, pp. 165–166, 202–203, and 220–221. See also pp. 207, 222–226. To a certain extent Strauss was anticipated by Sabine, who noted that "Locke had to adopt into his social philosophy a large part of Hobbes's premises." Sabine also pointed out "the inherent contrariety of what he took from Hooker and what he took from Hobbes" (*A History of Political Theory*, pp. 525 and 531; see also pp. 533 and 535).

17. In Britain outstanding refutations of Hobbes were written by Whichcote, Culverwell, Henry More, John Smith, Ralph Cudworth, Shaftesbury, Clarke, and Cumberland. In France François d'Aube, Montesquieu, and the Abbé Claude-Marie Guyon, among others, defended the traditional conception of Natural Law.

18. John Plamenatz, *The English Utilitarians* (Oxford: Blackwell, 1949), p. 20.

19. Hobbes's attempt to place ethics on a foundation of geometry was first noted in 1686 by Leclerc in the *Bibliothèque universelle et historique*.

20. See William Hazlitt, *The Complete Works of William Hazlitt*, II, 123–191; XX, 69–83.

21. Strauss, *Natural Right and History*, pp. 249–251.

22. Sabine, *A History of Political Theory*, p. 529. Willmoore Kendall also noted that Locke's disagreement with Hobbes and other ethical hedonists was largely verbal, because "the law of nature is . . . a law which commands its subjects to look well to their own interests" (*John Locke and the Doctrine of Majority-Rule* [Urbana, Ill.: University of Illinois Press, 1941], p. 77).

23. See Kendall, *op. cit.*, pp. 66–67, 106, and 112.

24. A. P. D'Entreves, *Natural Law*, pp. 52–53. Ernest Barker stated that

in Gierke's great study of the modern natural law "the Natural Law which is in question is a secular Natural Law." It is noteworthy that as the eighteenth century unfolded, the term "natural law" was replaced by "natural rights" in many treatises on jurisprudence.

25. Thomas Gilby, *St. Thomas Aquinas* (New York: Oxford University Press, 1951), p. 364.

26. John C. H. Wu, "Natural Law and Our Common Law," *Fordham Law Review*, XXIII (March, 1954), 21–22.

27. Strauss, *The Political Philosophy of Hobbes*, p. 164.

28. In France, reinforced by Cartesian scientific philosophy, the deism of Voltaire and Diderot was extended into atheistic materialism by such *philosophes* as Holbach, Helvetius, La Mettrie, and Meslier. These *enragé* admirers of Locke, together with the separate influences of Spinoza and Rousseau, completed the circle back to Hobbes, whose influence upon French thought in the eighteenth century was perhaps second only to that of Locke. The *philosophes* did not merely believe in materialism; they openly and defiantly professed their atheism. In their writings the term "Natural Law" was generally replaced by "law of nature" or "natural rights." Like Hobbes and Locke they appealed to "nature," but their universal moral law was assimilated into or annihilated by the "law of nature" pervading the Newtonian universe of the deists or the Spinozist universe of the pantheists.

29. "Hobbes used a traditional vocabulary unsuited to his political theory, and it was precisely this vocabulary that the utilitarians abandoned. That is why the difference between them appears so much greater than it is" (Plamenatz, *The English Utilitarians*, p. 16).

30. "Since the nineteenth century, readers of Locke have found it hard to understand why . . . he stated his doctrines in terms of natural law" (Strauss, *Natural Rights and History*, p. 246).

31. For Hobbes on natural right, see Strauss, *Natural Right and History*, pp. 166–202; for Locke on natural right, see pp. 202–251.

32. Sir Frederick Pollock, *History of the Science of Politics* (New York: J. Fitzgerald, 1883), pp. 111–112.

Notes to Chapter Three

1. Henry T. Buckle, *The History of Civilization in England*, ed. John M. Robertson (New York: E. P. Dutton and Co., 1904), pp. 259–260 and 263.

2. John Morley, *Edmund Burke: A Historical Study* (London, 1867), pp. 150–152.

3. *Ibid.*, pp. 309–310.

4. John Morley, *Burke* (London, 1879), pp. 165, 215, and 211. In 1917 Morley recorded that he once defended himself against Lord Acton's

charge that he had no "large principles" by claiming adherence to Burke's "higher expediency" (John Morley, *Recollections* [New York: The Macmillan Co., 1917], I, 232–233).

5. Francis W. Hirst, *Early Life and Letters of John Morley* (New York: The Macmillan Co., 1927), II, 211.

6. William Lecky, *A History of England in the Eighteenth Century* (New York, 1891), V, 476.

7. Sir Leslie Stephen, *English Thought in the Eighteenth Century* (London, 1881), II, 225–226. See also pp. 106, 253, and 280.

8. Charles E. Vaughan, *Studies in the History of Political Philosophy Before and After Rousseau* (New York, 1925), II, 2, 5, and 19. See also pp. 6–7, 9–10, and 13–16.

9. Charles E. Vaughan, *The Romantic Revolt* (London: William Blackwood and Sons, 1923), p. 147.

10. Vaughan, *Studies in the History of Political Philosophy* . . . , II, 10, 14, 23–24, 28–29, and 37.

11. *Ibid.*, pp. 3–4, 11, and 54.

12. John MacCunn, *The Political Philosophy of Burke* (London: Edward Arnold, 1913), p. 193. For MacCunn's argument that Burke believed in "natural rights" in theory but not in practice, see pp. 194–199.

13. *Ibid.*, pp. 195–209. This distinction is fundamental in MacCunn's analysis, yet he does not try to explain why Burke said "natural rights" if he really meant "civil rights."

14. "From a utilitarian philosophy Burke deduced an anti-democratic political theory. . . . The utilitarian morality led Burke to social views which were profoundly different from those to which it led Bentham" (Elie Halévy, *The Growth of Philosophic Radicalism* [New York, 1928], pp. 158 and 161; see also pp. 153–157, 159–161, 181, and 223). "Priestley, Burke, and Bentham are in harmony in their utilitarianism, Burke developing the doctrine in the form of a philosophy of expediency" (Lois Whitney, *Primitivism and the Idea of Progress* [Baltimore: The Johns Hopkins Press, 1934], pp. 196–197). "Like the utilitarians who had formulated their famous doctrine of the 'greatest happiness of the greatest number' . . . Burke fully recognized the importance of happiness to the welfare of the nation" (Annie M. Osborn, *Rousseau and Burke* [London: Oxford University Press, 1940], p. 133; see also pp. 134–145). "The utilitarian principle . . . recurs in Burke, though not in a narrowly schematic form" (John A. Lester, "An Analysis of the Conservative Thought of Edmund Burke," Ph.D. thesis, Harvard University, 1943, p. 64; see also p. 201). "The repudiation of natural rights was implicit not only in his utilitarian conviction that the end of government is the happiness and welfare of the people governed, but also in his reliance on experience and in his rejection of all abstract doctrines of political theory. . . . Burke's opposition to the theory of natural rights and to the use of nature as the norm in political theory was . . . a conviction unshaken during his whole career"

(Henry V. S. Ogden, "The Rejection of the Antithesis of Nature and Art in English Political Writings, 1760–1800," Ph.D. thesis, University of Chicago, 1936, p. 85; see also pp. 83, 86, 113, 116, 137–138, 146, and 155).

15. John H. Randall, *The Making of the Modern Mind* (Boston: Houghton Mifflin, 1940), p. 432.

16. George Sabine, *A History of Political Theory* (New York: Henry Holt, 1937), pp. 607–614.

17. See the *Catalogue of the Library of the Late Right Hon. Edmund Burke,* Sold by Auction by Mr. Evans, No. 93 Pall-Mall, on Thursday, Nov. 7, 1833 (London, 1833). Among 664 items are the following works which contain discussions of the Natural Law: *Aristotle on Government; Ciceronis opera philosophica,* 2 vols.; *Ciceronis epistolae ad familiares; Ciceronis opera,* 11 vols.; *Ciceronis orationes;* Cicero, *De natura deorum;* Cicero, *De republica; Ciceronis opera,* 4 vols.; Cicero's *Worthy Booke of Old Age;* Epictetus' *Manuell;* Bacon, *Abridgment of the Law;* Bacon, *On the Laws and Government of England;* Grotius, *On War and Peace,* ed. Barbeyrac; *Pufendorfius de lege naturali;* Pufendorf's *Law of Nature and Nations,* 2 vols.; *Works* of the Author of *The Whole Duty of Man;* Vattel, *Droit des gens,* 2 vols.; Vattel's *Law of Nations,* 2 vols. All of these works were published before the death of Burke in 1797. However, it is important to note that 221 of the volumes offered for sale were published *after* Burke's death.

18. Arthur L. Woehl, "Burke's Reading," Ph.D. thesis, Cornell University, 1928, pp. 111–112. See also *The Speeches of the Rt. Hon. Edmund Burke* (London: Longman, Hurst, Rees, Orme, and Brown, 1816), I, 151 and 328. Hereinafter this work will be cited as *Speeches.*

19. "Burke met a man after his own heart in Cicero . . . the only man at all like Burke for richness, expansiveness, and variety of mind in all the ancient world" (Woodrow Wilson, *Mere Literature* [Boston, 1896], pp. 113–114). See also *The Dictionary of National Biography* on Burke, p. 17. With his friend Windham, Burke discussed problems in semantics in Cicero's work. See William Windham, *The Diary of the Rt. Hon. William Windham, 1784–1810,* ed. Mrs. Henry Baring (London, 1866), pp. 65–66.

20. See John A. Lester, "An Analysis of the Conservative Thought of Edmund Burke," p. 120. See also E. J. Payne, *Burke's Select Works* (Oxford, 1878), II, xxxvii–xxxviii. Hereinafter this work will be cited as *Select Works.*

21. Burke, *Speeches,* IV, 223. See also pp. 224–227, 229, and 255.

22. See Woehl, "Burke's Reading," pp. 66, 133–134, 202–203, and 205.

23. "The student of *Esprit des Lois* will recognize its influence in every one of Burke's masterpieces" (Morley, *Burke,* p. 50). For Burke's important use of Vattel, see *Speeches,* II, 255; IV, 151; and especially his *The Policy of the Allies* in *The Works of the Rt. Hon. Edmund Burke* (London: Henry G. Bohn, 1854), III, 431 and the Appendix, 458–466. Unless designated otherwise, hereinafter all references to the works of Burke will be

from the Bohn edition of 1854, in six volumes. Each reference will be identified by its particular title, or a shortened form of the title, rather than as *Works*.

24. See Lord Acton, *Essays on Freedom and Power* (Boston: The Beacon Press, 1949), p. 252.

25. For details on these and other reviews see Thomas W. Copeland, "Edmund Burke and the Book Reviews in Dodsley's *Annual Register,*" *PMLA*, XLV (June, 1942), 446–468.

26. Burke, *Annual Register* (1760), p. 263.

27. Burke, *Speeches*, I, 172.

28. Woehl, "Burke's Reading," pp. 203–205. For Burke's use of digests of English common law see p. 206.

29. Burke, *Speeches*, IV, 202. This speech, a report on the causes of the duration of Hastings' trial, is saturated with English common, canon, statutory, and criminal law and procedure from the time of Richard II to 1794.

30. Burke, *Speeches*, III, 536–537. See also Thomas Macknight, *History of the Life and Times of Edmund Burke* (London, 1858), I, 67; III, 568; Woehl, "Burke's Reading," pp. 65–66.

31. See Burke, *Speeches*, I, 61 and 158.

32. See Wilson M. Hudson, "An Index to the Works of Edmund Burke," Ph.D. thesis, University of Chicago, 1947, pp. 83–84. See also Burke, *Speeches*, I, 78, 92, and 300; II, 34–35; III, 246; IV, 137, 176, 191, 202–203, 208, 232, 451, 473, and 483. See also *Correspondence of the Rt. Hon. Edmund Burke, 1744–1797* (London: Francis and John Rivington, 1844), I, 280. Hereinafter this work will be cited as *Correspondence*.

33. Morley, *Burke*, pp. 22–23. See also pp. 24–27.

34. See Burke, "A Letter to Sir Hercules Langrishe," pp. 311, 315. Hereinafter this will be cited as "Letter to Langrishe." See also Burke, "On the Penal Laws Against Irish Catholics," p. 289. Hereinafter this will be cited as "Laws Against Irish Catholics."

35. Burke, "Letter to Langrishe," p. 343. For a detailed account of this English system of persecution, see Morley, *Edmund Burke: A Historical Study*, pp. 180–186 and 191–193.

36. Burke, "Letter to Langrishe," pp. 305 and 317. See also pp. 303–307, 319, 331–338. See also Burke, "Tract on the Popery Laws," p. 24. Hereinafter this will be cited as "Popery Laws."

37. Burke, "Popery Laws," p. 34.

38. *Ibid.*, pp. 48 and 45.

39. Burke, *Speeches*, I, 151. See also p. 328. Yet as in American affairs, Burke rested the practical side of his case for Ireland on moral prudence rather than on abstract right: "I do not put the thing on a question of right" ("Letter to Langrishe," p. 334).

40. Burke, "Popery Laws," pp. 21–22 and 29–30. To enforce this appeal to Natural Law Burke quoted Cicero's *De legibus.*

41. Burke, "Popery Laws," pp. 32–33.

42. *Ibid.*, p. 21.

43. Burke, *A Letter to Richard Burke*, p. 80. See also "Letter to Langrishe," p. 324.

44. Burke, "Popery Laws," p. 22.

45. For example, see Morley, *Edmund Burke: A Historical Study*, pp. 135–152.

46. Burke, *Speeches*, I, 20. This idea recurs frequently in Burke's speeches on American affairs.

47. *Ibid.*, pp. 303–304.

48. House of Representatives of Massachusetts to Conway, Feb. 13, 1768, Almon, *Prior Documents*, pp. 181–182.

49. Burke, *Speeches*, IV, 136. See also I, 214, 237, and 257.

50. *Ibid.*, I, 16–17. See also p. 327. The king had so corrupted the House of Commons, Burke lamented, that "the ground and pillar of freedom is . . . held up only by the treacherous underpinning and clumsy butresses of arbitrary power" (p. 195).

51. *Ibid.*, 110. See also p. 111.

52. *Ibid.*, 295. See also pp. 20 and 298.

53. For these passages see respectively Burke, *Speeches*, I, 176 and 233; *Correspondence*, IV, Appendix, 493, 474, 476–477, 488–489, 490–493; *Speeches*, I, 270; and *Correspondence*, IV, Appendix, 495.

54. Boswell, *Life of Samuel Johnson* (New York: E. P. Dutton, 1949), I, 320.

55. Morley, *Burke*, p. 81.

56. Burke, *Speeches*, I, 35–37 and 70–74. See also pp. 75–76 and 79.

57. *Ibid.*, p. 78.

58. Burke, *Speech on the Reform of Representation in the House of Commons*, p. 145.

59. Burke, *Speeches*, III, 414; IV, 57 and 66.

60. *Ibid.*, I, 84 and 88.

61. *Ibid.*, III, 360. See also p. 51.

62. Burke, *Correspondence*, IV, 463.

63. See Dixon Wecter, "Adam Smith and Burke," *Notes and Queries*, CLXXIV (April 30, 1938), 310–311; Alfred Cobban, *Edmund Burke and the Revolt Against the Eighteenth Century* (London, 1929), pp. 189–197; William C. Dunn, "Adam Smith and Edmund Burke; Complementary Contemporaries," *The Southern Economic Journal*, VII (Jan., 1941), 330–346.

64. Halévy, *The Growth of Philosophic Radicalism*, pp. 230–231 and *passim;* Harold Laski, *Political Thought in England from Locke to Bentham* (New York: Henry Holt, 1920), p. 236.

65. Burke, *Two Letters to Gentlemen in Bristol*, pp. 51–52.

66. Burke, "Thoughts and Details on Scarcity," p. 89. Hereinafter this will be cited as "Thoughts on Scarcity." See also pp. 92 and 107–108. See

also *Letters on a Regicide Peace,* pp. 315–316. Hereinafter this work will be cited as *Regicide Peace.* See also "A Second Letter to Sir Hercules Langrishe," p. 58.

67. *Ibid.,* p. 83.

68. *Ibid.,* p. 100.

69. Burke, *Speeches,* II, 413 and 409.

70. *Ibid.,* p. 410.

71. *Ibid.* A fragment on monopoly found among Burke's papers is worth noting here: " 'Monopoly' is contrary to 'Natural Right.' Monopoly is the power . . . of exclusive dealing in a commodity . . . which others might supply if not prevented by that power. No monopoly can, therefore, be prescribed in; because contrary to common right. . . . The State, representing all its individuals, may contract for them; and therefore may grant a monopoly" (*Correspondence,* IV, Appendix, 459; see also pp. 460–462; *Speeches,* IV, 310).

72. *Ibid.,* pp. 412–413. See also pp. 428, 476, 478, 486–487, and 490.

73. For a good account of this fraud, see Morley, *Edmund Burke: A Historical Study,* pp. 205–207.

74. Burke, *Speeches,* III, 162. See also p. 163. This passage may be interpreted as a reference to *physical* rather than *moral* laws of nature, in which case the reference is merely an analogy.

75. *Ibid.,* IV, 356. See also p. 357; *Speeches,* II, 446–447; III, 66.

76. *Ibid.,* pp. 354, 472, 479, and 367. In securing absolute rule, Burke noted that Hastings acted on a principle of sovereignty centered in power alone: "He declares that in a division between him and the Nabob 'the strongest must decide.' " (*Speeches,* II, 434). The same applied in divisions with England: "Here Mr. Burke read from parts of the defence of Mr. Hastings, passages, stating, that whenever he thought the laws of England militated against the interests of the Company, he was at liberty to violate them" (*Speeches,* IV, 476–477).

77. *Ibid.,* pp. 357–358.

78. *Ibid.,* pp. 374–375. For other examples in Indian affairs of Burke's attacks on the theory of sovereignty based upon arbitrary power, see *Speeches,* II, 429, 431–432, 434, 446–447, 460, 473, 475–476; III, 57, 68, 74, 86, 99, 175–176, 223–225, 266, 280; IV, 307, 313, 328, 354–363, 368, 374–375, 475–476, 478–479, 489–491, and 499.

79. *Ibid.,* IV, p. 354.

80. *Ibid.,* pp. 366–367. See also p. 481.

81. *Ibid.,* p. 477.

82. See Burke, *Correspondence,* IV, 24, Appendix, 519, 544, and 547. See also *Regicide Peace,* pp. 155 and 215.

83. For the various theories concerning M. Dupont's identity, see Thomas Copeland, *Our Eminent Friend Edmund Burke* (New Haven, Conn.: Yale University Press, 1949), pp. 190–245. Professor Copeland's own theory is doubtful.

84. See Burke, *Correspondence*, III, 102–121, especially pp. 107–117.

85. Burke, *Speech on the Army Estimates*, p. 275. See also pp. 276–278. Burke's italics.

86. Burke, *The Policy of the Allies*, p. 453.

87. For the division of public opinion between Burke and his opponents, see Samuel Bernstein, "English Reactions to the French Revolution," *Science and Society*, IX, No. 2 (1945), 147–171.

88. William Wilberforce, *Diary* (London, 1897), I, 284.

89. Quoted by James Prior, *Life of the Rt. Hon. Edmund Burke*, 5th ed. (London: Henry G. Bohn, 1854), p. 315.

90. Burke, *Correspondence*, IV, 356 and 359.

91. "Le succès de cette publication avait été immense; trente mille exemplaires s'étaient vendus dans une seule année, et tous les peuples de l'Europe avaient pu lire cette oeuvre remarquable, traduite dans toutes les langues des son apparition. . . . La première traduction française, faite d'après la 3e édition anglaise, parut à Paris en 1790. Le manuscrit fut distribué, par parties, à trois imprimeries et imprimé en huit jours. On fit cinq éditions de cette traduction de 1790 à la fin de 1791" (René Bazin, "Edmund Burke et la révolution," *Revue de l'Anjou* [nouvelle série], IV [Jan., 1882], 33).

92. Jean Baptiste Cloots, *Adresse d'un Prussien à un Anglais* (Paris, 1790), p. 12. See also p. 49.

93. Quoted by Donald C. Bryant, *Edmund Burke and His Literary Friends* (St. Louis: Washington University, 1939), p. 42.

94. Carl B. Cone in "Pamphlet Replies to Burke's *Reflections*," *Social Science Quarterly*, XXVI (June, 1945), 22–34, made use of twenty-one replies. Ernest Barker noted "some forty answers to the *Reflections*." In the course of my studies on Burke I have discovered and read forty-eight replies to the *Reflections* and Burke's other writings on French affairs.

95. Burke, *Reflections on the Revolution in France*, pp. 368–369. Hereinafter this work will be cited as *Reflections*. See also p. 370. Charles E. Vaughan dismissed this passage as "a mere metaphor," and F. J. C. Hearnshaw condemned it as "resounding nonsense." H. V. S. Ogden stated that "Burke was imbued with the importance of the differences between peoples, and for him the contract is an *ex post facto* abstraction of particular validity, not an initiating act of universal application." Ogden concluded by agreeing with Vaughan: "A contract between the dead, the living and the unborn is only a contract by metaphor." John A. Lester called this passage "the work of Burke's moral idealism," a criticism too abstract to be meaningful. He too failed to mention the Natural Law. It is ironical that the positivist Morley, who also never mentioned the Natural Law in Burke, recognized in a general way, and apart from any consideration of contract, that the ultimate basis of Burke's politics lay in a "mysticism" that transcended a naturalistic explanation of life: "At the bottom of all his thoughts about communities and governments there lay a certain mys-

ticism. It was no irony, no literary trope, when he talked of our having taught the American husbandman 'piously to believe in the mysterious virtue of wax and parchment.' He was using no idle epithet, when he described the disposition of a stupendous wisdom, 'moulding together the great mysterious incorporation of the human race.' To him there actually was an element of mystery in the cohesion of men in societies, in political obedience, in the sanctity of contract; in all that fabric of law and charter and obligation, whether written or unwritten, which is the sheltering bulwark between civilization and barbarism. When reason and history had contributed all that they could to the explanation, it seemed to him as if the vital force, the secret of organization, the binding framework, must still come from the impenetrable regions beyond reasoning and beyond history" (*Burke*, p. 165). This was the closest Morley ever came to recognizing the sovereignty of Natural Law in Burke's political philosophy.

96. Pufendorf, *Of the Law of Nature and Nations* (Oxford, 1703), p. 117. Pufendorf's italics.

97. Burke, *Reflections*, pp. 307–309.

98. *Ibid.*, p. 370.

99. *Ibid.*, pp. 364–366.

100. Burke, *Speeches*, I, 114. See also *Annual Register* (1767), pp. 290 and 293–294.

101. Burke, *Reflections*, p. 493. See also p. 492; *Letter to Richard Burke*, p. 80.

102. *Ibid.*, p. 422. See also p. 423.

103. *Ibid.*, p. 377. See also pp. 378–379.

104. *Ibid.*, p. 331. Burke again distinguished between "the pretended *rights of man*" and "the rights of the people" in his *An Appeal from the New to the Old Whigs*, p. 95. Hereinafter this work will be cited as *New to the Old Whigs*. Burke's distinction recurs in *The Policy of the Allies*, p. 417; *Letter to a Noble Lord* (hereinafter cited as *Noble Lord*), p. 150; *Regicide Peace*, p. 305.

105. *Ibid.*, p. 444. See also pp. 452, 454, and 467.

106. *Ibid.*, p. 334. My italics.

107. *Ibid.*, p. 332.

108. *Ibid.*, p. 335.

109. Burke, *New to the Old Whigs*, p. 79. See also pp. 80–81.

110. Burke, *Noble Lord*, p. 137. See also pp. 138–139.

111. Burke, *Regicide Peace*, pp. 168, 172, and 176–177. See also pp. 178, 185–186, 206–207, 406, 414–415; *Preface to M. Brissot's Address*, pp. 524–526. Burke denied that prescription applied to recent conquests: "A recent wrong . . . can plead no prescription. It violates the rights upon which not only the community of France, but those on which all communities are founded . . . principles which are as true in England as in any other country" (*Regicide Peace*, p. 219).

112. *Ibid.*, pp. 211, 216, 304, and 400.

113. Burke, *Speeches*, IV, 73.

114. Burke, *Letter to William Elliot*, p. 75.

115. Burke, *Regicide Peace*, p. 207. Burke's basic conviction that "God is the all-wise but mysterious Governor of the world" is a recurring theme in this work. See pp. 236, 277, 322, 326, and 353.

116. Burke, *The Epistolary Correspondence of Edmund Burke*, ed. Dr. French Laurence (London, 1827), p. 241. Hereinafter this work will be cited as *Laurence Correspondence*.

117. *Ibid.*, pp. 106–107.

118. William Hazlitt, *The Spirit of the Age*, in *The Complete Works of William Hazlitt*, ed. P. P. Howe (London, 1930), II, 100. For Burke's letter to Mackintosh see Robert M. Mackintosh, *Memoirs of the Life of Sir James Mackintosh* (Boston: Little Brown, 1853), I, 88–90. Hazlitt's account agrees with that of Lois Whitney, *Primitivism and the Idea of Progress*, pp. 224–226. For a different account of the origin of Mackintosh's lectures, see B. Sprague Allen, "Minor Disciples of Radicalism in the Revolutionary Era," *Modern Philology*, XXX (1923–1924), 294.

Notes to Chapter Four

1. Hobbes, with his theory that nations are related to each other as individuals in his hypothetical "state of nature," was the one great exception to this assumption. Although Hobbes used the language of "Natural Law," his theory of international law is purely contractual, expedient, secular, and utilitarian. By contending that international law derived primarily from national civil laws and self-interest, Pufendorf arrived through different means at a theory almost identical with that of Hobbes.

2. "Apparently following Suarez, Grotius derives the law of international relations primarily from the law of nature, and secondarily from the *jus gentium* by which the law of nature is supplemented" (Arthur Nussbaum, *A Concise History of the Law of Nations* [New York: The Macmillan Co., 1947], p. 104).

3. For the dual use of "law of nations" in the works of Suarez and Grotius, see Nussbaum, *A Concise History of the Law of Nations*, pp. 64–72 and 92–112. The international conception was generally stressed.

4. William Blackstone, *Commentaries on the Laws of England*, Chitty ed. (New York, 1832), I, 29.

5. Henry St. John Bolingbroke, "The Idea of a Patriot King," in *The Works of Lord Bolingbroke* (Philadelphia, 1841), II, 379. The last sentence indicates how Bolingbroke, as a patriot, deist, and logician, could appeal to the Natural Law and yet invert the whole moral basis of political sovereignty. Bolingbroke made not merely constitutional law, but civil conventions, statutory laws, and even the arbitrary decrees of his "patriot king" the ultimate basis of just rule. Like Burke he used the vocabulary

of Natural Law, but he arrived at a Hobbist theory of sovereignty, of will over law, which completely contradicted Burke. For the vital differences in their conceptions of Natural Law, see Eldon M. Talley, "The Concept of Natural Law in the Thought of Bolingbroke and Burke," M.A. thesis, Fordham University, 1948.

6. Even statutory laws were derived from Natural Law: "All civil laws . . . either presuppose or include the chief heads of the Law of Nature . . . neither are these in the least injured or impaired by the particular ordinances, which each commonwealth finds a necessity of superadding, for its separate interest and benefit" (Samuel Pufendorf, *Of the Laws of Nature and Nations* [Oxford, 1703], p. 106).

7. See Burke, *Speeches,* III, 217–218; IV, 476.

8. *Ibid.,* IV, 480.

9. Burke, *Regicide Peace,* p. 214. The idea of "the Commonwealth of Europe" occurs frequently in this work. See pp. 203, 206, 215, 219, 233, 244, 253–254, 323–324, 364, 373, and 433.

10. James Mackintosh, *A Discourse on the Law of Nature and Nations* (London, 1799), p. 21. See also pp. 4, 17, and 35.

11. Burke, *A Letter to the Sheriffs of Bristol,* p. 6. Hereinafter this work will be cited as *Sheriffs of Bristol.*

12. Burke, *Speeches,* I, 398. Burke insisted that the method of warfare conducted by the Indians was utterly lawless and uncivilized, and that Britain was bound by the rules of war which governed all civilized nations.

13. *Ibid.,* p. 414.

14. *Ibid.,* II, 248. For Burke's second account of the St. Eustatius affair, see *Annual Register* (1781), pp. 101–106. The universal confiscation of private property, wrote Burke, "drew upon us . . . the odium of all Europe" (p. 105). William Lecky said that the events and treachery that followed the capture of St. Eustatius "ought to bring a blush to the cheek of every English historian" (*A History of England in the Eighteenth Century* [New York, 1891], IV, 179–182).

15. *Ibid.,* pp. 256–258. See also pp. 259–269, 313–328. Written authorities were for Burke the least binding evidence of the law of nations. Although Burke quoted Vattel more than any other writer on international law, his own conception of the law of nations was far more consciously connected with traditional Natural Law. Twenty-three years before Burke condemned Britain's behavior at St. Eustatius, he had attacked Frederick of Prussia for pillaging the private property of the conquered Saxons: "When a country is entirely possessed by any power, and claimed as a conquest, the rights of war seem to cease, and the people have a claim to be governed in such a manner as becomes a just prince" (*Annual Register* [1758], p. 64).

16. *Ibid.,* p. 260. Later Burke noted that the Marquis de Bouillé, in

seizing British possessions, "treated the conquered with tenderness and humanity" (*Speeches*, II, 326).

17. *Ibid.*, p. 259. For Burke's other appeals to the law of nations in colonial affairs, particularly in the exchange of prisoners after Cornwallis surrendered, see *Speeches*, I, 131–132; II, 295–311.

18. *Ibid.*, IV, 6.

19. *Ibid.*, p. 85.

20. *Ibid.*, p. 95.

21. *Ibid.*, p. 93. See also p. 100. Lord Acton, a staunch defender of the French Revolution, conceded that on this vital point Burke was right: "The French Revolution . . . involved international consequences. It condemned the governments of other countries. If the revolutionary government was legitimate, the conservative governments were not. They necessarily threatened each other. By the law of its existence, France encouraged insurrection against its neighbors. . . . The Convention which . . . promised brotherhood to populations striking for freedom, was impolitic, but was not illogical. . . . Nobody imagined that the new system of international relations could be carried into effect without resistance or sacrifice, but the enthusiasts of liberty, true or false, might well account it worth all that it must cost, even if the price was to be twenty years of war. This new dogma is the real cause of the breach with England, which did such harm to France" (*Lectures on the French Revolution* [London: The Macmillan Co., 1920], pp. 317–318).

22. *Ibid.*, pp. 107–108. See also p. 109.

23. *Ibid.*, p. 140.

24. Lord Acton suggests how Marat's belief in the Hobbist "state of nature," interpreted optimistically, supplied in part the theoretical basis of the Reign of Terror: "Marat was obedient to a logic of his own. He adopted simply the state of nature and the primitive contract, in which thousands of his contemporaries believed. The poor had agreed to renounce the right of savage life and the prerogative of force, in return for the benefits of civilization; but finding the compact broken on the other side, finding that the upper classes governed in their own interest, and left them to misery and ignorance, they resumed the conditions of barbaric existence before society, and were free to take what they required, and to inflict what punishment they chose upon men who had made a profit of their suffering" (*Lectures on the French Revolution*, pp. 226–227). Identifying his "state of nature" with the "law of nature," Marat wrote his own draft of the "Rights of Man," in which he avowed, said Acton, "that, by the law of nature, a man may do what he likes in the pursuit of happiness, and, to elude oppression, may oppress, imprison, and destroy" (*Lectures on the French Revolution*, p. 113; see also pp. 241–242). Burke knew that anarchy in international affairs had begun in the early 1770's with the violations of Corsica and Poland, which he had condemned: "The

breach that has been now made, in those compacts that unite states for their mutual benefit, establishes a most dangerous precedent; it deprives, in a great measure, every separate power in Europe, of that security which was founded in treaties, alliances, common interest, and public faith. It seems to throw nations collectively into that state of nature, in which it has been supposed that mankind separately at one time subsisted, when the security of the individual depended singly upon his own strength" (*Annual Register* [1772], preface).

25. Burke, *Speeches*, IV, 120.

26. *Ibid.*, pp. 150–151.

27. Burke, *Correspondence*, III, 226. See also pp. 508–509. The same doctrine had been advanced by Burke to justify the interest of France in the American cause, and in December 1787, during the Dutch Patriot-Court conflict, Burke had said that the defeat of the French party in Holland was within Britain's legitimate self-interest. See *Speeches*, III, 310.

28. Burke, *Speeches*, IV, 151. As early as 1772–1774, Burke had attacked the theory of noninterference when, out of jealousy for France, Britain had refused to help her prevent the partition of Poland. He had castigated Britain for placing a narrow national self-interest above social justice, and had warned that noninterference was a novel innovation which might some day destroy the balance of power in Europe. See *Annual Register* (1772), pp. 1–45; *Parliamentary History* (May 18, 1774), XVII, 1341. In 1791 even Mackintosh had admitted that all Englishmen, friends and enemies of the Revolution, agreed its influence could not be restricted to France, that it would alter the whole social order of Europe. See *Vindiciae Gallicae* (London, 1791), p. 358. Lecky agreed with Burke: "It was idle to say that French affairs did not concern Englishmen, when they were steadily and persistently held up as a model" (*A History of England in the Eighteenth Century*, V, 487; see also pp. 519–521).

29. *Ibid.*, p. 153.

30. Burke, *Regicide Peace*, p. 153. See also pp. 213, 220; *Reflections*, pp. 307–308.

31. *Ibid.*, p. 178. See also pp. 182–186.

32. *Ibid.*, pp. 206, 233–234. Acton's comment on the impending emigré invasion is worth noting here: "Already Burke had written: 'If ever a foreign prince enters into France, he must enter it as into a country of assassins. The mode of civilized war will not be practiced; nor are the French, who act on the present system, entitled to expect it' " (*Lectures on the French Revolution*, p. 213). Acton interpreted Burke's words not as an indicative fact on how a Royalist-Jacobin war would be fought, but as an imperative command on how the antirevolutionary forces should conduct themselves. For Burke's other appeals to the law of nations in French affairs, see *Thoughts on French Affairs*, pp. 348–349; *The Policy of the Allies*, p. 431, and particularly Burke's Extracts from Vattel's *Law of Nations*, Appendix, pp. 458–466.

33. *Ibid.*, p. 216.

34. *Annual Register* (1767), p. 295; *Regicide Peace*, p. 425.

35. Burke, *Reflections*, p. 307. See also p. 306.

36. See Burke, *Sheriffs of Bristol*, p. 10.

37. Burke, *Reflections*, p. 423. Burke's speeches in parliament are filled with statements that statutes should conform to the spirit of Magna Carta, the common law, and the constitution.

38. *Ibid.*, p. 310.

39. Burke, *New to the Old Whigs*, p. 109.

40. Burke, *Correspondence*, IV, Appendix, 465.

41. Burke, *Reflections*, p. 307.

42. *Ibid.*, pp. 308–309.

43. *Ibid.*, p. 320. See also p. 467. MacCunn has a fairly good account of "civil vicinity" in *The Political Philosophy of Burke* (London: Edward Arnold, 1913), pp. 16–37.

44. Burke, *Correspondence*, IV, 186.

45. William Windham, *The Diary of the Rt. Hon. William Windham, 1784–1810*, ed. Mrs. Henry Baring (London, 1866), p. 371.

46. Burke, "A Letter to a Member of the National Assembly," p. 548. For the next two quotations see p. 549. Hereinafter this will be cited as "To the National Assembly."

47. For example, see John Morley, *Burke* (London, 1879), pp. 168–169, 172–174; Sir Leslie Stephen, *History of English Thought in the Eighteenth Century* (London, 1881), II, 280; Lecky, *A History of England in the Eighteenth Century*, V, 460–461, 464, 468–469, 490, and 517; George Sabine, *A History of Political Theory* (New York: Henry Holt, 1937), pp. 611–614. For a legalistic approach to this problem see Victor M. Hamm, "Burke and Metaphysics," in *Essays in Modern Scholasticism*, ed. Anton C. Pegis (Westminster, Maryland: The Newman Bookshop, 1944), pp. 206–221.

48. Burke, *Speeches*, III, 48.

49. Burke, *Observations on "The Present State of the Nation,"* pp. 258, 270, and 280.

50. See Burke, *Thoughts on the Causes of the Present Discontents*, pp. 307, 310, 315–316, 320, 324, 337, 365, and 376. Hereinafter this work will be cited as *Present Discontents*.

51. Burke, *Speeches*, I, 276 and 287.

52. Burke, *Sheriffs of Bristol*, pp. 25–29.

53. *Ibid.*, pp. 29–30. My italics.

54. See for example, Burke, *Speeches*, I, 457.

55. Burke, *Reflections*, pp. 282 and 332–333. My italics. In his reply to Burke, Priestley confessed his bewilderment over Burke's "paradoxical" distinction between abstract metaphysical theory and concrete moral practice in politics: "One of the most curious paradoxes in this work [*Reflections*] is that the rights of men . . . are all extremes, and in proportion as they are metaphysically true, they are morally and politically false. Now by

metaphysically true can only be meant *strictly* and *properly* true, and how this can be in any sense *false,* is to me incomprehensible" (Joseph Priestley, *Letters to Edmund Burke Occasioned by His Reflections* [London, 1791], p. 25; Priestley's italics). The anonymous author of *Another Sketch of the Reign of George III, 1780–1790* (London, 1791, p. 34) also conceived of politics as a purely theoretical science based upon mathematical reasoning: "It is to be observed, that the terms abstract, philosophy, metaphysics, etc. have been much confounded of late, and endeavoured to be brought into disrepute by those who could only expect to succeed in perverting reason, by confounding terms. The author of the letter upon the French Revolution, speaking of rights, etc. says, their abstract perfection is their practical defect: now, abstract perfection can only arise from practical excellency, and it is . . . from contemplation and knowledge of individuals alone, that we are able to combine various qualities, so as to complete and harmonize any system whatever, whether of mechanics or of ethics, and the effects and the value of a system so framed, may be precisely ascertained, by resolving it into its elementary parts." The basic tenet of positivism, that the assumptions and methods of physical science can validly be applied to man, is clearly evident in this passage. This theme runs through many of the replies to Burke's *Reflections.*

56. *Ibid.,* pp. 454–455. In 1769 Burke had condemned Grenville's speculative reasoning: "It looks as if he had dropped down from the moon, without any knowledge of the general nature of this globe or of its inhabitants" (*Observations on "The Present State of the Nation,"* p. 363).

57. Burke, *Speeches,* IV, 55.

58. *Ibid.,* I, 328.

59. Burke, *Reflections,* p. 444. For Burke's other attacks on geometric politics, see pp. 335, 443, 452, 454, 467, and 509.

60. Burke, *Sheriffs of Bristol,* p. 33. Almost the whole of this brief work is a pure expression of Burke's principle of prudence.

61. Burke, "Letter to Langrishe," p. 340.

62. Burke, *Reflections,* p. 334. Italics mine.

63. Burke, *Speeches,* IV, 139–140.

64. Burke, *Reflections,* p. 295.

65. Burke, *Speeches,* III, 48.

66. St. Thomas Aquinas, *Summa theologica,* Id. at Q. civ, A. 3 ad 1.

67. Thomas Gilby, *St. Thomas Aquinas* (New York: Oxford University Press, 1951), p. 364.

68. Burke, *Correspondence,* II, 276. See also *Speeches,* IV, 224.

69. Burke, *New to the Old Whigs,* p. 16. See also "Letter to Langrishe," pp. 317–318.

70. Burke, *Speeches,* IV, 55–56. See also pp. 58–59, 309, 323–324; I, 278, 285, and 353.

71. *Ibid.,* II, 11.

72. Jeremy Bentham, *Defence of Economy Against the Late Mr. Burke* (London, 1817), p. 32.

73. Burke, *Regicide Peace*, p. 326.

74. Burke, *Correspondence*, III, 118–120. See also p. 121.

75. See Mary Gladstone Drew, *Acton, Gladstone and Others* (London: Nisbet and Co., 1924), p. 29; John Acton, *Essays on Freedom and Power*, ed. Gertrude Himmelfarb (Boston: The Beacon Press, 1949), pp. xxxvii–xxxviii.

76. Quoted by Sir George O. Trevelyan, *The Early History of Charles James Fox* (London: Longmans, Green and Co., 1881), p. 192.

77. Burke, *Regicide Peace,* p. 192. However, see also pp. 158, 192, and 224.

78. *Ibid.,* p. 236.

79. For these examples and others of Burke's appeals to prudence, see *Reflections*, pp. 286, 430, 440, 453, 474; *Sheriffs of Bristol*, p. 41; *Regicide Peace*, p. 224; *Speeches*, I, 113, 189–190, 270, 323, 327, 345, 352, and 413; II, 57, 198, 213, 433, and 481; III, 48, 462, and 539; IV, 6–7, 13–14, and 55–56; *Correspondence*, III, 118.

80. Burke, *Speeches*, II, 62. See also p. 63.

81. *Ibid.,* III, 50.

Notes to Chapter Five

1. Burke, *A Vindication of Natural Society*, p. 47. See also "A Letter from Montesquieu to the Author of the View of Bolingbroke's Philosophy," *Annual Register* (1760), p. 189.

2. John Morley, *Burke* (London, 1879), p. 13. "Irony is a dangerous weapon . . . and in after-life Burke had frequently to explain that he was not serious" (Augustine Birrel, *Obiter Dicta* [London: Duckworth and Co., 1913], pp. 235–236).

3. See Thomas W. Copeland, "Burke's Vindication of Natural Society," *Transactions of the Bibliographical Society*, second series, XVIII, in *The Library*, ed. F. C. Francis (New York: Oxford University Press, 1938), 461–462. Copeland points out that the preface explaining the satire was not first published in 1765, as Prior, Morley, and Murray had said, but in the second edition of 1757. Burke's satire was also included in Dodsley's collection of tracts, *Fugitive Pieces* (London, 1761).

4. Burke, *A Vindication of Natural Society* (1765 ed.), preface, p. 3.

5. William Godwin, *Political Justice* (Dublin, 1793), I, 10.

6. Elie Halévy, *The Growth of Philosophic Radicalism* (New York, 1928), pp. 215–216.

7. John B. Bury, *The Idea of Progress* (New York: The Macmillan Co., 1932), pp. 181–182.

8. Woodrow Wilson, *Mere Literature* (Boston, 1896), p. 119.

9. Burke, *A Vindication of Natural Society*, p. 21. See also p. 20.

10. James Bryce, *Studies in History and Jurisprudence* (Oxford, 1901), p. 590.

11. Burke, *Speeches*, IV, 328.

12. John A. Lester, "An Analysis of the Conservative Thought of Edmund Burke," Ph.D. thesis, Harvard University, 1943, p. 157. See also p. 129. However, see also pp. 179–180.

13. Arthur L. Goodhart, *English Contributions to the Philosophy of Law* (New York: Oxford University Press, 1949), p. 24. See also George H. Sabine, *A History of Political Theory* (New York: Henry Holt, 1937), p. 609.

14. Leo Gershoy, *From Despotism to Revolution* (New York: Harper and Brothers, 1944), p. 233.

15. Charles E. Vaughan, *Studies in the History of Political Philosophy Before and After Rousseau* (New York, 1925), II, 9.

16. Morley, *Burke*, pp. 171–172.

17. Burke, *Speeches*, III, 475–476. In his *Speech on Conciliation* (p. 466), Burke had identified primitive natural rights as the fundamental principle of the most radical religious Dissenters, the principle which distinguished them sharply from both Catholicism and Anglicanism. But Burke was always careful to distinguish these revolutionary Dissenters from those who merely wished to practice their private faith in peace.

18. Burke, *Speeches*, IV, 5–6 and 51. See also pp. 8–9 and 52. Mackintosh stated that "all theories which suppose the actual existence of any state antecedent to the social, might be convicted of futility and falsehood" (*Vindiciae Gallicae* [London, 1791], p. 206). This rejection of the state of nature may well have been the basis of Mackintosh's eventual agreement with Burke concerning the French Revolution. Burke's position toward the state of nature is excellently summarized in an anonymous work written in his defense: "These internal enemies to our happy constitution meditate its destruction, as an infringement on the natural rights of man . . . those enviable rights which our painted ancestors enjoyed in common with the beasts of the field and the fowl of the air. . . . The teachers of the Rights of Man should recollect the difference between a civilized state and a state of nature. . . . They say that all men are born equal. This is their text. . . . . They infer that because all men are born equal, which however, is granting what they cannot prove, they must remain so" (*A General Reply to the Several Answerers of a Letter to a Noble Lord* [London, 1796], pp. 30–31 and 43–44). No scholar on Burke has ever mentioned this important anonymous pamphlet, written in defense of Burke's pension and position toward the French Revolution. From internal evidence it could have been written by Burke himself. A copy of this pamphlet is to be found in the New York Public Library. George Dallas, a contemporary of Burke, agreed with him that his pamphleteer enemies during the French Revolutionary period were essentially primitivists: "These men of the woods, or modern philosophers, wish to recall us to the shivering solitude of pastoral life" (*Thoughts upon Our Present Situation* [Dublin, 1793], p. 10).

19. Burke, *Reflections,* pp. 331–332. Burke's italics.

20. Burke, *New to the Old Whigs,* p. 95. Burke's italics. Vaughan agreed with Burke's criticism of the revolutionists' state of nature: "The truth is that the Revolutionists have never made up their mind whether the individual they have in view . . . is the individual as we know him in the civil state, or the individual as he must have been in the state of nature. All their principles point to the latter" (*Studies in the History of Political Philosophy Before and After Rousseau,* II, 49). For Vaughan's full account on this point see pp. 38–44.

21. Burke, *New to the Old Whigs,* p. 86. See also "Letter to Langrishe," p. 311.

22. Burke, *Speeches,* III, 476.

23. *Ibid.,* IV, 359. See also p. 479.

24. Burke, *Reflections,* p. 349.

25. "Mr. Burke objected much to that false refinement (which he called it) of this age, which had banished gilding from the ornamental parts of buildings. . . . He said he considered it as one of the many instances of the vanity of this age, that man should suppose he could improve all nature, and yet be so fastidious as to object to many good and generally approved ornaments of art" (Mrs. Crewe, "Extracts from Mr. Burke's Table-Talk at Crewe Hall," *Miscellanies of the Philobiblon Society* [London, 1862–1863], VII, 31 and 42–43; see also pp. 32–33).

26. Burke, *Reflections,* p. 376. Burke's italics.

27. Burke, "To the National Assembly," pp. 527–528.

28. Burke, *Reflections,* pp. 334–335. See also pp. 282, 306, 437–438, 440, 452, 454–455, 515; *Regicide Peace,* pp. 255–256; *New to the Old Whigs,* pp. 28–29, 109–111; *The Policy of the Allies,* p. 419; *On the Duration of Parliaments,* p. 133.

29. Burke, *An Abridgment of History,* p. 294. See also pp. 295–305, 414, and 416. I shall demonstrate the importance of manners and laws in Burke's conception of the relation of Church and State.

30. *Ibid.,* p. 196. See also pp. 279–280 and 354.

31. Quoted by Burke, *Reflections,* p. 438. For an analysis and refutation of St. Étienne's primitivism, see John Gifford, *A Plain Address to the Common Sense of the People of England* (London, 1792), pp. 13 ff.

32. Burke, *A Vindication of Natural Society,* preface, p. 4.

33. John Locke, *Second Treatise on Government,* VIII, 101.

34. Leo Strauss, *Natural Right and History* (Chicago: University of Chicago Press, 1953), p. 230.

35. Willmoore Kendall, *John Locke and the Doctrine of Majority-Rule* (Urbana, Ill.: University of Illinois Press, 1941), p. 74.

36. Ernest Barker, *Essays on Government* (London: Oxford University Press, 1951), p. 98. See also p. 97.

37. Locke, *Second Treatise on Government,* VIII, 120. See also Kendall, *op. cit.,* pp. 104–107. "There is indeed such emphasis on the public good in

the 'Essay,' that Locke's thought may justly be termed 'Utilitarian' in the broadest sense of the word" (Henry V. S. Ogden, "The Rejection of the Antithesis of Nature and Art in English Political Writings, 1760–1800," Ph.D. thesis, University of Chicago, 1936, p. 5; see also pp. 6–7).

38. Strauss, *Natural Right and History*, p. 248.

39. *The Spirit of John Locke on Civil Government* (Sheffield, 1793), preface, p. viii.

40. See Ogden, *op. cit.*, pp. 7, 15–16, and 18–32.

41. Ogden, *op. cit.*, pp. 107–128.

42. See Mary Wollstonecraft Godwin, *A Vindication of the Rights of Man* (London, 1790), pp. 11, 40–41, 36, 60–61, 64–65, 12, 17–18, and 20.

43. See Mrs. Catherine Macaulay Graham, *Observations on the Reflections of Burke* (London, 1791), pp. 23 and 30. All italics are Mrs. Graham's. See also pp. 4 and 19, 30 and 33.

44. "W. C.," *A Short Essay on Whigs and Tories* (London, 1791), p. 3. See also pp. 4–11, 12, 16–17, and 23.

45. See Joseph Towers, *Thoughts on the Commencement of a New Parliament, with Remarks on the Letter of the Rt. Hon. Edmund Burke, on the Revolution in France* (Dublin, 1791), pp. 2–3, 49, 100, 62–65, 75–78, and 113.

46. Charles Pigott, *Strictures on the New Political Tenets of Edmund Burke* (London, 1791), pp. 84–86. See also pp. 58–63, 70, 72–73, and 80–81. As Arthur O. Lovejoy has said, it may be doubted that Rousseau was a primitivist, and that he really favored an intermediary simple civil society somewhere between a state of nature and the too complex civil society of Europe. See "The Supposed Primitivism of Rousseau's *Discourse on Inequality*," in *Essays in the History of Ideas* (Baltimore: The Johns Hopkins Press, 1948). Nevertheless, the desire to return to any supposed or real simple civil society is quite as revolutionary as the doctrine of primitivism. Pigott's belief that man's depravity originates in government as such differs from Rousseau's position only as revolutionary primitivism differs from revolutionary simplicity. Several other critics of Burke also appealed to Rousseau to justify revolutionary simplicity.

47. Thomas Paine, *Rights of Man*, Part I (London, 1791), pp. 17, 26, and 75; Part II, pp. 10, 26, 41, and 45. See also Part I, pp. 46, 78–79, 120–121; Part II, pp. 12–13. Sir Leslie Stephen suggested how the close parallel between Paine's political and religious theories is related to his antithesis of nature and art: "Paine's doctrine may be given in two words. Kings, like priests, are cheats and impostors. The dawn of the 'Age of Reason' implies the disappearance of royalty from politics as of superstition from religion. Democracy corresponds in the one sphere to Deism in the other. It is the teaching of pure unsophisticated Nature, and the new gospel is the effectual counterblast to all the nonsense with which statesmen have for their own base purposes imposed upon the people whom they enslaved. These doctrines are laid down as absolutely and unhesitatingly as the

axioms of a geometer; and Paine is, in all sincerity, incapable of understanding that there can be any other side to the question" (*History of English Thought in the Eighteenth Century* [London, 1881], II, 262). Halévy has pointed out that to Paine "democracy is the nearest approach to a society without government," a theory dear to the heart of Paine. Halévy added: "Paine would not have objected to this view that the democratic regime is the nearest approach to the state of nature" (*The Growth of Philosophic Radicalism*, pp. 129–130).

48. Paine, *Rights of Man*, Part I, pp. 47–51.

49. *Ibid.*, pp. 55–56. See also p. 131. "His [Paine's] doctrine of natural rights at times involves an antithesis of nature and art by making the state of nature a primitive or pre-political state" (Ogden, *op. cit.*, p. 122; see also pp. 123–128).

50. Joseph Priestley, *Letters to Edmund Burke Occasioned by His Reflections* (London, 1791), p. 25. "Lurking beneath the radical part of Priestley's thought is the antithesis of nature and art. Civil society is contrasted with an imaginary state of nature, and natural liberty is presented as at least a theoretical good" (Ogden, *op. cit.*, p. 50).

51. Mark Wilks, *The Origin and Stability of the French Revolution* (London, 1791), p. 28. See also pp. 29 and 30–70.

52. *The Political Crisis* (London, 1791), pp. 5–8.

53. *Ibid.*, pp. 20–21, 72, and 119. See also pp. 73 and 114–116.

54. Sir Brooke Boothby, *Observations on the Appeal from the New to the Old Whigs* (London, 1792), pp. 91–93. Boothby's italics.

55. Francis Stone, *An Examination of Burke's Reflections* (London, 1792), pp. 2–3, 43, 48–50, and 63. For other examples of appeals to the simplicity of the Saxon constitution, and its connection with the primitive "rights of man," see pp. 3–4, 13, 26, 29, 36–37, 45, 53–54, 57, 59–65, 68, 70–71, 101, 179–181, and 185–186. Granville Sharp and Major Cartwright also advocated a return to simple Saxon institutions.

56. *Ibid.*, pp. 176–177. See also pp. 200, 206. This revolutionary idea is the climax point in Stone's attack on Burke's supposed Catholicism (pp. 8, 67–68, 88–89, 105–106, 120, and 163), and on the Church hierarchy in France (pp. 80–81, 158–162). Stone's antithesis of nature and art reveals the usual dislike of an aesthetic appeal in religious worship: "As a plain building, free from ornament, is better calculated to promote spiritual worship, than the gorgeous finery of modern churches, a wise man will think 'ribbands and laces and national cockades' more worthy objects of expenditure than the embellishment of temples with pictures, with images, with shewy gilt ginger-bread altar-pieces. . . . To these splendid temples, which can have no other tendency than to introduce gross sensual ideas into pure spiritual worship, a wise man prefers a decent unornamented place of worship for his God" (pp. 177–178). This antiaestheticism is a commonplace among Burke's critics, and is derived from their inbred Puritanism.

57. *Ibid.*, pp. 171–172. See also p. 188. "The order of nobility," wrote Stone, "is a trespass on the natural equal rights of men," and Burke, by being "a zealous advocate for the gewgaw trappings . . . of royalty," and through his defense of chivalry and aesthetic ornaments, is an enemy of natural rights. See pp. 33–34, 57, 61, 88, 91, 136, 138–153, 154–156, 162–163, and 171–172.

58. *Ibid.*, p. 88. See also pp. 89–90.

59. *Ibid.*, pp. 61–62. See also pp. 65, 68, 70–71, and 90.

60. George Rous, *Thoughts on Government; Occasioned by Mr. Burke's Reflections* (London, 1791), p. 30.

61. George Rous, *A Letter to Burke in Reply to His Appeal from the New to the Old Whigs* (London, 1791), p. 19.

62. *Ibid.*, pp. 20–21. Rous's italics.

63. *Six Essays on: Natural Rights, Liberty and Slavery, Consent of the People, Equality, Religious Establishments, the French Revolution* (London, 1792), pp. 1–4. Author's italics.

64. Elie Halévy has shown that in many vital points the seventeenth-century religious Dissenters held the same doctrines as the eighteenth-century political radicals. See *The Growth of Philosophic Radicalism*, pp. 137–138.

65. For example, William Hazlitt noted that Wordsworth during his revolutionary period made an antithesis between nature and art: "His poetry is founded on setting up an opposition . . . between the natural and the artificial. All the traditions of learning, all the superstitions of age, are obliterated [in trying] to return to the simplicity of nature. Kings, queens, priests, nobles, the altar and the throne, the distinctions of rank, birth, wealth, power . . . are not to be found here" (*The Spirit of the Age* in *The Complete Works of William Hazlitt*, ed. P. P. Howe [London, 1930], II, 87). See also Basil Willey, "Wordsworth and the Locke Tradition," in *The Seventeenth Century Background* (New York: Columbia University Press, 1950), pp. 296–309.

66. See Halévy, *The Growth of Philosophic Radicalism*, pp. 39, 42, 57, 77–78, 114–116, 143, 146–147, 170, 179–180, 182–185, 190, 196–197. In stating how the Natural Law is perceived, even Blackstone, who certainly revered precedents, was deeply influenced by the eighteenth-century zeal for simplicity and utility: "God has not perplexed the law of nature with a multitude of abstracted rules and precepts, as some have vainly surmised, but has graciously reduced the rule of obedience to this one paternal precept, 'that man should pursue his own true and substantial happiness.' This is the foundation of what we call ethics, or natural law" (*Commentaries on the Laws of England*, Chitty ed. [New York, 1832], I, 27). Burke's critic, Francis Stone, in discussing the new code of law made by the French National Assembly, drew out the logical consequences of this emphasis on abstract simplicity: "If their code of law be sufficiently short, simple and clear, I should hope the professions of advocates and attornies might be abolished" (*An Examination of Burke's Reflections*, p. 194).

Notes to Chapter Six

1. Charles E. Vaughan, *The Romantic Revolt* (London: William Blackwood and Sons, 1923), p. 134.

2. "That conception of reason, as a creative faculty, which we have seen to be implicit in the ideas of Burke . . . lay at the very heart of the romantic movement" (Vaughan, *The Romantic Revolt*, p. 330). The fullest study of Burke's supposed identification with the romantic movement is Alfred Cobban's *Edmund Burke and the Revolt Against the Eighteenth Century* (London, 1929).

3. Basil Willey, *The Eighteenth Century Background* (New York: Columbia University Press, 1950), p. 249.

4. Burke, *Reflections*, pp. 427–428.

5. Arthur P. I. Samuels, *The Early Life, Correspondence and Writings of the Right Hon. Edmund Burke* (Cambridge, Eng.: At the University Press, 1923), pp. 29–30. See also pp. 28, 128–129. Hereinafter this work will be cited as *The Early Life*. As a student at Trinity College, Swift had objected to Burgersdicius on the same grounds as Burke. In *A Tale of a Tub* (Section IX), Swift castigated the impudence of rational logicians in a manner which anticipated Burke: "For what man, in the natural state or course of thinking, did ever conceive it in his power to reduce the notions of all mankind exactly to the same length, and breadth, and height of his own? Yet this is the first humble and civil design of all innovators in the empire of reason."

6. Burke, *Correspondence*, III, 410. Burke acknowledged that the British constitution permitted noncorporate groups and individuals to petition the House of Commons.

7. Arthur Woehl, "Burke's Reading," Ph.D. thesis, Cornell University, 1928, p. 56.

8. Burke, *Speech on Representation of the Commons*, p. 145. Burke's italics.

9. Burke, *Speech on Conciliation with the American Colonies*, p. 483. See also p. 491. Hereinafter this work will be cited as *Speech on Conciliation*. See also *Speech at Bristol Previous to the Election*, p. 128; *Speech on Economical Reform*, pp. 56–69.

10. For these quotations see *Regicide Peace*, p. 275; *Sheriffs of Bristol*, p. 39; *Reflections*, pp. 367 and 359; *Noble Lord*, p. 118; *Present Discontents*, p. 378. Burke may have had in mind Burton's quotation, "homo solus aut deus aut daemon," *The Anatomy of Melancholy*, Vol. I, sect. 2, mem. 2. Bacon's "Essay on Friendship" and Aristotle's *Politics*, I, 2, 14, also contain this idea.

11. Burke, *Speeches*, III, 226.

12. Burke, *Present Discontents*, p. 372.

13. Burke, *Speech on Representation of the Commons*, p. 147. See also *Reflections*, pp. 439–440. Elie Halévy has summarized this point well:

"Between an ancient opinion which has not been shaken by long experience through generations, and a new idea, born in the brain of a solitary thinker, the presumption is in favour of the ancient idea" (*The Growth of Philosophic Radicalism* [London, 1928], p. 163). For other examples of Burke's belief that man is most wise as a corporate being, see *Correspondence*, II, 257 and 277; III, 98, 106–108, 114, and 212; *Speeches*, I, 34, 69, 71, 102–103, 146, 323; II, 42, 50, 165, 169, and 268; III, 12, 17, 33–36, 45–47, 53, 248, 250, 261, 360, 459, and 482; IV, 57, 105–106, and 309.

14. "He [Burke] knew that man had affections and passions and powers of imagination, as well as hunger and thirst and the sense of heat and cold. He took his idea of political society from the pattern of private life, wishing, as he himself expresses it, to incorporate the domestic charities with the orders of the state. . . . He knew that the rules that form the basis of private morality are not founded in reason, that is, in the abstract properties of those things which are the subjects of them, but in the nature of man, and his capacity of being affected by certain things from habit, from imagination, and sentiment, as well as from reason" (William Hazlitt, "Character of Mr. Burke," in *The Collected Works of William Hazlitt*, ed. A. R. Waller and Arnold Glover [London, 1902–1904], VII, 306).

15. John Lester, "Analysis of the Conservative Thought of Edmund Burke," Harvard Univ. Ph.D. thesis, 1943, p. 74. Lester thought he found the source of Burke's faith in emotion in "the moral sense tradition" (p. 37), in the Scotch moral philosophers who followed Shaftesbury. Yet the "benevolent theory of morals" put forth by Francis Hutcheson, Shaftesbury's chief disciple, has many principles in common with Locke's ego-centered conception of human nature. It is significant that Hutcheson's phrase, "the greatest happiness of the greatest number," anticipated both the language and the utilitarian principles of Bentham. The "common sense" moral philosophy of Thomas Reid and the intuitionalist principles of Dugald Stuart were also strongly influenced by empirical assumptions. Dr. Price, Burke's chief "natural rights" enemy in the tradition of Locke, was an intuitionalist in his moral philosophy. The ethical theories of the Scotch moralists reveal the same inconsistencies with an empirical theory of knowledge as are found in Locke. Like the "natural rights" theorists who opposed Burke after 1789, they never distinguished clearly between a normative and descriptive conception of nature. The truth is that Burke's normative moral principles were centered in Ciceronian "right reason," rather than in Shaftesbury's "moral sense." Lester concluded that despite his skepticism toward speculative reason Burke's psychology followed the tradition of Locke. See "The Background in Eighteenth-Century Psychology," pp. 36–72, and "The Psychology of Edmund Burke," pp. 73–115. An understanding of the vital differences between the classical Natural Law and the revolutionary "natural rights" theory would have prevented many errors in Lester's otherwise excellent thesis.

16. Wilson Hudson, "An Index to the Works of Burke," Ph.D. thesis,

University of Chicago, 1947, p. 11. Hudson's italics. See also pp. 12–13.

17. Burke, *Speech on Warren Hastings in India,* May 30, 1794.

18. Burke, *Noble Lord,* p. 136.

19. Lester, *op. cit.,* p. 82. See also pp. 78 and 98.

20. Wilson O. Clough, "Reason and Genius—an Eighteenth Century Dilemma," *Philological Quarterly,* XXIII, 1 (Jan., 1944), 45. There are at least four grave errors in Clough's analysis of Burke's aesthetic theory: (1) Burke was always far more horrified at systematic *logical* reason than at "unreason" or divergence from mere logic. Clough failed to distinguish between Ciceronian "right reason," in which Burke believed, and the Hobbist or Lockian mathematical reason which was the basis of eighteenth-century rationalism. (2) Burke never held in any degree an "atomistic" theory of man. (3) Burke never isolated man's "sensory equipment" from reason, nor did the combination of senses and reason (not to mention emotion) teach him that nature "methodized" need be "static." (4) Burke considered the senses neither the source of "indisputable facts" nor the sole "power" in determining aesthetic responses found in reason. Divine revelation was the norm for moral facts and the foundation of all social and political principles, and as for aesthetic responses, Burke wrote: "I am afraid it is a practice much too common in inquiries of this nature, to attribute the cause of feelings which merely arise from the mechanical structure of our bodies, or from the natural frame and constitution of our minds, to certain conclusions of the reasoning faculty on the objects presented to us; for I should imagine, that the influence of reason in producing our passions is nothing near so extensive as is commonly believed" (*On the Sublime and Beautiful,* p. 79).

21. Arthur L. Woehl has proved that among other works of Locke "the *Essay Concerning Human Understanding* . . . Burke certainly read." See "Burke's Reading," p. 147. See also p. 26 and E. J. Payne, *Burke's Select Works* (Oxford, 1878), II, 329–330.

22. Burke, *On the Sublime and Beautiful,* pp. 68–70. The arguments Burke advanced to support his aesthetic and moral dualism are well worth reading. See pp. 68–74.

23. *Ibid.,* pp. 70–71. See also pp. 72–74.

24. Burke, *Reflections,* pp. 352–353. See also *Speeches,* II, 418–419; III, 456.

25. Burke, *Sheriffs of Bristol,* pp. 13–14.

26. Burke, *Reflections,* p. 359.

27. *Ibid.,* pp. 353–354. See also pp. 359 and 413–414.

28. Adam Smith, *Wealth of Nations* (London, 1896), II, 293.

29. Sir Brooke Boothby, *Observations on the Rights of Man* (London, 1791), p. 181.

30. Halévy, *The Growth of Philosophic Radicalism,* p. 213.

31. Burke, *Correspondence,* III, 448. See also pp. 478–479, 523; IV, 321–322.

32. Burke, *Two Letters to Gentlemen in Bristol,* pp. 51–52. Burke's italics. See also pp. 53–54 and *Speech at Bristol Previous to the Election,* pp. 134–137; *Speeches,* I, 297; *Correspondence,* II, 211–220.

33. Burke, *Reflections,* p. 412. See also p. 413.

34. Burke, *The Conduct of the Minority,* pp. 493–494. See also *Regicide Peace,* p. 318.

35. Burke, "Popery Laws," p. 21. For other examples of Burke's belief in man's divinely ordained nature, see *Regicide Peace,* pp. 164 and 216; *Reflections,* p. 333; *Present Discontents,* pp. 309–310; *Speech on Conciliation,* p. 467; *Two Letters to Gentlemen in Bristol,* p. 52.

36. Burke, *Correspondence,* I, 331. See also pp. 332–333.

37. *Ibid.,* III, 512. For further instances of the theme of man's common and inevitable infirmity, see *Correspondence,* I, 375; II, 195; *Present Discontents,* pp. 307, 381; *Sheriffs of Bristol,* pp. 14 and 38; *Reflections,* pp. 354, 414; *Regicide Peace,* p. 397; *Letter to William Elliot,* p. 75; *Speeches,* I, 51, 69, 71, 105, 113, 118, 157, 202, 272; II, 165, 171, 344; III, 44, 331, 335, 383, 527; IV, 215, 303, and 381.

38. Burke, *Speech at Bristol Previous to the Election,* p. 130.

39. Burke, *Speech on the Duration of Parliaments,* p. 132. See also pp. 133–135. "To the Deity must be left the task of infinite perfection, while to us poor, weak, incapable mortals, there is no rule of conduct so safe as experience" (*Speeches,* IV, 23). By "experience" Burke meant man's corporate experience through history and not merely immediate individual empirical observation and rational reflection. See also *Speech on the Reform of Representation,* pp. 144–145; Mrs. Mary Leadbeater, *The Leadbeater Papers* (London, 1882), I, 116–117.

40. Burke, *Correspondence,* III, 117. See also p. 116.

41. Burke, *Speeches,* I, 82. See also III, 60.

42. Burke, *Correspondence,* III, 41–42. See also *Speeches,* IV, 303.

43. *Ibid.,* p. 39. To Hastings's friend, Capt. Mercer, Burke wrote in February 1790: "It is plain, you would think every thing justified by your warm good intentions."

44. Burke, *Speeches,* II, 337; III, 488–489. See also I, 54, 307, 357; II, 445; III, 64–65, 421, 477; IV, 5, 43, 66, 337, and 374.

45. Samuels, *The Early Life,* p. 216. For other examples of Burke's adherence to the Anglican tradition, see Woehl, "Burke's Reading," pp. 82–83, 141, and 151; E. J. Payne, *Burke's Select Works,* I, xlii and xxx–xxxvi; II, xxiii, 314, 316, 352–353, and 383; III, 365.

46. Woehl, "Burke's Reading," p. 157.

47. Mrs. Crewe, "Extracts from Mr. Burke's Table-Talk at Crewe Hall," *Miscellanies of the Philobiblon Society,* VII (London, 1862–1863), 55.

48. For an excellent analysis of Butler's theory of man, see Albert Lefevre's two articles, "Self-Love and Benevolence in Butler's Ethical System," and "Conscience and Obligation in Butler's Ethical System," in *Philosophical Review,* IX (1900), 167–187 and 395–410. Lefevre agreed with Henry

Sidgwick (*History of Ethics*, 5th ed. [London, 1902], pp. 194 ff.) that Butler's ethical system is dualistic, and the antithesis of the eighteenth-century utilitarian pleasure-pain calculus. Mario Einaudi, in "The British Background of Burke's Political Philosophy," *Political Science Quarterly*, XLIX (Dec., 1934), 576–598, has shown Burke's indebtedness to Butler. Some observations have also been added by John A. Lester, *op. cit.*, pp. 65–67 and 83–84.

49. Burke, *Correspondence*, III, 453.

50. Burke, "Popery Laws," p. 45. Burke has in mind the histories of Temple and Clarendon. This inversion of "the known order of nature" was a common assumption in English policy toward Ireland. Burke always rejected the theory that force would establish a just order in Ireland. See *Correspondence*, I, 42–43, 337–338; II, 271–272; IV, 31–34, 75–79, 396–398, and 449; *Laurence Correspondence*, pp. 206–208, 215–216, and 236.

51. Burke, *Correspondence*, II, 195.

52. Burke, *Sheriffs of Bristol*, p. 38.

53. Burke, *New to the Old Whigs*, p. 5. See also *Observations on "The Present State of the Nation,"* pp. 294–295.

54. See Burke, *Correspondence*, I, 293–295, 296–298, 300–302, 373–374, 381–383, 487–489; II, 196–197; IV, Appendix, pp. 526–531, 550–551; *Speeches*, I, 212, 215–217, 226–229, 409; II, 66, 487; III, 319–320, 340, 531–532; IV, 441.

55. See Samuels, *The Early Life*, pp. 43, 51, 126, 162, and 167.

56. Ross Hoffman and Paul Levack, *Burke's Politics* (New York: Alfred A. Knopf, 1949), pp. xiv–xv.

57. For Burke's remarks on man's corruption in politics, see *Present Discontents*, pp. 313 ff.; *Speech on the Duration of Parliaments*, p. 141; *Sheriffs of Bristol*, p. 21; *On the Affairs of India*, pp. 80–81, 107, 169; *On the Nabob of Arcot's Debts*, pp. 138 ff., 160–161, 173, 176, 185, 188, 192, 194, and 196.

58. Burke, *Reflections*, p. 410. See also pp. 417–418.

59. *Ibid.*, p. 353.

60. Burke, *Present Discontents*, p. 332. See also p. 336. See also Mrs. Mary Leadbeater, *The Leadbeater Papers*, II, 116.

61. Burke, a review of "Essays on the Importance of an Inquiry into the Human Mind," *Annual Register* (1764), p. 192.

62. Burke wrote to his friend Dupont in October 1789 that anything which "destroys our social nature . . . transforms us into something little better than . . . wild beasts" (*Correspondence*, III, 106).

63. See Arthur Samuels, *The Early Life*, pp. 30 and 82–83. "Pascal's *Thoughts* were known to him while at Trinity" (Mrs. Mary Leadbeater, *The Leadbeater Papers*, II, 59–60).

64. See for example Burke, *Correspondence*, I, 278, 489–490; II, 346; III, 127; IV, 36.

65. The strong Stoicism which characterized Burke's religious piety was

revealed at age sixteen, in a letter to Shackleton, when a flood which confined him to his room occasioned some reflections on man's ambiguous state and proper attitude toward his limitations: "I considered how little man is, yet in his mind how great! He is lord and master of all things, yet scarce can command anything. He is given a freedom of his will, but wherefore? Was it but to torment and perplex him the more? How little avails the freedom, if the objects he is to act upon be not as much disposed to obey as he is to command? What well laid and what better executed scheme of his is there, but what a small change of nature is sufficient to defeat and entirely abolish? If but one element happens to encroach a little on the other, what confusion may it not create in his affairs! What havoc! What destruction! The servant destined to his use confines, menaces, and frequently destroys this mighty, this feeble lord. I have a mind to go abroad today—my business and my pleasure require it; but the river has overflown its banks, and I can't stir without apparent danger to my life. What, then, shall I do? Shall I rage, fret, and accuse Providence of injustice? No, let me rather lament that I do not what is always right; what depends not on the fortuitous changes of this world, nor the blind sport of fortune, but remains unalterably fixed in the mind; untouched though this shattered globe should fall in pieces, and bury us in the ruins" (Samuels, *The Early Life*, p. 84).

66. For these passages see Burke, *On the Sublime and Beautiful*, p. 50; *Two Letters to Gentlemen in Bristol*, p. 52; *Regicide Peace*, pp. 321-322; *Laurence Correspondence*, p. 34. See also pp. 56, 253, and 301. For other examples of Burke's Stoicism see *Correspondence*, I, 386; II, 166; III, 356-357, and 449; IV, 380-381, and 421; *Speeches*, I, 98 and 346; "Thoughts on Scarcity," p. 89; "Popery Laws," p. 21.

67. In a general way several scholars have suggested that Burke's political philosophy derived its ultimate moral basis and spirit from his Stoical Christianity. Ross Hoffman wrote: "On this bed rock of humble submission to the Mind that has made the world and man Burke based his political philosophy" (*Burke's Politics*, p. xiv). "For Burke the divine authorship of human nature is a fact never questioned, a fact on which the political philosopher may proudly build his creed. . . . There is something genuinely medieval in his firm conviction that all human affairs, great and small, are under the supreme and constant guidance of God" (John A. Lester, *op. cit.*, pp. 119 and 81; see also pp. 107 and 114).

68. Burke, *Speeches*, I, 337. William Hazlitt understood that Burke's conception of man went far beyond his merely biological needs: "He saw in the construction of society other principles at work, and other capacities of fulfilling the desires, and perfecting the nature of man, besides those of securing the equal enjoyment of the means of animal life. . . . He thought that the wants and happiness of men were not to be provided for, as we provide for those of a herd of cattle, merely by attending to their

physical necessities. He thought more nobly of his fellows" (*The Collected Works of William Hazlitt*, VII, 306).

69. Burke, *Regicide Peace*, p. 116. See also Samuels, *The Early Life*, pp. 68 and 84; *Reflections*, p. 375.

70. Burke, *Correspondence*, II, 172.

71. See Morley, *Burke*, pp. 158–160.

72. See Burke, *Speeches*, I, 158–161.

73. Burke, *Correspondence*, II, 18–19.

74. Burke, *Speech on the Middlesex Election*, p. 127.

75. Burke had stated in his "Popery Laws" that "equity grows out of the great rule of equality, grounded upon our common nature."

76. Thomas Cooper, *A Reply to Mr. Burke's Invective Against Mr. Cooper and Mr. Watt in the House of Commons* (Manchester, 1792), p. 79.

77. Thomas Paine, *Rights of Man*, Part I (London, 1791), p. 49. See also p. 50.

78. William Belsham, *Examination of an Appeal from the New to the Old Whigs* (London, 1792), p. 63.

79. Benjamin Bousfield, *Observations on Edmund Burke's Pamphlet on the French Revolution* (London, 1792), pp. 37–38.

Notes to Chapter Seven

1. Burke, *The Policy of the Allies*, p. 456. See also pp. 425 and 455; *Regicide Peace*, pp. 204–205.

2. Burke, *Speech on the Petition of the Unitarians*, p. 115.

3. Burke, *Reflections*, p. 420. See also pp. 421 and 430.

4. Burke, *An Abridgment of English History*, pp. 232, 300, and 215.

5. *Ibid.*, 238. See also pp. 196, 244–247, and 416–417.

6. *Ibid.*, pp. 239, 241, and 253.

7. *Ibid.*, p. 253. For Burke's thesis that the Church fostered social manners through religion, and abated the ferocity of the barbarians by making them more mild and sociable, see pp. 184–187, 194–196, 215, 217, 233, 238–241, 244, 247, 254–255, 290, 294, 332, 367, and 416. See also *Sheriffs of Bristol*, p. 11; *Reflections*, p. 311; *The Policy of the Allies*, p. 426; *Address to the British Colonists in North America*, p. 480; *Letter to Henry Dundas*, p. 523; *Sketch of the Negro Code*, pp. 527–530.

8. *Ibid.*, p. 306. See also pp. 308 and 347.

9. Burke, *Reflections*, p. 370. See also pp. 372 and 375; *An Abridgment of English History*, pp. 244 and 247.

10. *Ibid.*, pp. 350–351.

11. This sketch was first printed in Dixon Wecter's *Edmund Burke and His Kinsmen* (Boulder, Colo.: University of Colorado, 1939), pp. 12–16.

12. Burke, *Reflections,* pp. 349–351. See also pp. 348 and 352; *An Abridgment of English History,* pp. 309 and 331–332.

13. See Burke, *Regicide Peace,* p. 215. See also *An Abridgment of English History,* p. 309.

14. Burke, "Popery Laws," p. 23.

15. Burke, *Regicide Peace,* p. 214. See also p. 215; *Reflections,* pp. 420–421 and 430; *Speech on the Relief of Protestant Dissenters,* p. 110; *An Abridgment of English History,* p. 309.

16. Burke, *Letter to William Smith* (1795), p. 52.

17. Burke, "Popery Laws," p. 32.

18. See Robert H. Murray, *Edmund Burke, A Biography* (London: Oxford University Press, 1931), pp. 72 and 292–293.

19. James A. Froude, *The English in Ireland in the Eighteenth Century* (New York, 1881), III, 24.

20. Burke, "Letter to Langrishe" (1792), p. 313. Burke's italics. Among the "positive doctrines" which Anglicanism retained from Roman Catholicism was the principle that reason is superior to will in the nature of God and man. For this principle in Burke's political philosophy, see Ernest Barker, *Essays on Government* (London: Oxford University Press, 1945), p. 230.

21. Burke, *Speech on the Affairs of Ireland,* p. 88. Burke's italics. See also "Laws Against Irish Catholics," p. 292; "Letter to Langrishe," p. 313.

22. Burke, *Speech at Bristol Previous to the Election,* p. 145.

23. Burke, *Reflections,* pp. 371–372. See also p. 358; "Letter to Langrishe," p. 340.

24. Burke, *Speech on the Acts of Uniformity* (1772), p. 96.

25. Burke, "Letter to Langrishe," p. 309. Burke's italics.

26. Burke, *Speech on the Relief of Protestant Dissenters,* p. 113.

27. Burke, *Speech on the Petition of the Unitarians,* p. 126. For a different treatment of Burke's Anglicanism as it relates to his political philosophy, see Alfred Cobban, *Edmund Burke and the Revolt Against the Eighteenth Century* (London, 1929), pp. 238–241, 244–245, 258, and 262.

28. Robert M. Hutchins, "The Theory of the State: Edmund Burke," *The Review of Politics* (April, 1943), p. 145.

29. Burke, *Regicide Peace,* p. 207. See also *An Abridgment of English History,* p. 236.

30. Burke, *Reflections,* p. 354.

31. *Ibid.,* p. 370. See also *Sheriffs of Bristol,* p. 31.

32. Burke, *Regicide Peace,* p. 407.

33. For Burke's use of this analogy, see *Regicide Peace,* p. 152.

34. Burke, *Reflections,* pp. 368–369. See also *New to the Old Whigs,* pp. 79–80; *The Conduct of the Minority,* p. 498.

35. For an excellent summary of these essential differences, see Ernest Barker, "The Theory of the Social Contract in Locke, Rousseau and Hume," in *Essays on Government* (London: Oxford University Press,

1951), pp. 86–119. Barker's failure to distinguish between the classical and Scholastic Natural Law and the seventeenth- and eighteenth-century revolutionary "rights of man" invalidates parts of his article.

36. No scholar has yet noted the close connection between Burke's conception of the social contract and his belief in the classical and Scholastic Natural Law. As I noted in Chapter Three, note 95, Vaughan, Hearnshaw, Ogden, and Morley dismissed Burke's great passage on the social contract as a mere rhetorical flourish. To date, the most valid statement of the true significance of the contract to Burke has been expressed by Ernest Barker: "The idea of the divine concordance of the Universe, which includes the State in its scheme, haunted the mind of Burke. Not only does it occur in the *Reflections* of 1790 . . . where he speaks of the 'eternal society . . . connecting the visible and invisible world, according to a fixed compact sanctioned by the inviolable oath which holds all physical and all moral natures, each in their appointed place': it already appears in his speech of 1783 on the East India Bill. . . . It is also, and finely, expressed in his *Appeal from the New to the Old Whigs* in 1791 . . . where he speaks of the predisposed order of things in which, by a divine tactic, we are all disposed and marshalled to act the part which belongs to the place assigned us. The underlying philosophy . . . is fundamentally Catholic or Thomistic (though Burke himself was a loyal member of the Church of England); or again it may be said to find its analogies, though not its sources, in the philosophy of Suarez and the other theologians of the Counter Reformation" (*Essays on Government*, p. 218).

37. Burke, *An Abridgment of English History*, p. 281.

38. *Ibid.*, pp. 311, 340–342, 349, 354, and 357. See also *Reflections*, pp. 305–308, and *New to the Old Whigs*, p. 65.

39. *Ibid.*, p. 402. See also pp. 386–387, 389, 398–399, 401, and 403–406.

40. Burke, *Speech on the Army Estimates*, p. 277.

41. Burke, *Reflections*, p. 368.

42. Burke, *Speech on the Reform of Representation*, p. 153.

43. See *ibid.*, and *Speech on the Duration of Parliaments* and *Speech on the Economical Reform*, especially pp. 56 ff.

44. Burke, *Reflections*, p. 395.

45. Burke, *Speech on the Economical Reform*, p. 106.

46. See Burke, *Present Discontents*, pp. 313 ff., especially pp. 324–325. See also *An Address to the King*, pp. 460–476.

47. Burke, *Speech on Fox's East India Bill*, p. 180.

48. Burke, *New to the Old Whigs*, p. 34. See also pp. 17, 35, 46, and 66; *Reflections*, pp. 299 and 397.

49. Burke, *Present Discontents*, p. 331.

50. Burke, *Speech on the Economical Reform*, p. 61. See also pp. 70–71; *Speech on the Conclusion of the Poll*, p. 448.

51. Burke, *Letter to William Smith*, p. 52.

52. Burke, *Speech on the Repeal of the Marriage Acts*, p. 170.

53. Burke, *Present Discontents*, p. 323. See also *Speech on the Nabob of Arcot's Debts*, p. 188.

54. Burke, *An Abridgment of English History*, p. 406. See also *A Vindication of Natural Society*, pp. 25–26; "Letter to Langrishe," p. 303. Burke's distrust of aristocracy as a basis for government was constant throughout his life. In his *Present Discontents* he stated that if the British constitution was to be altered he preferred to see it "resolved into any other form, than lost in that austere and insolent domination."

55. See Burke, *Speech on the Repeal of the Marriage Acts*, p. 170.

56. See Burke, *The Conduct of the Minority*, p. 500.

57. See Burke, *Speech from the Throne*, pp. 252–253, 259, 262. See also *The Conduct of the Minority*, pp. 500–503; *Speech on the Middlesex Election*, p. 127.

58. Burke, *Present Discontents*, p. 348. See also p. 380; *Speech on the Conclusion of the Poll*, p. 447.

59. Ernest Barker pointed out that Burke and St. Thomas Aquinas both accepted "the divine concordance of the universe." In addition to this implicit faith in the sovereignty of Natural Law, Barker noted other vital principles common to Burke and St. Thomas: "The 'spirit of religion' meant far more for Burke than a vesture or decoration. It was the inmost essence of his theory of politics. Already in his *Thoughts on the Cause of the Present Discontents*, which goes back to the year 1770, he is professing a theory of government which had already been enunciated by St. Thomas Aquinas. St. Thomas, who has been called by Lord Acton 'the first Whig,' developed a theory of government (or *potestas*) according to which the *principium*, or essence, of power was an emanation or delegation proceeding from God . . . but the *modus* or constitutional form of power was determined, and the *exercitium* or actual enjoyment of power was conferred, by the people. This was a combination of a doctrine of the divine right of authority with a doctrine of its popular origin. Burke made the same combination, in practically identical terms. . . . How Burke came to know and to use the theory of St. Thomas is a problem which deserves investigation. In the *Reflections* he also uses the same Thomistic terminology, when he speaks of the Bill of Rights of 1689 as 'not changing the *substance*, but regulating the *mode* and describing the *persons*' vested with the exercise of power" (*Essays on Government*, pp. 224–225). For the other points common to Burke and St. Thomas, see pp. 218–219, 226, and 230.

60. Burke, *Speech on the Economical Reform*, p. 58.

61. Burke, *Speech at Bristol Previous to the Election*, p. 167.

62. Burke, *Speech on the Duration of Parliaments*, p. 134. For another account of Burke's attitude toward the people, see Ernest Barker, *Essays on Government*, pp. 198–201.

63. Burke, *Letter to Charles J. Fox* (1779), p. 450.

64. For a more extensive account of the function of the House of Commons, see *Present Discontents*, pp. 347 ff.

65. Burke, *Letter to William Elliot*, p. 80. See also *New to the Old Whigs*, pp. 60–61; "To the National Assembly," p. 552.

66. Burke, *Speech on the Army Estimates*, p. 280. See also *Speech on the Middlesex Election*, p. 126. Burke's principle of divided but combined powers implied a conviction that each branch of the state should be independent within the constitution. It is possible that Burke voiced these combined principles while he was still an undergraduate at Trinity College, Dublin: "I will venture to affirm, what is an allowed truth, as in the grand, so in the lesser subordinate communities, the safety of the whole depends on the proper balance of power among the parts; and in this balance consists in the mutual independency of the parts; by which independency I mean an absolute uninfluenced freedom in their councils and proceedings; nevertheless every part is answerable to the rest for the consequences of these proceedings, so far as they affect the whole" ("Free Briton," in Arthur Samuels, *The Early Life, Correspondence and Writings of the Rt. Hon. Edmund Burke* [Cambridge, Eng.: At the University Press, 1923], pp. 334–335; see also p. 380). The authenticity of Burke's authorship of the "Free Briton" has been doubted. There is no doubt, however, that Burke believed in the independence of each branch of the British state. In February 1788, in a speech during Hastings' trial, Burke analyzed the nature and extent of independent power, its origin as a trust from God, and its responsibility through conscience to divine law: "The King in this country is undoubtedly unaccountable for his actions. The house of Lords . . . if it should ever abuse its judicial power, and give such a judgment as it ought not to give, whether from fear of popular clamour on the one hand, or predilection to the prisoner [Hastings] on the other; if they abuse their judgments, there is no calling them to account for it. And so, if the Commons should abuse their power, nay, if they should have been so greatly delinquent as not to have prosecuted this offender, they could not be accountable for their acts, because we exercise a part of the supreme power. But are they less criminal, less rebellious against the Divine Majesty?" (*Works*, XIII, 171).

67. Burke, *Speech on the Conclusion of the Poll*, p. 448. See also *Two Letters to Gentlemen in Bristol*, p. 47.

68. Burke, *Reflections*, p. 309. See also *New to the Old Whigs*, p. 110.

69. Burke, *Regicide Peace*, p. 254.

70. Burke, *Present Discontents*, p. 368. See also *Speech on Conciliation*, p. 500; *Reflections*, pp. 448–449 and 518.

71. Burke, *Speech on the Army Estimates* (1790), p. 274.

72. Burke, *Present Discontents*, p. 314.

73. *Ibid.*, p. 369.

74. *Ibid.*, p. 313. See also pp. 316, 318–324, and 329; John MacCunn, *The Political Philosophy of Burke* (London, 1913), p. 153.

75. Because Burke made a case for "virtual" rather than "actual" representation, and said some things favorable to the character of Louis XVI, it has been argued seriously by Robert M. Hutchins that his political

philosophy "makes a case for absolute monarchy" ("The Theory of Oligarchy: Edmund Burke," *The Thomist,* Maritain Vol. [New York: Sheed and Ward, 1943], p. 67).

76. Burke, *Speech at Bristol Previous to the Election,* p. 163.

77. See *New to the Old Whigs,* pp. 25–29. See also *The Conduct of the Minority,* p. 500.

78. Burke, "Thoughts on Scarcity," p. 107. Burke's italics.

79. Burke, *Speech on Reform of Representation,* p. 149.

80. Burke, *Speech on the Petition of the Unitarians,* p. 115. See also *An Abridgment of English History,* pp. 357–358.

81. Burke, *Reflections,* p. 371. See also *An Abridgment of English History,* p. 359; *Regicide Peace,* p. 422; *A Vindication of Natural Society,* p. 9.

82. For a different interpretation of Burke's conception of Church and State, see John MacCunn, *op. cit.,* pp. 122–143 and 144–189.

83. See Burke, *Noble Lord,* pp. 142–143. For Burke's consistency on this vital point between the American and French revolutions, see also *Speech on Conciliation,* p. 453.

84. Burke, *Reflections,* p. 452. See also pp. 402, 443–444; *The Policy of the Allies,* pp. 418–422.

85. Burke, *Regicide Peace,* p. 397. See also pp. 153, 168, 219–220; *New to the Old Whigs,* pp. 80 and 106; *Letter to William Elliot,* pp. 75–77; *Noble Lord,* pp. 142–144; *Speech on the Reform of Representation,* p. 149.

86. Burke, *Present Discontents,* p. 347. See also p. 348.

87. Burke, "Thoughts on Scarcity," p. 108.

88. Burke, *Regicide Peace,* p. 208. See also *Correspondence,* III, 138–139; *Speech on the Relief of Protestant Dissenters,* p. 106.

89. Burke, *Sheriffs of Bristol,* p. 11.

90. Burke, *Regicide Peace,* p. 210. See also p. 211.

91. Burke, *Reflections,* p. 350. See also pp. 311, 350, and 416. For other examples of how manners are related to laws throughout English history, see *An Abridgment of English History,* pp. 280, 294–295, 375, 417, 421. See also *Regicide Peace,* pp. 213–215, 404, 424, 428–429, and 433; *New to the Old Whigs,* p. 7.

92. Burke, *Regicide Peace,* p. 404.

93. See, for example, Thomas Paine, *Rights of Man,* Part I (London, 1791), pp. 26, 46; G. R. S. Taylor, *Modern English Statesmen* (London, 1920), pp. 154–155, 163–165, and 170. A. J. Grieve, in his notes to the Everyman edition of the *Reflections,* is typical in his error: "Burke's lament over the departed age of chivalry is of a piece with the universal longing for the good old times, a longing which is as old as it is untrue."

94. See Burke, *Speech on the Army Estimates,* p. 272.

95. Burke, *Reflections,* p. 350.

96. Burke, *Thoughts on French Affairs,* p. 358. See also *Letter to William Elliot,* pp. 74–75; *The Present State of Affairs,* pp. 397–407.

97. *Ibid.*, p. 360. However, see also *New to the Old Whigs,* pp. 101–103, and *Regicide Peace,* pp. 351 and 378–379.

98. *Ibid.*, p. 360.

99. See Burke, *The Policy of the Allies,* p. 448.

100. *Ibid.*, Appendix, p. 464. See also pp. 440–441; *Speech on the Army Estimates,* pp. 270, 275, 277; *Regicide Peace,* p. 226.

101. Burke, *Regicide Peace,* p. 311. See also p. 242.

102. *Ibid.*, p. 303. See also pp. 291 and 304.

103. Burke, *New to the Old Whigs,* p. 110. See also pp. 29, 108–111; *Sheriffs of Bristol,* p. 4; *To the British Colonists in North America,* pp. 482–483; *A Vindication of Natural Society,* pp. 34–35.

104. Burke, *Letter to William Smith,* p. 53. See also *Noble Lord,* p. 132; *Speech on the Relief of Protestant Dissenters,* p. 107; *Second Reading for Relief of Protestant Dissenters,* pp. 103–104; *Speech on the Acts of Uniformity,* p. 95.

105. See Burke, *An Abridgment of English History,* p. 318, and *Reflections,* p. 368. See also *Reflections,* pp. 364–365 and 371.

106. Burke, "Letter to Langrishe," p. 310. For an account of the important relationship between the king and the Church of England, see pp. 310–316.

107. Burke, *Letter to Richard Burke,* p. 72. See also *Speech on the Relief of Protestant Dissenters,* p. 112.

108. Burke, *Noble Lord,* pp. 137–138. This carefully revised passage illustrates the characteristic complexity of Burke's prose style. Burke frequently appealed to the total nature of man, so that the essential passages in his argument generally contain an image or figure to appeal to the senses, a philosophical idea to satisfy the mind, and an emotion centered in the instincts or moral sensibility—all bearing upon dramatic action.

Notes to Chapter Eight

1. Non-Calvinist Protestants, such as Pufendorf, generally held to a doctrine of grace which gave a superiority to the divine intellect rather than the divine will: "The things forbidden by the Natural Law are not therefore Evil because God hath forbidden them, but God therefore forbad them, because they were in themselves Evil: And on the other hand, the things enjoined by the same Law, are not made good or necessary by God's enjoining them; but were therefore enjoined by God, because they were in themselves simply good and necessary" (Pufendorf, *Of the Law of Nature and Nations* [Oxford, 1703], p. 97).

1a. East Lansing, Mich.: Michigan State College Press, 1950.

2. Richard Hooker, *Of the Laws of Ecclesiastical Polity* (Oxford, 1868–1876), I, ii, 5.

3. *Ibid.* In the words of Pufendorf, "God cannot but observe His prom-

ises" (*op. cit.,* p. 99). Burke's contemporary, William Blackstone, agreed on this vital point with Hooker and Pufendorf: "These are the eternal, immutable laws of good and evil to which the Creator Himself in all His dispensations conforms" (*Commentaries on the Laws of England,* Chitty ed. [New York, 1832], I, 27).

4. The idea of an absolute power which makes law is common to both the Calvinists and to Hobbes. God's commands are as absolute to the former as those of the "mortal God," the Leviathan, are to the latter. See Mosse, *The Struggle for Sovereignty in England,* p. 176.

5. Henry de Bracton, *Tractatus de legibus,* f. 5b.

6. Several excellent brief accounts of this famous encounter between the king and Coke are readily available. See Roscoe Pound, *The Spirit of the Law* (Boston, 1909); Rene A. Wormser, *The Law* (New York: Simon and Schuster, 1949), pp. 286–290; John C. H. Wu, *Fountain of Justice* (New York: Sheed and Ward, 1955), pp. 92–93.

7. Mosse, *op. cit.,* p. 171. See also p. 172.

8. For this vital point see Margaret A. Judson, "Growth of the Theory of Parliamentary Sovereignty in England, 1640–1660," Ph.D. thesis, Harvard University, 1935.

9. Burke, *New to the Old Whigs,* p. 30. Burke's insistence that his position toward the revolutions of 1688, 1775, and 1789 was consistently constitutional forms one of the major themes of this important work.

10. Burke, *Speech on the Duration of Parliaments* (1773), p. 134.

11. Burke, *Correspondence,* II, 340.

12. Burke, *Speech at Bristol Previous to the Election* (1780), p. 167. In recognizing that God Himself may not be "competent to alter the essential constitution of right and wrong," Burke implicitly accepted Hooker's conception of the divine contract, and the superiority in God of right reason or law to will or power.

13. *The Political Crisis,* p. 25. Belief in the absolute right of popular sovereignty runs through almost every reply to Burke's *Reflections.* For example, Thomas Paine wrote: "That which a whole nation chooses to do, it has the right to do." "The nation . . . has the right of changing its whole form of government" (*Rights of Man,* Part I, 12, and Part II, 130). "Despite their variety of expression, these writers all meant essentially the same thing—that the will of the people was the supreme law. The revolutionaries and the reformers of the period needed no other doctrine than this, for if it were accepted, political reforms must follow" (Carl Cone, "Pamphlet Replies to Burke's *Reflections*," *Social Science Quarterly,* XXVI [June, 1945], 27).

14. Lord Acton agreed with Burke on this vital point: "It is bad to be oppressed by a minority, but it is worse to be oppressed by a majority. For there is a reserve of latent power in the masses which, if it is called into play, the minority can seldom resist. But from the absolute will of an entire people there is no appeal, no redemption, no refuge but

treason" (*Essays on Freedom and Power* [Boston: The Beacon Press, 1949], p. 40). Among others, Sabine has pointed out that Locke, unlike Burke, contradicted his theory of individual "natural rights" by making majority will the basis of civil liberty and law. See for example Locke's *Of Civil Government*, Book II, sect. 96. Sabine's criticism of Locke is well taken: "If an individual's rights are really indefeasible, it is no better for him to be deprived of them by a majority than by a single tyrant; apparently it did not occur to Locke that a majority could be tyrannous" (*A History of Political Theory* [New York: Henry Holt, 1937], p. 533). This basic contradiction is also found in practically every reply to Burke's *Reflections*. English radicals such as Price, Paine, and Priestley frequently appealed to Locke and used the terminology of "nature" and "rights," but the utilitarian element in their thought put a premium on numbers and made majority or popular will the basis of their conception of political sovereignty. "New Whig" liberals, such as George Rous, James Mackintosh, and Charles J. Fox, were invariably utilitarians, and wished to reform parliament through representation based upon numbers. In France the Jacobins were involved in the same contradictions. They frequently appealed to "the rights of man," which they held to be universal and unchangeable, yet drew their theory of political sovereignty from *la volonté générale,* as popularized by Rousseau.

15. Burke, *Thoughts on French Affairs,* p. 352. See also pp. 353 ff., especially pp. 376–378. For other examples of Burke's argument against the sovereignty of absolute popular will, see also *New to the Old Whigs,* pp. 13–14, 44–45, 76–85, 93, and 108–109.

16. This important point has been established beyond any doubt by Eric Thompson in *Popular Sovereignty and the French Constituent Assembly, 1789–1791* (Manchester: Manchester University Press, 1952). In the preface to this book Thompson wrote: "Towards the end of the eighteenth century in France, the concept of the sovereignty of the 'general will' of the people had been widely disseminated amongst the mass of the people. It is true that the more elaborate treatment of the nature of the sovereign power, which had been contained in the works of Rousseau and other major treatises published during the second half of the century, was probably little known outside a small circle of intellectuals. But the concept of popular sovereignty itself had been popularised in thousands of pamphlets."

17. Burke, *The Conduct of the Minority,* p. 497. See also pp. 498–500.

18. "The origin of this phrase *la volonté générale* is uncertain. Montesquieu had used it as early as 1748 in the *Esprit des lois.* In 1755 it was used almost simultaneously by Diderot and Rousseau, the former in his article on Natural Law and the latter in his *Discourse on Political Economy.* It was, of course, Rousseau who gave it its most detailed development, particularly in the *Contrat Social.* In the years which followed the publication of this latter work, the term became popularised . . . by second-

and tenth-rate writers, and by pamphleteers to such an extent that not only had the term itself become a *cliché,* but the concept of the sovereignty of the 'general will' had become a leading tenet of the current *mystique.* It was repeated *ad nauseam* in the pamphlets which appeared during 1788 and 1789. It is to be found in many of the *cahiers* which reached Versailles. From 1789 onwards it became a constant phrase on the lips of the Palais Royal orators; it was repeated endlessly in the popular journals and in the speeches of deputies in the Assembly itself. It was constantly heard in the Jacobin Club and in the branches later established by it throughout the country" (Thompson, *op. cit.,* pp. 34–35).

19. "Robespierre's political views . . . were greatly influenced by the teachings of Rousseau's *Le Contrat Social"* (Thompson, *op. cit.,* p. 19; see also p. 18). Even moderate members of the National Assembly attributed to Rousseau its "rights of man" doctrines: "As for the Declaration [of August 1789] itself, is it other than a contract made between all the members of the community, according to Rousseau's ideas? Is it more than the enunciation of the clauses and conditions of this contract?" (Paul Janet, *Histoire de la science politique,* II, 457). Needless to say, scholars have attributed the origin of the Declaration of Rights to many other sources.

20. Quoted by Thompson, *op. cit.,* p. 5.

21. "As early as June, 1789, the deputies of the Nobility and the higher Clergy had been hustled, insulted and occasionally maltreated on entering and leaving the Assembly. Any opposition to the more revolutionary motions proposed by the Left, any defence of the attitude of the King or of the privileged Orders, aroused catcalls and threats in the Assembly itself, the names of the offending deputies being listed and later publicised and denounced in the popular clubs which were rapidly formed from 1789 onwards, as also in the Palais Royal, and such speakers were invariably blacklisted in the revolutionary journals. On one occasion a particular motion was initially opposed by some 300 deputies. Under pressure of visitors to the Assembly, the opposition was decreased to 90 deputies, and finally to one, and he was compelled to escape by an unguarded door. As Malouet remarked, on July 14th the reign of terror had already begun. De Ferrières wrote, 'Liberty has ceased to exist, even in the National Assembly itself.' The property, the families and even the lives of the deputies of the Right were frequently in danger" (Thompson, *op. cit.,* p. 24; see also pp. 53–55).

22. Thompson, *op. cit.,* p. 33. See also p. 34.

23. *Ibid.,* p. 51.

24. For Burke's prophecy that the attempt of the French revolutionists to achieve a simple, direct, uniform and unimpeded will of the prevailing majority would end in military dictatorship, see *Reflections,* pp. 482 and 489.

25. To the charge that he was an enemy to republican forms of govern-

ment, Burke wrote of himself: "He said nothing to give the least ground for such a censure. He never abused all republics. He has never professed himself a friend or an enemy to republics or to monarchies in the abstract. He thought that the circumstances and habits of every country . . . are to decide upon the form of its government. There is nothing in his nature, his temper, or his faculties, which should make him an enemy to any republic modern or ancient" (*New to the Old Whigs*, p. 36).

26. Burke, *Speech at Bristol Previous to the Election*, p. 163.

27. Burke, *Correspondence*, III, 147.

28. Burke, *Reflections*, p. 353. See also pp. 245 and 406.

29. Leland J. Thielemann has shown how, in their theory of human nature and the social contract, "the liberal philosophers of the eighteenth century disclosed unwittingly the indirect debt which democratic theory owed to Thomas Hobbes" ("The Tradition of Hobbes in Eighteenth-Century France," Ph.D. thesis, Columbia University, 1950, p. 114). Thielemann's description of how Hobbes influenced Rousseau's theory of political sovereignty throws considerable light on the chief criticism Burke made against the Jacobin interpretation of the general will. According to Thielemann, Spinoza, who "took most from Hobbes," put popular will where Hobbes had placed monarchical will (pp. 40–42). "Spinoza . . . held that man's rights in society were the same as they were in the state of nature, coeval with his power. It was in the Spinozist form that the Hobbesian concept of natural right was preserved in Rousseau's conclusion of the *Discours sur l'inégalité*. The difference between Rousseau and Hobbes was Benedict Spinoza" (p. 299). "Diderot, in criticizing Hobbes' theory of contract and defense of monarchical absolutism, took Locke's implicit suggestion that the legislative power should be superior to the executive, and advanced a theory of sovereignty centered in the infallible common sense of the *volonté générale*" (see pp. 202–220). "From this position it was but a short step that Rousseau had to take in order to bring the contractual implications of the *volonté générale* back to *jus civile* and Thomas Hobbes" (p. 221). "The similarities between Rousseau's and Hobbes' conception of the scope of sovereignty have frequently been pointed out, and it is indeed clear that the absolute power Hobbes had attributed to the sovereign was not a point of difference between them. . . . Hobbes had acknowledged the legitimacy of a democratic as well as an aristocratic and monarchic *Leviathan*. . . . Civil liberty, for Rousseau as for Hobbes, did not mean the inviolate freedom of the individual but the freedom of the community. Justice was defined by the sovereign and to speak of rights against the community was an absurdity. . . . To limit the sovereign power, by definition, was to destroy it" (pp. 312–314; see also p. 357). "Even Rousseau had outlined a very unsocial contract in demanding a surrender of all individual rights to the self-governing community" (p. 264). "Rousseau denied that he had postulated the absolutism of civil authority. . . . In the end, he seems to have been content . . .

that in any case the most general *de facto* will was the most just. . . . The human race . . . was forced to turn to the collective will, in the confidence at least that it was against nature that a man should willingly do harm to himself. Here unmistakably was Hobbes' society of gamesters; what they all agreed upon could be injustice to none" (pp. 319–321). "Not even Leviathan state presented plans for such a total submergence of the individual to the purposes of the sovereign community as those Rousseau envisioned. . . . Those who refused to obey the General Will would be constrained, and this operation meant nothing more than that men would be forced to be free. . . . The most inviolable law of nature, Rousseau wrote in the *Pologne,* was the law of the stronger. . . . In this fundamental realism Rousseau was standing in the long shadow of Thomas Hobbes" (pp. 330, 343–344, and 346–347). Many other scholars have agreed that Rousseau's conception of sovereignty was that of a "democratic totalitarian." See for example, Ernst Cassirer, *The Question of Jean-Jacques Rousseau,* ed. Peter Gay (New York: Columbia University Press, 1954), p. 8 and *passim*. See also Harald Hoffding, *Jean Jacques Rousseau and His Philosophy* (New Haven, Conn.: Yale University Press, 1930), pp. 132–136.

30. John Acton, *Essays on Freedom and Power* (Boston: The Beacon Press, 1949), p. 159. That the Jacobin conception of sovereignty was held by Dr. Price, Burke's original antagonist in French affairs, is clearly evident in the following criticism of Burke: "Burke objected to the implications which Price, quite logically and moderately, drew from the idea of the sovereignty of the people. If one assumed that principle, then Price's statements could not be refuted. One cannot escape the admission that if the will of the people is supreme, then anything the people will is legal. Burke's philosophy could not stand before that single idea" (Carl Cone, "Pamphlet Replies to Burke's *Reflections,*" *Social Science Quarterly,* XXVI [June, 1945], 27).

31. Woodrow Wilson, *Mere Literature* (Boston, 1896), p. 156.

32. Burke, *Speeches,* I, 153.

INDEX

SELECTED ANN ARBOR PAPERBACKS

works of enduring merit

For a complete list of Ann Arbor Paperback titles write:
THE UNIVERSITY OF MICHIGAN PRESS / ANN ARBOR